Idle Haven

CALIFORNIA STUDIES IN
URBANIZATION AND ENVIRONMENTAL DESIGN

Idle Haven

COMMUNITY BUILDING
AMONG THE WORKING-CLASS RETIRED

by Sheila K. Johnson

UNIVERSITY OF CALIFORNIA PRESS

BERKELEY LOS ANGELES LONDON 1971

University of California Press
Berkeley and Los Angeles, California
University of California Press, Ltd.
London, England

ISBN: 0-520-01909-1
Library of Congress Catalog Card Number: 72-145786

Printed in the United States of America

for Chal

Acknowledgments

I should like to acknowledge with gratitude the assistance and encouragement I have received from a number of people during my graduate training and the research and writing of this study. Professors Elizabeth Colson, Herbert E. Phillips, and Margaret Clark were not only excellent and stimulating teachers, but they made many valuable suggestions about my work while it was in progress. Margaret Clark was also instrumental in introducing me to the Adult Development Research Program at San Francisco Medical Center, where I spent two pleasant and interesting years as a trainee. This traineeship (funded by NICHD grant HD-00238-02) came at a crucial time, since it provided the necessary financing for my research and also brought me into contact with others who were doing research on the problems of aging. As a result, I received a valuable post-graduate education in this fascinating field, and I found numerous sympathetic and knowledgeable listeners on whom to test my own ideas and vent my field-work frustrations. Among these listeners (and givers of advice) were, in particular, Marjorie Fiske Lowenthal, Donald L. Spence, and Frances M. Carp, all of them on the staff of the training program in Adult Development and Aging at the time that I was there.

My greatest debt, however, is to my husband, Chalmers Johnson, to whom this work is affectionately dedicated. In an age when women are clamoring for liberation (from men or from themselves, I sometimes wonder), it is only fair to acknowledge publicly that I would probably never have earned a Ph.D. or completed this study without his assistance and encouragement. Throughout my more than ten years as an off-and-on graduate student he cheerfully paid my registration fees, book bills, and library fines, to say nothing of providing a very comfortable roof over my head. He was also my best social science teacher, most honest critic, and most loyal fan. If the demands of his career sometimes interfered with my own studies—for example when we went to Hong Kong for a year and to Tokyo for a year—it was never less than a pleasure to defer to them. In short, if my work was not completed as rapidly as I might have wished and may not be quite as good as I had hoped, the responsibility rests solely with me.

Contents

Tables

Figures

1. Introduction

This study had its inception one Sunday morning in January, 1965, when I read a San Francisco newspaper supplement devoted to mobile homes. "SOCIABILITY! WHY PEOPLE GO FOR MOBILE PARKS" one of the headlines proclaimed. In the story that followed a satisfied lady resident of a mobile-home park was quoted as saying that "It is like being on Main Street all over again."

At the time I was a graduate student in social anthropology and I was just finishing a seminar paper about conflict resolution in small face-to-face communities as contrasted with large urban centers. For the first time it occurred to me that within these large urban centers there might also be neighborhoods or enclaves which

functioned very much like the small villages that were the stock-in-
trade of anthropological fieldwork.[1]

Who were these people who moved into mobile-home parks for
the sociability, companionship, and neighborliness that they apparently hadn't found in other city neighborhoods? Were they, perhaps,
"displaced" villagers—people who had grown up in small towns and
who had never gotten used to the greater anonymity of urban life?
In California, I learned, many of the people who lived in mobile-
home parks were retired. Were these parks perhaps a form of
retirement community? What sorts of life styles were developing in
mobile-home parks and how self–contained were they? What sorts
of uses did their residents make of the surrounding urban environment?

Like most graduate students, I was too busy with seminar
papers and course requirements to pursue these questions at once,
but I did save the newspaper supplement. I returned to it in the
spring of 1967, when I was beginning to think about possible dissertation topics. One day I mentioned casually to a friend that I
was interested in mobile-home communities and the style of life
developing in them. He asked me whether I had ever heard of the
Wally Byam Caravan Club—an association for people who own
Airstream travel trailers and who gather all over the country for
rallies and caravan-like trips. My friend thought that the social characteristics of Wally Byam Club members and the social patterns
within the club might resemble those of the more stationary residents of mobile-home parks.

On an impulse, I wrote a letter to the Airstream Company saying that my husband was about to retire and that we were thinking
of buying an Airstream and were particularly interested in the Wally
Byam Club. I received a very cordial reply and was put on the
company's and club's mailing lists. From one of the publications
that I began to receive I learned that the club's 1967 "International
Rally"—an annual mid-summer event that draws as many as 3,000
trailers from all over the United States, Canada, and Mexico—would
be held in Santa Rosa, a community about 60 miles north of the
San Francisco Bay Area. I decided to conduct a small sociological

---

[1] I was still a rather new graduate student and had not yet read Herbert
Gans's *The Urban Villagers* (1962) or Michael Young and Peter Willmott's
Family and Kinship in East London (1962), from whom I might have learned
the same thing.

survey at that rally, and during the ten days that some 2,100 Airstream trailers were gathered near Santa Rosa on an abandoned airstrip, I managed to interview a random sample of seventy households (sixty-nine couples and one widower).

The results of this survey are described in Appendix I, but briefly stated, they bore out my friend's surmises. Most of the people I interviewed were retired—the median age for men was 66; for women, 60. Most of the people had a high school education or less, and the majority of the men had been either skilled blue-collar workers (e.g., in construction, steel, carpentry, or electrical work) or in retail businesses (e.g., selling construction materials, automobiles, livestock feed, or insurance) or farmers and ranchers. In terms of their age and social class they were very similar to the people I later interviewed in mobile homes; in fact, there is a good deal of overlap. Of the seventy Airstreamers I interviewed, six lived in mobile homes (and another eight lived year-round in their Airstream trailers); of the 200 family units in the mobile-home park I studied, thirty-three owned travel trailers (four of them Airstreams) or campers. In terms of income, the average Airstream owner was somewhat more affluent than the average mobile-home park resident; and, not unexpectedly, the mobile-home park contained a great many more widows and single men and women than the Wally Byam Club.

As a result of my survey in Santa Rosa, I realized that a study of mobile-home parks would involve not only the literature on urban neighborhoods, suburbia, and small communities in highly industrialized societies, but also the literature on working-class families and their way of life, and the literature on aging. The latter, in particular, took me outside the interests of most social anthropologists and anthropology courses, and led to my becoming an interne in the newly formed, interdisciplinary Adult Development Program headed by Marjorie Fiske Lowenthal.[2] The staff of the Adult Development Program, in addition to introducing me to the field of gerontology and teaching me a great deal about research methods, was very hospitable to my proposal to do a "village" study of a mobile-home park.

In this manner what began as a simple question—"Who lives in

---

[2] This research and training body is affiliated with the University of California's San Francisco Medical Center and largely financed by the National Institute of Child Health and Human Development.

these mobile-home parks and why?"—developed into a case study of
community building among elderly, working-class, white urban
Americans. Much has been written, recently, about the silent majority, and certainly the residents of most mobile-home parks could
be considered charter members of that fraternity. But while they
may have been silent, they have by no means been inactive. Frightened by urban violence and prevented by their low incomes from
moving into safer and more congenial neighborhoods, these individuals have nevertheless managed to create secure and homogeneous enclaves within the urban environment. This achievement is
all the more remarkable in that it occurred spontaneously, without
federal aid programs, urban planners, or even much assistance or
awareness on the part of mobile-home manufacturers and mobile-
home park owners. Now that the achievement has become better
known, in fact, there is a real danger that it may be wrecked by those
seeking to tamper with it: whether they be liberal zealots wanting
to integrate the parks racially, or social welfare zealots wanting to
segregate the parks still further on the basis of age and indigence,
or business zealots wanting simply to make the greatest possible
amounts of money out of parks in the shortest possible amounts of
time regardless of community values, or urban renewal zealots wanting to zone the parks out of existence because they are deemed
"unsightly."

All of these, plus still other threats exist, and therefore mobile-
home parks are likely to continue evolving over time. For the present, however, they constitute an interesting and viable form of community that has developed in response to certain acute social
problems. These problems include the needs of the elderly in a
highly youth-oriented, age-graded society; urban violence and
anomie in our at once expanding and yet declining metropolises;
and the pincer-like pressures felt by working-class Americans caught
between an increasingly militant lower class and a wealthy, liberal
upper middle class that often allies itself with the lower class ideo-
logically without in any way risking its own comforts or status.[3]

---

[3] As Stewart Alsop noted in an article entitled "The Wallace Man," one
of Wallace's most effective arguments against the upper-middle class liberal
was that out of 535 members of Congress, only six sent their children to
Washington's public schools (Newsweek, October 21, 1968). Other popular
articles that contain similar analyses of the pressures currently experienced by
working-class Americans include Peter Schrag (1969), "The Troubled American" (1969), and Richard Rogin (1970).

Mobile home parks solve a number of these problems although in the process of doing so they have created some new ones of their own. This study is an attempt to analyze one particular, but hopefully representative, park with an eye toward explaining who lives there and why, and also exploring some of the benefits and drawbacks to life in such a community.

Although Idle Haven was chosen to be representative of a large number of "adult" parks, the universe from which it was selected was limited in certain ways. To begin with, when in the fall of 1968 I began to look for a suitable park, I limited my choice to parks that had been in existence for at least five years. Mindful of Suzanne Keller's warning that patterns of neighboring can be affected by the newness of a community—a period of initial frenzied neighboring usually gives way to a more stable pattern of "restricted interaction, selectivity, and withdrawal" (Keller, 1968:68)—I was anxious to study social relationships in a stable, well-established park. At the same time, I also wanted a park that was new enough to have recreation facilities and a community hall. I further limited my choice by only looking at parks that had about 200 spaces—large enough to have a formal social structure, yet small enough for people to operate on a face-to-face basis and for me to interview everyone personally; and I restricted my choice to "adult" parks (i.e., parks that exclude children under 16) since these constitute the most prevalent type of park in California and appear to account for most of the spontaneous upsurge in mobile-home park living. Finally, I wanted to study a park within the metropolitan, urban area in order to study what uses the residents made of urban facilities and what their ties were to the community outside their own small enclave.

There were, at the time, approximately 150 mobile-home parks in the San Francisco Bay Area if one took into account the peninsula as far south as Sunnyvale and the East Bay Area as far south as San Jose, as far north as Martinez, and as far east as Concord. There were no mobile-home parks within San Francisco itself, nor were there any in Berkeley or Oakland. Using the 1967 Woodall's Mobile Home Park Directory, I compiled a list of about twenty seemingly suitable parks within an hour's driving of my home in Berkeley, and I then visited most of these parks. After narrowing the list down to five, I began to approach the managers of these parks in order to explain my study and to ask for their cooperation. A mobile-home park, unlike a subdivision or a neighborhood, is a private community, with a fence around it, a manager, and—in many cases—a sign that reads "Private Property: Permission to Pass Revocable at Any Time." Uninvited outsiders, such as door-to-door salesmen, are usually denied access to the park; and even the residents' personal guests must register with management if they stay overnight. It is therefore imperative for anyone entering a mobile-home park to have the tacit or explicit consent of its management.

The first manager to whom I explained my study denied me access to his park. He said that many people had moved into the park in order not to be bothered by door-to-door salesmen, and nothing could persuade him that I was not selling anything and that I would not bother people who were unwilling to be interviewed. When I finally proposed attending a residents' association meeting in order to let the residents themselves decide whether they wanted to participate in my study, the manager bluntly refused me permission. Of course, this type of screening function has important positive and negative value for the community (aside from its impact on researchers), and it will be discussed more fully in Chapter 3.

My second attempt to gain access to a mobile-home park was much more successful. The lady manager was bright and self-confident, and she had been in charge of the park since its inception 5 years earlier. (The manager who had refused me access had been on the job less than a month, which probably accounted for some of his rigidity and his desire not to offend anyone in the park.) Moreover, the manager of this second park was personally interested in my study and in the fact that it might "improve the image of mobile-home residents" and lessen the opposition by city councils and planning boards to the building of more parks. She readily assented to my plan for gaining the cooperation of people in the park: I would put a letter in everyone's mailbox explaining the nature and purpose of the study and announcing that I would attend the next residents' association meeting in order to introduce myself and answer any questions or objections. While we sat and talked in the community hall she also gave me a copy of the park's mimeographed monthly newsletter and introduced me to some of the residents who wandered in to chat or drink a cup of coffee.

Two days later, the first Wednesday of January 1969, I put a mimeographed letter in the residents' mailboxes, and that evening I attended the park association's monthly meeting. To my disappointment, only about thirty-six people (out of approximately 360 residents) turned out for the meeting, although it later became clear that this was the usual attendance at this particular event. Most of the thirty-six were leaders or socially active people in the park, however, so that I gained the cooperation of an influential group. The greatest objection raised to the study at this meeting was the fact that I was affiliated with the notorious University of California at Berkeley (not only inasmuch as I was a graduate student there but also because my husband was a Berkeley professor). The Berkeley campus, at that time, was in the midst of a strike over the issue of whether Eldridge Cleaver would be allowed to lecture in a student-initiated course. One lady in the park had phoned the manager shortly after receiving my letter in her mailbox and had said that if I had anything to do with that awful place she would refuse to be interviewed by me.

I had already learned in Santa Rosa that hippies, blacks, and campus riots were not popular with the people I would be interviewing; and in my letter I had stressed my affiliation with the San Francisco Medical School and the Adult Development Program rather than with Berkeley. Later on I brought my husband to several park breakfasts and dinners in order to demonstrate that not all Berkeley professors were wild-eyed, long-haired radicals; he also gave a free lecture to a park association meeting and was well received. I myself tried to dress conservatively (even dowdily) and on various occasions brought my mother and mother-in-law to the park—again, in order to demonstrate that I had solid, respectable family ties. But some suspicion doubtless remained—in part, just the normal working-class suspicion of "pointy-headed intellectuals"—and I never had the nerve to put a Berkeley campus parking sticker on our second car, which caused a great deal of car-juggling in our family.

I began interviewing people exactly a week after speaking at the association meeting. During the period when I had been visiting mobile-home parks around the Bay Area I had been repeatedly struck by their quiet, self-enclosed atmosphere; like Ronald Frankenberg in the Welsh village that he called "Pentrediwaith" I often looked at the rows of mobile homes and wondered how one could ever know what went on inside them (Frankenberg, 1966:16). I had therefore decided to combine interviewing with participant observation. I had spent part of the fall of 1968 constructing a questionnaire—cobbled together out of questions asked in other people's surveys, questions I myself had asked in Santa Rosa, and questions that my background reading had suggested as ones that might possibly yield productive answers. Because of the difficulties I anticipated in finding a suitable mobile-home park that would permit me to conduct a study, I did not make an effort to find a second park in which to "pre-test" my questionnaire. Thus, aside from having tried it out on some friends and relatives (none of whom lived in a mobile home and who therefore had to invent answers to many of the questions), I had no idea how good the questionnaire was or how long it would take to administer. To my horror, my first interview—with two loquacious sisters, retired school teachers who had indicated a strong interest in my research—lasted nearly four hours!

As I went on with my interviews I soon noticed several questions that did not produce significant responses, and these I omitted from the questionnaire almost at once. Even with these omissions, the interviews varied enormously in length and completeness. With some people, certain questions triggered interesting and lengthy discussions, so that I then had to rush through the rest of the questionnaire, sometimes choosing only the most important questions, in order not to take an inordinate amount of time. Some of these discussions were so clearly gossipy "asides" that I ostentatiously had to lay down my pen in order to indicate that we were now talking "off the record." Nevertheless, like all anthropologists, I wrote up such additional information after every interview, either sitting in my car or at home that evening, along with a general assessment of the interview, the individual, and his home environment.

My general practice, for the first few months, was to arrive in the park around noon and to interview one or two individuals, depending on the length of the interviews. I only occasionally made appointments ahead of time—for example, when someone met me at the door and said, "I'm busy this afternoon, but how about tomorrow?" Usually I simply called on people and asked whether they were free to talk for a while. I began by calling on people whom I had met socially in the recreation hall and I also followed up leads furnished by the interviews themselves. "Have you interviewed my neighbor, old Mrs. So-and-so," someone would ask. If I hadn't, the chances were that I would soon. Sometimes I also got good advice about opportune times to visit people. "Mr. Blank [a neighbor] is a very nice man but he drives a truck all night and so he sleeps during the day. Mondays are his day off and that's a good time to catch him." Toward the end of my interviewing, I saw a lot of people on weekends in order to reach those who worked during the week.

Because I was attempting to interview everyone and because many of the people I was interviewing knew and were in daily contact with each other, I expected that there would be gossip about my questionnaire. One woman, who was very difficult to draw out (it was the only interview during which an individual turned *up* the television set instead of turning it off!), apparently gave such a bad report of me to her clique of four or five friends that the entire group refused to be interviewed. More frequently, people warned me at the start of an interview that they would not answer any of the "personal" questions that they had heard I asked. Many of these people then went on to answer every question, some even commenting at the end of the interview that they had found it very interesting. All in all, of the 200 "units" in the park, I encountered only nine outright refusals. There were a number of people who made excuses to me so often that I finally quit bothering them and marked them down as "probable refusals;" and there were a few people whom I did not try to interview because they were extremely ill, or recently bereaved, or on extended vacations. There were also some people who moved out of the park before I got around to interviewing them, and in such cases I did not interview the new tenants who replaced them. Over a period of six months, I thus conducted 146 interviews, although I met virtually every resident in the park or obtained some second-hand information about him. My data indicate that the people I interviewed do not differ substantially from those I missed; both groups appear to contain similar proportions of the retired and the working, the married and the unmarried, and the socially active and inactive.

I found only one instance of an answer being rehearsed because of prior knowledge of the question. This instance involved the question, "Do you happen to know the name of the mayor of ———— [the town in which the mobile-home park is located]?" which was designed to tap people's awareness of and ties to the larger community in which they lived. One couple answered this question (correctly) and then admitted that the night before they had had dinner with a close friend in the park—a woman I had interviewed that same previous day—who had told them the question to see whether they could answer it. They couldn't, and so she had supplied them with the answer.

At the same time that I was interviewing people in the park, I was also attending social functions as a participant observer. Herbert Gans felt that in Levittown he could not combine both roles and that he would not have been accepted as a neighbor and a genuine participant had he also been conducting formal interviews (Gans, 1969:xii-xxvi). In my own case, the situation was somewhat different. I was never a resident of the park, although many people assumed that I must be and others often asked me when I was going to buy a mobile home and move in. I attended the monthly social functions so religiously that, like Gans, I was often complimented on my faithfulness, particularly when attendance was low. However, not being a permanent resident, I never became a part of any friendship or leadership clique, and this slight social distance probably made it easier for me to conduct interviews. I also found that my role as interviewer was the only one readily understood by people; it gave me an excuse for being in the park every day. When I sat around for an afternoon drinking coffee or playing bridge, I was "taking a break" or "just being lazy." Had my sole research effort been directed toward such *ad hoc* occasions, people would probably have become acutely suspicious and uncomfortable in my presence.

It was understood that I wanted to see and participate in some of the park's social gatherings in order to "get the feel of the mobile-home way of life," but I think only a very few people realized that my attendance at such events was a major part of my research. I never openly took notes unless it was something that I knew people would expect me to copy down—such as the number of tenants who had joined the park's association. Nevertheless, the fact that I was not wholly trusted was sometimes made evident by the sudden suspension of conversation when I joined a group. And one day when I was strolling about the park and had stopped to chat with a lady who was transferring some soil from her garden to some potted plants, another lady bicycled past and cheerfully called out, "Now, now, Mrs. Johnson; you know that's not the kind of dirt you're after!"

In addition to the occasional problems caused by my being both an interviewer and a participant observer, there were advantages and disadvantages to conducting all the interviews myself. At first I was so acutely sensitive to snubs, that even normal put-offs, such as "I'm busy just now," could paralyze me for days. I gradually learned to take refusals in my stride and to cope with instances of hostility and rudeness, but I continually had to guard against self-censorship in conducting interviews. I wanted to be liked by these people; I knew I would continue to meet them socially; so that when I sensed resistance to a certain line of questioning my first impulse was to stop and tactfully change the subject. Particularly after I had been in the park for a long time, I found that I already knew some of the people so well that it was hard to maintain the facade of impersonal questioner. I also became excruciatingly bored. To hear the same answers cropping up again and again may be good from a statistical standpoint, but it certainly deadens the brain.

The advantages of conducting one's own interviews, however, more than outweigh the disadvantages. It gave me an opportunity to meet everyone privately, in his own mobile home, and to evaluate not only what he said but how he said it and how he looked when he said it. There is, of course, ample room for misinterpretation in this process, but at least all of the data is being filtered through a single mind. In the Adult Development Program, where extensive life histories were being taken by a number of interviewers and then evaluated by others, I was often struck by the fact that an individual whose interview we had read and who seemed to us to be vain, spoiled, and neurotic, would be described by the interviewer as charming, outgoing, and self-possessed. Who was right, I always wondered; perhaps if we had met the person we would have agreed with the interviewer. Charm is not a quality readily conveyed in words, even by novelists.

Being my own interviewer and knowing at least vaguely what sorts of data I was looking for, I could also probe and deviate from the questionnaire when it seemed desirable. Someone being asked a series of straightforward questions—Do you have any relatives in this area? Do you have any friends in this area? Do you have any friends in the park?—cannot be expected to know that the interviewer is actually trying to get a picture of his social connectedness. A widow who had answered "no" to all of the above questions, and who had given me a mental picture of complete social isolation, suddenly revealed, when I asked a totally different question—Are you ever gone from the park for long periods of time?—that she drove quite frequently to Oregon to see her brother. Such sudden impression reversals made me wonder whether a questionnaire is not simply a series of buttons that one pushes, hoping some, or one, of them will open a small window into another's social and personal being. Of course, some people are so well defended that no question-

naire can give an indication of their lifestyle. The two most notorious alcoholics in the park—individuals whom neighbors had warned
me not to interview at all—both gave me sober, pleasant interviews
that held no clue to their usual condition.

One final note about interviewing. I found the women decided-
ly easier to interview than the men. Perhaps this was because I am
a woman and because I interviewed many more women than men:
eighty-seven interviews were with women, twenty-five with men,
and thirty-four with couples. (It should be noted that in thirty-six
cases—widows, divorcées, and unmarried daughters living with
their mothers—I had no choice but to interview a woman.) In general I found it easier to establish rapport with women and I found
them, with several notable exceptions, to be much easier to draw
out. Most of the men—except for bartenders and salesmen—were
either extremely taciturn or seemed to be simply unused to expressing themselves verbally. I attributed this to the fact that most of the
men I interviewed were blue-collar workers, whereas their wives
were often both better educated and, if employed, working at white-
collar jobs. However, Marjorie Lowenthal has assured me that even
with white-collar and professional samples, interviewers find the
women more verbal. This has led her to wonder whether sociological
research may not resemble gossip in form and content and therefore
make it more congenial to women than men in our culture.

In addition to interviewing residents for six months and participating in park activities for a year, I also attended the monthly
meetings of two organizations that are concerned with mobile-home
life. One of these is the Golden State Mobilehome Owners League
(GSMOL) which, in mid-1969, had a membership of 23,500 California families who live in mobile homes, and which maintains a
paid lobbyist in Sacramento. The GSMOL organizes chapters in
mobile-home parks (the park I studied had such a chapter) and it
holds monthly regional meetings which are attended by chapter
officials, regional and state officers, and any individual members
who care to attend. Beginning in September, 1968, I attended the
meetings of Region 1 for approximately one and one-half years. In
addition to learning a good deal about some of the common problems facing mobile-home owners, I also had an opportunity to visit
a number of parks, since the monthly meetings circulated around
the region, meeting in a different park's recreation hall each time.
The other organization whose local meetings I attended was the
Western Mobilehome Association (WMA), whose membership con-

sists of mobile-home park owners and which also lobbies with the state legislature. I was taken to one WMA meeting by the manager of the park I was studying, and after explaining the nature of my study I was invited to attend the monthly meetings of this group. I also attended a day-long workshop for park owners and operators in the Bay Area.

The hospitality and frankness of such organizations, and the personal friendship and trust of individuals, always place the social scientist under a moral obligation. He has heard things that are for "internal consumption" only; he has been told some private gripes; and he has seen some family quarrels. To write about these things is a breach of confidence, and yet to leave them out is both to falsify reality and to invite the secret scorn of "insiders" who know what has been omitted. I have tried to write an honest account; in all cases my descriptions of incidents and my choice of anecdotes have been guided by sociological purposes rather than by malice or fortuity. The exact location of the park and its real name have been changed. All personal names have also been changed, and in some cases personal attributes have been somewhat altered to protect the privacy of informants. Nevertheless, I could not invent a whole new social structure for the park, and residents of the park who read this study will doubtless recognize some of their friends and neighbors. I hope they will not be unduly startled by that shock of recognition.

2. The Park and the People

Idle Haven Mobile Home Park is located on the eastern side of San Francisco Bay. The suburban community within which it is situated flows, without clear boundaries, into the string of communities known collectively, and colloquially, as the East Bay. The East Bay as a whole is sometimes regarded as a suburb of San Francisco—part of the metropolitan web that has San Francisco as its center. But Oakland and San Jose have large business and industrial centers of their own, and many of the smaller East Bay communities see themselves as suburbs of these towns instead. Among the employed men living in Idle Haven, some commuted to San Francisco, some to San Jose, some to Oakland, and some lucky few worked only a short distance from where they lived.

Idle Haven itself is well situated between two major freeways leading to San Francisco and the rest of the East Bay. Near the access points of both freeways, each about two miles from Idle Haven, are extensive shopping centers, including clothing stores, furniture stores, branches of Sears and Montgomery Ward, banks, cinemas, and all the other appurtenances of modern urban life. Only about two blocks from Idle Haven, within easy walking distance of all but the most elderly and ailing of its residents, is a smaller shopping complex that includes a supermarket, laundromat, liquor store, doughnut shop, and barber and beauty shops. There are two good hospitals and several Protestant and Catholic churches within a mile or two of the park.

Across the street from the entrance to Idle Haven and surrounding the park on three sides are tract houses not much different in size and appearance from many of the larger mobile homes. Nor do the residents of these tract homes differ much from the residents of Idle Haven except in age: they are generally younger and have school-age children, but they hold the same sorts of jobs—as sheet-metal workers, truck-drivers, machinists, construction workers, and the like—and they drive the same assortment of pick-up trucks bearing bumper strips that proclaim "When Guns Are Outlawed, Only Outlaws Will Have Guns," or "America! Love It or Leave It!" Some of these tract dwellers are the sons and daughters of couples living in Idle Haven, and many of them plan to move into mobile homes as soon as their own children are grown, or when they retire.

But Idle Haven also differs from the surrounding tract neighborhoods. For one thing, it has a 6-foot high fence around it and a prominent sign at the entrance reading "Private Property, Permission to Pass Revocable at Any Time." The fence is required by a state law dating from a time when "trailer parks" were considered so unsightly that they had to be hidden from public view. Today the fence serves a very different function, particularly from the standpoint of park residents. Although it still hides the park from public view, thereby promoting a sense of community and solidarity within, it is more highly prized for the fact that it shuts out the rest of the world. Within the confines of the fence, residents feel secure from most of the dangers of urban life: muggers, burglars, hit-and-run drivers, vandals, disturbers of the peace. On Halloween, for example, the entrance to the park is blocked by a row of long tables from which candy is dispensed by a committee of park residents, but children from the surrounding neighborhood are prevented from trick-or-treating within the park.

Within the confines of the park one can also be relatively assured that one's neighbors will abide by certain moral and social
standards. Every park has a list of rules and regulations that tenants
must abide by or risk being evicted. Among the rules of Idle Haven
is one prohibiting loud talking, television playing, or other noise
between the hours of 10 p.m. and 8 a.m., and noisy parties or intoxi-
cation at any time. Dogs, cats, and other pets must be kept "under
control" at all times, either indoors or on a leash on their own lots,
and dogs must be taken to relieve themselves outside rather than in
the park. Every tenant is expected to keep his lot neat and clean;
"lawns must be watered, mowed, trimmed, and kept weed-free;"
patio furniture must be "suitable" and not consist of discarded
couches or overstuffed chairs; and dirty or unsightly mobile homes
are not permitted to remain in the park. Needless to say, these rules
are not quite as draconian in practice as they appear on paper. However, they do exist and the fact that management can enforce them
means that one need not personally antagonize one's neighbor in
keeping him up to the mark.

Idle Haven occupies about seventeen acres, cross-hatched by
eleven streets. Since the park is a self-enclosed entity, cars do not
drive through it on their way to somewhere else, and the streets
are generally very quiet, used only by residents and the occasional
visitor or delivery truck. The streets are narrow and without side-
walks, and because residents both walk and bicycle through the park
the speed-limit for cars is 10 miles per hour. The mobile homes
which line these streets sit on lots about a third the size of a conventional city lot. There is usually a narrow strip of land to the
left of the mobile home and a paved driveway to the right of it; at
the back is another small strip of land, partly occupied by a tool
shed. Despite, or perhaps because of the limited amount of ground
available to them, some people garden avidly, cultivating every
square inch for flowers, trees, shrubs, lawns, and even vegetables.
Others have planted their spot in rocks and plastic flowers and do
not garden at all.

The mobile homes themselves range in size from 10 feet wide
and about 40 feet long to 24 feet wide and 60 feet long, although
there is now talk of building 36-foot wide mobile homes as well as
two-story models. The term "mobile home" is generally used to distinguish anything over 10 feet wide that must be towed to its site
by a special truck, from the 8-foot wide smaller "travel trailer" that
can be pulled on the road by a car. However, the term "mobile

home" has also come into vogue in an effort to dissociate modern mobile-home parks from their shabbier World War II ancestors, the trailer parks. Trailers were being built as early as the 1920s—usually home-made wooden structures on old Ford chassis—and being used by sportsmen and by people such as construction workers who traveled from job to job and lived at the construction site far from any sort of housing. During World War II, however, great labor migrations and the wartime housing shortage forced many people to live in trailers and produced, for the first time, extensive trailer parks in and around large cities. These trailers were not self-contained—that is, they had no toilet or bathing facilities—and the early trailer parks were generally messy encampments, clearly temporary in nature.

After the war, as the housing stock began to expand, many trailer dwellers moved into new apartments and tract homes. But others found they had grown to like the convenience of their compact trailers, and manufacturers were rapidly eliminating the discomforts of trailer life. Bathrooms were installed and natural gas rather than butane came into use for heating and cooking. In response to these internal changes, more elaborate trailer parks were built with underground sewage and gas mains. Trailers grew in width from 8 feet to 10 and 12 feet, and many of these latter models came with "pop-out" or "expando" sections that made the living room as much as 16 feet wide. Some units came with double expando sections—that is, with a front section pulled out to make the livingroom wider and a back section extending the bedroom. Owners of such units usually built a porch between the two pop-out sections, thereby creating on-site what the industry was soon to copy in its "double-wides."

A "double-wide"—the most common type of mobile home on the market today—consists of either two 10-foot wide sections or two 12-foot wide sections, trucked out separately to a mobile-home park and then joined together on the site. At present the largest mobile home on the market is 24 feet wide, but obviously the principle of joining 10- or 12-foot sections could be extended to produce 30- or 36-foot wide mobile homes as well. Since many of the parks built in the 1950s and early 1960s cannot accommodate mobile homes this wide on their lots, the principle of the earlier expando is also being applied upwards, and a prototype has been built of a 12-foot wide, two-story mobile home that is trucked to its site in a collapsed state and then extended to its full height.

Mobile homes this large, which must be dismantled and hauled by truck in several sections, are obviously not very mobile. Of the twenty-nine new residents in Idle Haven during 1969, for example, eighteen bought used mobile homes already set up within the park, and only eleven moved in new mobile homes. Of the twenty-five new residents in 1968, thirteen bought units already in the park and twelve brought new units with them. Not only do many people prefer to sell their mobile homes rather than attempt to move them, but the population of mobile-home parks is far more stable than most people suspect. In Idle Haven the average annual turn-over for 1965-69 has been 15 per cent, or thirty families per year; by the end of 1969, there were still fifty-one families in the park who had been there since it opened in early 1964. Departures from the park are due to deaths (there has been an average of seven deaths in the park per year), decisions to move to another park—often in a recreation area or a less populated part of the state—and decisions to move back into another type of housing. Of the twenty-nine vacancies that occurred in 1969, two were due to deaths, eleven were the result of moves to other parks, and eleven were caused by moves to other types of housing (the causes of five vacancies were unknown).

Who are the people currently living in mobile homes, and what sorts of pleasures and problems does this type of housing entail? Why do they move into mobile-home parks? What kind of social patterns exist in such parks and what kind of implications do they have for urban life as a whole? To ask these questions is, in turn, to raise others—either directly or by implication. For example, how representative is Idle Haven of other mobile-home parks in the Bay Area, in California, or in the United States as a whole? There are some statistics from other sources that can shed light on this problem. However, the question of *why* people move into a particular type of housing (or vote for a certain man, or buy a given brand) can be answered in several different ways. For example, one can ascertain the sociological characteristics of a given population—age, income, religion, education, and occupation—and then interpret behavior in terms of these characteristics, or one can *ask* people why they behave in a given way. The former method explores the impact of structural differentiation within the social system on human behavior, whereas the latter focuses on individual purpose. Of course, the two approaches often complement each other. One may conclude, for example, that mobile-home inhabitants have a lower than average income and have this corroborated by the many people who say that they moved into mobile homes because they could not afford the upkeep, payments, or property taxes on an ordinary home.

The analysis of social patterns within the park—such as patterns of friendship, leadership, neighboring, participation, aid and trade —is also open to several different approaches. According to ecologists, social patterns in a community can best be explained in terms of the *physical* properties of that community. Thus, the self-enclosed nature of a mobile-home park, the population density, the length of residence of individuals and their exact location within the park would be cited to explain who was friendly with whom and why certain individuals and not others became leaders. Such ecological concepts can provide some interesting insights into human behavior —particularly in a small and homogeneous community.[1] Nevertheless, there are likely to be many intervening variables affecting such things as friendships and the degree of participation in the park's activities; and these intervening variables are best expressed in terms of sociological characteristics or personal choice. As Herbert Gans has noted:

> ". . . number, density, and heterogeneity . . . are ecological concepts which describe human adaptation to the environment. However, they are not sufficient to explain social phenomena, because these phenomena cannot be understood solely as the consequences of ecological processes. . . . Ecological explanations of social life are most applicable if the subjects under study lack the ability to make *choices*, be they plants, animals, or human beings" (1962b:639).

Since mobile-home parks are voluntarily created communities, it is particularly important to study not merely the possible ecological impact that the community may have on its residents, and the shared social characteristics of the residents, but also the element of rational choice that led these particular people to choose this particular way of life. The balance of this chapter will be devoted to the social characteristics of the residents of Idle Haven, but Chapter 3 will turn to questions of personal choice and need as expressed by the residents, and later chapters will return to ecological factors as these affect friendship, participation, and leadership.

One of the most arresting characteristics about the residents of

---

[1] See, for example, the excellent study by Leon Festinger, Stanley Schachter, and Kurt Back (1967, paper ed.).

Figure 1 - AGE DISTRIBUTION

Males

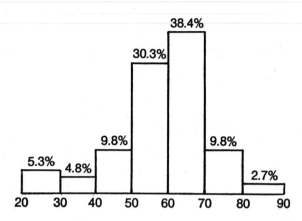

Females

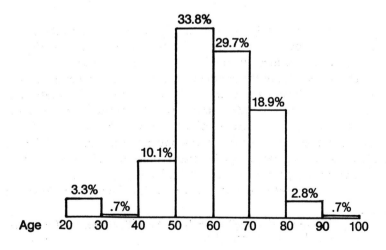

Idle Haven is their relative homogeneity of age. Although the mobile-home park was not designed as a retirement community, half of the men and slightly more than half of the women are over 60 years old (Figure I). Part of the age structure of Idle Haven is, of course, determined by policy; as an "adult park" it admits no children under 16 and this tends to exclude couples in their 20s and 30s. In the interview group there was a huge age gap among the women, only two of whom fell between the ages of 24 and 44. Idle Haven did have five very young couples resident at the time of the study (three of them included in the interviews), but two of these had their first child while living in the park and were planning to move.

The age structure of Idle Haven is not typical of mobile-home residents in the United States as a whole, but it does appear to be typical for California. For the nation as a whole a government survey found that 49.4 per cent of the heads of household in mobile homes were under 35 years of age, 29.4 per cent were between 35 and 54, 11.8 per cent were between 55 and 64, and 9.3 per cent were 65 years or older (HUD, 1968:82). This survey also found that the young mobile-home resident was typically a blue-collar worker living in a small town rather than a large city or metropolitan area. In these small towns there are generally few new houses being built, and larger, older houses are often not suited to the needs of a young, small family.

> "The young man who, with his wife, and perhaps a baby, comes to such a town to take a factory job is likely to find that available housing consists of a few small apartments and large old houses with many more rooms than his family requires, judging from the data on vacant units" (HUD, 1968:68).

In California, on the other hand, a recent survey found that 54 per cent of all mobile-home residents were over 50 years of age (WMN, Sept. 8, 1969:10). This same survey also found that 49.5 per cent of the California residents of mobile homes were retired; in Idle Haven the percentage of retired was 46.6.

The household composition of the 146 "units" interviewed in Idle Haven was as follows:

Married couples	100
Widows	28
Divorcées	4
Widowers	1
Bachelors	2
Couples with widowed mother	2
Divorced man and son	1
Son and widowed mother	2
Daughter and widowed mother (in one case, two daughters)	3
Two bachelors	1
Widow and male boarder	1
Widow and unmarried sister	1
Total	146
Number of men	112
Number of women	148

Six of the 102 couples interviewed claimed to have a teenager still living with them, but in all but two of these cases the son or daughter was between 18 and 21 and either lived at home only intermittently or moved out altogether while the study was in progress. When Idle Haven was first opened there were about eighteen teenagers in the park, and since the park was new and everyone was trying hard to get acquainted, the teenagers managed to form a close-knit group that held parties, went to the beach together, and—in one case—led to a marriage. All but two of these "original" teenagers have since moved out of the park, and the few new teenagers who have moved in after the park was established have generally kept to themselves and not even met their cohorts. (The same was true of the young couples in Idle Haven; none of them knew each other, probably because they did not live adjacent to each other in the park and did not participate in any park activities, where they might have had an opportunity to meet.) Several parents who had moved into the park since 1964 and who had had a teenage son or daughter living with them for a brief period said that their children had moved to apartments of their own because they had actively disliked living in Idle Haven—"There wasn't enough room to horse around;" "His friends couldn't come by on their motorcycles and lounge on the front porch;" "He was afraid that driving in at all hours of the day and night would disturb the neighbors." In other words, the tone is set by the over-60 majority living in the park.

Of the 102 married couples interviewed, fifty-seven had only been married once, and a number of these couples had been married for as long as 40 to 50 years. However, for forty-five of the couples interviewed their present marriage was either the second (or third) for one or both of the partners. Many of these second marriages were also of 20 or more years' standing, indicating that the earlier marriages must have been broken when the partners were relatively young. Of the ninety individuals involved in these remarriages, 26 per cent had been widowed, 13 per cent had never before been married (but their partners had been), and 61 per cent had been divorced. This is typical for working-class couples. August Hollingshead has commented, with regard to similar findings, that:

> "The family cycle is broken prematurely in the working class about twice as frequently as it is in the middle classes. Community studies indicate that from one-fourth to one-third of working-class families are broken by divorce, desertion, and death of a marital partner, after a family of procreation has been started but before it is reared. . . . In Elmtown I found that 33 per cent of the working-class families (class IV) had been broken after fifteen and more years of marriage" (1953:290).

Family relationships will be discussed in greater detail in the following chapters, but a number of observations regarding second marriages may shed some light on why many of these couples choose to live in mobile homes. Working-class couples generally have their children while still young and, regardless of whether the marriage is broken, the child-bearing period is likely to be short, as it is among all classes in the United States. Thus many working-class women who find themselves divorced at 35 years of age have virtually grown children. When they remarry—either a divorced man or a widower—they cannot see the point of buying a house "for just the two of us" and yet they may want to "own something" rather than living in an apartment. A mobile home is an ideal answer. It is interesting to note that while many of these women marry for the second time while they are still of childbearing age, almost none of them chooses to have another family by the second husband. Among the couples interviewed there were only three in which there were both children by the previous marriages and joint children. Yet there were thirty couples in the sample who had had children by a previous marriage but who, *as a couple,* were childless. Many of these partners seemed to be extremely close to each other, and this is no doubt an important factor in their ability to live together amicably in what is sometimes a very small mobile home.

The private, romantic nature of many of these second, childless marriages is mirrored in another unusual phenomenon: the marriage in which the woman is 10 or more years older than the man. Among the couples interviewed in Idle Haven there were seven such instances. The most interesting case involved a woman, aged 46, and a man, aged 35, who had been married for 14 years. The woman had married for the first time when she was 15, and she had had her first child when she was 16, her second when she was 18, and her last child when she was 20. At the age of 30 she was divorced and a year later she married her second husband, who was then 21 but who looked "old for his age." She had bought a mobile home after her divorce and she and her young husband continued to live in it while he was "getting established" and helping to raise her two younger children (the oldest married at virtually the same time that the mother remarried). This couple now lives very much as a middle-class couple might in the years before starting a family; they go out a lot together—dancing, camping, and waterskiing on weekends and vacations—except that they occasionally stay home to look after the visiting grandchildren. As Peter Townsend has noted, the narrowing of the span of years between generations has produced some important changes in family structure—for example, an individual may have both grandparents and great-grandparents alive for a considerable part of his lifetime and this may lead to certain role substitutions (Townsend, 1968:255–57). In the family just described and others like it, the woman's grandchildren appear to take the place of the children the young husband might have had and also of what could have been the woman's own "menopausal child."

The surviving children for the survey population of Idle Haven as a whole (that is, including widows, divorcées, and single individuals) are tabulated in Table I. These percentages differ significantly from those of a much larger survey of people aged 65 and over recently completed in the United States. According to that survey only 18 per cent of all men and women aged 65 and over are childless, and of those who have surviving children, 57 per cent have three or more (Shanas, et al., 1968:139–40). It may be that the percentages for Idle Haven are skewed by tabulating both partners of a couple, but one would expect that this would affect all the categories equally and that the general proportions of those who

have no children, one child, two children, and so forth would remain constant. The high percentage of childlessness is even more
marked when one considers that the population of Idle Haven does
not consist entirely of people aged 65 and over; about 40 per cent

TABLE I
Idle Haven Residents with and without Surviving Children[a]

Number of surviving children	Men	Women	Both
	per cent		*average*
None	30	23	26
One	21	30	26
Two	30	26	28
Three	12	14	13
Four	1	3	2
Five	4	3	3
Six	2	1	1

[a] Omitting three couples and two bachelors, all under 25 years of age.

of the residents are in their 40s and 50s, and some of those who
have only one child, may in fact, become childless before they
themselves reach 65. One couple and two widows in the survey
had already been rendered childless by the death of a grown child.

It seems probable that childlessness, or having only one child,
predisposes people in certain walks of life to move into mobile-home
parks. As in the case of late second marriages where no children are
expected, many such couples feel that an entire house for just the
two of them would be too costly and too large to maintain. At the
same time, they dislike apartments because they are noisy and "impersonal." Mobile-home parks solve both of these problems. Mobile
homes are quieter than apartments, with no shared walls and noises
from below or above, and "adult" parks also have quiet streets,
much favored by childless adults who dislike the noise of young
children and by elderly adults who have become sensitive to noise
of any kind. Only occasionally a lonely grandparent in Idle Haven
complained that "really, this place is too quiet; I like to hear young
voices, so long as they are happy and having fun." Even those who
thought the park was too quiet, however, acknowledged that they
would not want children living there; they argued that the lots were
too small and that children would be constantly infringing on

others' privacy—running on their lawns, breaking windows, or just
interrupting afternoon naps.

The less impersonal nature of mobile-home parks as compared
to apartments or ordinary neighborhoods is also likely to be of
special importance to older childless couples or single and widowed
individuals. Such people are more likely to need a source for casual
conversation; they are more likely to feel lonely (Shanas, *et al.,*
1968:285); and they are more likely to fear being incapacitated and
having no one available whom they can call on for assistance. The
need to make some formal arrangement to substitute for the care
that might otherwise come from children or other relatives is also
expressed in the choice of retirement homes and communities. The
director of one such Bay Area retirement home—an elegant apartment complex where individuals live in private apartments but eat
in a communal dining room and are guaranteed "lifetime" care should
they become disabled—says his facility is particularly popular with retired, unmarried schoolteachers.

Idle Haven and other "adult" mobile-home parks in California
and Florida (Hoyt, 1954), fulfill many of the same functions as retirement communities, but they cater to a different class of people.
This is not merely a question of income differentials, although the
apartment complex favored by school teachers, which necessitates a
joining fee of $12,000 to $33,000 and monthly payments of $250 to
$500, is well beyond the means of most of the people living in Idle
Haven. It is more a question of life styles. Some of the people in
Idle Haven who could have afforded condominium apartments or
houses in retirement communities, and who looked at such places
before buying a mobile home, said they did not like them: there
was too much "keeping up with the Joneses," or "not enough of the
kinds of things I like to do." Their discomfort in such surroundings
is an accurate reflection of the different class-based cultures that
exist in middle-class retirement communities as opposed to working-
class mobile-home parks.

Table II compares the occupations of all the men interviewed
in Idle Haven with a national sample of the heads of households of
two or more persons living in mobile homes and with the heads of
families in a national current (1967) population survey. Idle Haven
has even fewer professional people, managers and proprietors than
the national sample of mobile-home residents, and both Idle Haven
and the national sample have substantially fewer residents in these
categories than the national sample of the United States population

as a whole. If one reclassifies the retired men in Idle Haven on the basis of their former occupations, 70.6 per cent of all the residents fall into the blue-collar category (that is, craftsmen, foremen, operatives, and service workers) and 29.5 per cent wear (or wore) white collars (professionals, technical workers, managers, officials and proprietors [except farm], clerical and sales workers, and students). Among the blue-collar workers interviewed in Idle Haven, 15 per cent are, or have been, in construction work. Many of these individuals have lived in mobile homes since World War II, largely because of the transient nature of their occupation. However, the

TABLE II

Occupations of Male Mobile-home Residents
Compared with National Male-occupation Categories
(expressed in per cent of male population)

	Idle Haven[a]	National Mobile Home Survey[b]	U. S. Population Survey[b]
	per cent	*per cent*	*per cent*
Professional	1.8	7.1	10.9
Managers, Proprietors	2.7	8.1	15.0
Clerical and Sales	11.6	7.2	10.5
Craftsmen and Foremen	33.9	21.5	16.5
Operatives	9.8	21.4	15.7
Service Workers	3.6	4.8	6.2
Retired	33.9[c]	20.9[c]	20.5[c]
Students	2.7	0.0	0.0
Laborers and Farm Workers	0.0	8.9	4.7

[a] Occupations were classified using the U.S. Bureau of the Census, 1960 Census of Population, *Alphabetical Index of Occupations and Industries* (Washington, D.C.: Government Printing Office, 1960), rev. ed.

[b] U. S. Dept. of Housing and Urban Development, *Housing Surveys: Parts 1 and 2* (Washington, D.C.: Government Printing Office, November 1968), p. 89.

[c] The occupational category "Retired" of course offers no clue to the pre-retirement occupation and, hence, socioeconomic status of its members. It is a pity that neither the government's study of mobile home residents nor any other survey that I have seen asked retired residents what their pre-retirement occupation was. For a further breakdown of the Idle Haven statistics, see below and also Table XII, p. 184.

majority of the blue-collar residents hold or have retired from other jobs—as electricians, plumbers, pipe-fitters, machinists, mechanics, truck drivers, warehousemen, and the like—and their reasons for moving into a mobile home were not directly related to their work.

Most of the white-collar residents of Idle Haven are members of the lower middle class in terms of the types of jobs they hold and the educational levels they have attained. They include clerical workers, bookkeepers, business machine operators, and the like. For a number of these men their white-collar jobs represented a demotion rather than a step upward; some of them were highly paid blue-collar workers until an industrial accident or ill health forced them to take desk jobs. The proprietors include primarily men who have owned or managed grocery stores, print shops, or laundry and dry cleaning establishments. Even the professional people in the park have close ties to the working class. One, a professional musician in a small group, was a construction worker most of his life. Two others are retired civil and construction engineers. When I commented to one of these engineers that he was one of the few college-educated men in the park and wondered what he had in common with some of the other men, he replied that he had worked around such men all his life. As an engineer he had often been on project sites, checking out jobs and consulting with foremen and their work-crews.

Of the women interviewed in Idle Haven, 17.6 per cent had never been employed, 24.7 per cent were currently employed, and 57.7 per cent had been but were not currently employed. A few of the women who had worked had done so only briefly during World War II, but many more had worked for substantial portions of their lives. Of all the women who had ever worked, 10.3 per cent had held professional or managerial and proprietorial positions. The professions were primarily teaching and nursing; however, among the proprietors, a surprisingly large number of women had owned small businesses, such as fabric or dress shops, restaurants, or beauty parlors. By far the largest group of women, 55.5 per cent was working or had worked in clerical and sales positions; and the remaining 34.2 per cent had either worked in industry (on an assembly line) or in a service occupation (e.g., as a non-professional nurse, baby-sitter, or waitress).

Although for many individuals retirement or widowhood may mean a drop in social status—that is, in one's position and prestige—to say nothing of a drop in income, one's social class and the cultural preferences that accompany it are not so likely to change. Thus it is interesting to note that the retired men of Idle Haven do not constitute a disproportionate segment of the white-collar group. Had they done so, one might surmise that the retired had experienced a drop in their class ranking and that more were now living in blue-collar surroundings than when they were still employed. Similarly, the late husbands of the widows in Idle Haven included no greater proportion of professional or white-collar workers than the park as a whole, so that one cannot conclude that the widows experienced a change in class as a result of their widowhood.

Just as class affiliations are likely to remain stable throughout an individual's working life and into retirement, so too is social class likely to remain stable from generation to generation. As Lipset and Bendix (1959) have demonstrated, inter-generational social mobility in the United States is not as pervasive as is popularly believed. When parents in Idle Haven were asked about the occupations of their sons and their daughters' husbands, one encountered time and again the same spectrum of jobs found among the fathers: sheetmetal worker, truck driver, machinist, bartender, construction worker. Nevertheless, there was some upward mobility among the children of Idle Haven residents. Whereas in Idle Haven itself, 29.5 per cent of the men held white-collar jobs, among their sons 35 per cent held white-collar jobs. If one compares the occupation of the son with that of his father, one finds that 24 per cent of the sons of blue-collar workers held white-collar jobs. This latter percentage is somewhat lower than that in a national sample survey which found that 33 per cent of the sons of skilled and semi-skilled fathers held white-collar jobs (Lipset and Bendix, 1959:89). However, the Idle Haven findings support another of Lipset's and Bendix's conclusions: that there is more upward than downward mobility in the United States. Only 15 per cent of the sons of white-collar fathers held blue-collar jobs.

Interestingly enough, and despite popular assumptions about the prevalence of hypergamy, the daughters of Idle Haven residents were less socially mobile than the sons. Only 28 per cent of all the daughters had husbands who held white-collar jobs, and of the daughters who had blue-collar fathers only 18 per cent had married white-collar husbands. However, downward mobility among the daughters was identical to that of the sons. Only 15 per cent of the daughters of white-collar fathers had married blue-collar men. We shall return to some of these findings concerning the social class and

mobility patterns of children in Chapter 4, when we turn to the relationships between parents and their grown children.

Social class is not merely measured by one's occupation but
also by one's level of education, and of course the two are closely
related. A higher education makes it more likely that one will obtain
a white-collar job, and holding a white-collar job makes it more
likely that one's children, in turn, will go to college and hold white-
collar jobs. The educational levels of the residents surveyed in Idle
Haven are set forth in Table III. The percentages are very similar

TABLE III

Educational Level Attained by Residents of Idle Haven

Last grade completed	Men	Women
	per cent	*per cent*
8th or less	16.5	21.3
9th - 11th	24.7	23.6
12th	44.3	36.2
Some college	7.2	7.9
Four years of college or nurse's training	7.2	9.4
More than 4 years of college	0.0	1.5

to those of the government's study of mobile-home residents. This
study found that 7.5 per cent of the household heads living in
mobile homes had completed less than the eighth grade; 74.5 per
cent had completed anywhere from the eighth through the twelfth
grade; and 18 per cent had had one or more years of college (HUD,
1968:87). Compared to a national U. S. population sample, the
government study concluded that "the proportion of mobile home
heads with some high school education is higher than for the population in general but . . . there are relatively fewer college men in
mobile homes than in homes in the general population" (HUD,
1968:88).

It may be that the lower educational level of Idle Haven residents is partly a function of their age. Many respondents implied
this when they said regretfully, "Well, in my day one had to get out
and go to work . . ." or "In those days it wasn't so important to go to
college . . . ." Nevertheless, among all of their sons only 23 per cent
had had four years or less in college, and many of these sons had
white-collar, if not always college-educated, fathers. There was,
among the residents of Idle Haven, a genuine ambivalence toward

higher education. Those who had college-educated children or grandchildren were very proud of that fact, and many residents who had not gone to college tried to mitigate this lack by claims of "business college," home study courses, and the like. One man announced grandly that, considering how much more the schools taught people when he was young, he had the *equivalent* of a college education; this was a prelude to his admission that he had only finished the eighth grade.

At the same time this sort of reverence and desire for a college education is undermined by news of student riots, of Communists' being allowed to teach, and of the hippy drug scene around many campuses. "I hope my granddaughter *doesn't* go to college," one man said vehemently; "it can't do anything but harm her." Others wondered aloud what difference it would make if the universities and colleges were simply closed for a while. The fact that the children of the middle class are now rejecting as worthless the educational criteria that were (and still are) being used to keep blue-collar workers from holding certain types of jobs makes these blue-collar workers both angry and self-righteous. The behavior of college students—and the allegations they make against institutions of higher learning—merely confirm something most workers already suspected: that book-learning is really nonsense and those who have advanced degrees are, as Spiro Agnew put it, "effete snobs." But if a college education is so useless, they wonder, why are all the cards stacked against people who don't have one? Why do corporation executives and doctors and lawyers make $30,000 or $60,000 or $100,000 a year, when a hard-working machinist can consider himself lucky to make $10,000?

The problem of a low income is an important one for many but not all of the residents of Idle Haven. The income distribution in the park is set forth in Table IV, where it is compared with the percentages obtained by the government's nation-wide survey of mobile-home households. As the table reveals, Idle Haven has more people with yearly incomes of $4,000 or less, but it also has more people with yearly incomes over $10,000. The median household income in the government's study was $6,353, very similar to the median household income in Idle Haven, which was $6,760. Both of these fall below the median income for the U. S. population as a whole ($7,440).

Table IV also reveals that the income distribution curve for Idle Haven is bimodal, with high points occurring in the $2,001–

$4,000 and $10,001–$14,000 groups. The origins of this bimodal curve are clearly visible in Figure II, where the incomes are graphed

TABLE IV
Income Distribution Among Residents
of Mobile-home Parks

Annual Income	Idle Haven (N=138)	Gov't Survey of Mobile Homes
	per cent	*per cent*
Less than $2,000	9.5 (13)	5.7
$ 2,001 - $ 4,000	19.6 (27)	14.0
$ 4,001 - $ 6,000	15.2 (21)	25.9
$ 6,001 - $ 8,000	15.2 (21)	24.8
$ 8,001 - $10,000	15.9 (22)	15.1
$10,001 - $14,000	18.8 (26)	12.2[a]
$14,001 - $18,000	5.1 (7)	1.4[a]
$18,001 - $24,000	.7 (1)	.9[a]

[a] Government categories here are $10,000–$14,999; $15,000–$19,999; and $20,000 and over (HUD, 1968:91).

according to whether people are retired or still employed. Among the retired, 78 per cent have incomes below the median, whereas 89 per cent of the employed have incomes above the median. Of the forty households with incomes below $4,001 a year all but two (working widows) were fully retired, and all but eleven were single-person households. Of the thirteen cases of incomes below $2,000, all were single individuals.

These figures tell us something about the financial condition of people in Idle Haven, but perhaps more revealing are the sources of income, particularly among the retired. Ten of the householders interviewed (nine of them widows) were receiving Old Age Security benefits, or what the recipients generally referred to as "welfare." OAS payments are administered by the separate counties in California and in order to qualify one must pass a means test and have been a resident of California during the entire year preceding the application and for five out of the previous nine years (Pinner, *et al.*, 1959:15–21). Assets of the applicant cannot amount to more than $5,000 assessed value in real property and $1,200 ($2,000 for a couple) in personal property. Monthly payments to people who have qualified vary, depending on their other sources of income, and depending also on an variety of special needs for which extra amounts of money are granted. For example, someone who is unable to do his own housework may be granted an extra $20 a month to hire someone to come in once a week. One ailing widow in Idle Haven who could not do her own housecleaning or shopping received an extra $20 a month, with which she hired another widow in Idle Haven who was herself receiving OAS payments.

Most of the recipients of OAS benefits are widows or couples who have no source of retirement income other than social security payments. The men have usually been self-employed or have worked at a variety of jobs, none of which involved joining a union or contributing to a union pension plan. They managed to accumulate no savings, or their savings barely enabled them to buy a mobile home, or a major illness (or the death of the husband) had long

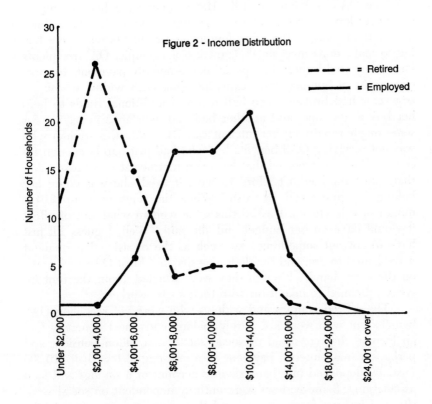

Figure 2 - Income Distribution

ago wiped out what little savings the family had accumulated. With OAS payments and social security combined, single individuals in Idle Haven had a monthly income of approximately $135 and couples of about $200. Although all of the OAS recipients interviewed owned their mobile homes, the major portion of their income still went to rent—spaces in Idle Haven cost from $75 to $95 a month, depending on the size of the mobile home—and to gas and electricity. The balance went for food and for small savings accumulated to pay the yearly license fee on the mobile home and insurance, if any. Medical bills were handled by Medicare. What few clothes these people needed were usually bought at a local "flea market" where used items of all sorts were sold. One neatly dressed widow proudly showed me her second-hand wardrobe and proceeded to tell me what she had paid for every item: there wasn't a thing that had cost more than a dollar.

The OAS recipients in Idle Haven may have been living on extremely low incomes, but they seemed to be less anxious about money than some of the other low-income residents who were trying to make ends meet on their own. For example, OAS recipients knew they could apply for special one-time-only payments to meet extraordinary but necessary expenses. One OAS widow whose refrigerator had broken down had received additional funds to help her buy a new one, and another had had assistance in paying for some major repairs on her ancient car. By contrast, a woman who was not receiving OAS benefits but who had just barely enough income to live on, reported that her oven thermostat was broken and that, since she couldn't afford to have it fixed, she was doing her baking "by guess and by gosh." When the rents went up $10 a month in Idle Haven, I asked this same woman what sort of effect it would have on her budget and she said, "Well, I guess I'll just have to cut out something else—such as the occasional permanent wave I used to get, and the daily newspaper." Most OAS recipients, on the other hand, although they were worried about the rent increase, planned to take it up with their social workers.

The retired couples and widows who were not receiving OAS benefits but who were just barely making ends meet generally had an income that consisted of social security, a union pension, and perhaps a small interest payment on a nest-egg of less than $10,000 (usually deposited in a bank savings account or a savings and loan association). Some widows were entirely dependent on social security and interest from savings, and these women were often in the most difficult position of all. Living on very tight budgets, they nevertheless dared not cut into the principal in their savings accounts for fear of depleting it. Yet in some cases their advanced age and a rational calculation of their life expectancy, combined with the fact that many had no survivors to inherit, would have made living on the principal a sensible course of action. But deep fears of running out of money and "having to go on welfare" kept them from trying this. By contrast, one widow who knew she would have to apply for OAS benefits after her husband's death and who was on bad terms with her upwardly mobile son, had first cashed in her life insurance policy and with the proceeds paid for a modest funeral for herself and then bought a huge and splendid color television set! It was a kind of "live now" gesture that the self-sufficient but low-income widows in the park would have been afraid to indulge in, although many could probably have afforded it.

The retired couples and widows who had incomes over $4,000 a year generally had some "investments," the most popular among working-class men and women being some form of real estate. Some couples had lived in one or more houses during their working years and continued to receive payments on the mortgages they still held. Others had bought several lake-front or wooded lots in a recreation area which they were now selling off or holding for future appreciation; and a number of individuals had at one time bought an apartment building, in which they had frequently lived as resident managers. With their advancing age, many of the people who had owned real estate had sold their holdings because looking after property had become too troublesome or, in the case of several couples who had owned apartment houses, because they did not want to face the eventuality of having to rent to Negroes.

Next to buying real estate, working-class individuals seem most prone to invest in mutual funds. Stocks and the stock market in general are regarded with some suspicion and fear, unless the stocks are in companies with which the individual has had some personal experience. For example, several of the better-off retired couples and widows owned stock in mobile-home manufacturing firms or shares in local mobile-home parks, or they owned some stock in the company for which they used to work. But stock brokers—much like bankers in earlier years—are regarded as remote and somewhat sinister figures who are not interested in dealing with the small investor. Mutual fund salesmen, by contrast, act more like insurance men, and many of them are adept at giving simple, illustrated talks about how mutual funds work and how much more lucrative investments in them are than putting one's money in a savings and loan company or buying life insurance. During the six months that I was interviewing people in Idle Haven, two mutual fund salesmen came to speak in the recreation hall—each at the invitation of a satisfied customer who was a resident in the park. Although mutual funds may be a good form of investment for some of the residents in Idle Haven, for the many who have only a limited amount of savings and no expectancy of earning more, it struck me as a dangerous come-on. Neither salesman who visited Idle Haven explained about the nature of front-loading funds (wherein the salesman's commission is deducted in advance) or mentioned that the typical sales commission on mutual funds is 8 per cent of the amount invested. Fortunately, the same widows who are cautiously living off their interest from savings without ever dipping into the principal, are probably also too cautious to reinvest their entire means of livelihood.

Among the residents of Idle Haven who are not retired, the average annual income of men ranges between $6,000 and $10,000. Of the twenty-eight couples interviewed who had incomes above $10,000, eighteen were cases in which both husband and wife were fully employed. Thus, most of the high incomes in the park can be explained by their being double incomes. Typically, the wife will earn between $4,000 and $6,000; but there were several instances in which a highly trained wife (e.g., a legal secretary or a data-processing clerk) earned about the same amount as her husband.

These income figures have an important bearing on the decision to live in a mobile home. As Chinoy (1965) has noted, most middle-aged working-class men realize that they have reached the top of the ladder insofar as income and job advancement are concerned: they realize that they will never make the jump into the managerial world and that further increments in salary will come only as a result of union demands and not as a result of job mobility. In fact, some men in their late 40s and 50s may face a serious decrement in salary long before they retire because an industrial accident or poor health may force them to take a less strenuous job. There were several men in Idle Haven who had been highly paid structural steel and construction workers when they were younger but who had spent or were spending the last 10 or 15 of their working years as union dispatchers or as white-collar workers at approximately half of their former pay. Given such working-class barriers to further financial improvement, it is not surprising that some middle-aged individuals decide to buy a $10,000 mobile home in order to pay it off well before they retire.

The data from Idle Haven reveal two distinct patterns of mobile-home purchasing which are related to whether or not the buyer is retired rather than to the over-all cost of the mobile home. Of those who were not retired, 69 per cent had financed their purchase of a mobile home, whereas of those who were retired when they bought their units (including widows who bought a mobile home after they were widowed) 87 per cent had paid cash. The national mobile-home survey reveals much the same pattern, for it found that of those with incomes of less than $2,000 a year (presumably including primarily retired individuals), 57 per cent had paid all cash for their units—a percentage not matched until one reaches the $20,000 or more income group, of whom 59.6 per cent had paid cash (HUD, 1968:132). The national survey as a whole reported that only 21.1 per cent of its sample had paid all cash for their mobile homes, whereas in Idle Haven 60 per cent of those interviewed had paid cash for the full purchase price—again reflecting the large number of retired individuals in Idle Haven. Typically the widowed or retired sold their homes, which they either owned outright or in which they had a large equity, whereas middle-aged buyers who were still working either used their savings for a down payment or sold a home in which they had a much smaller equity.

In Idle Haven half of the mobile homes surveyed cost between $6,000 and $10,000, with the median price being $8,133. The national survey found that the median price paid for mobile homes in 1966 was $5,585 and that 69 per cent of the mobile homes surveyed cost between $4,000 and $8,000 (HUD, 1968:72); however, there is no indication what percentage of these prices were paid for used mobile homes, which cost considerably less than new ones. In Idle Haven, two-thirds of the mobile homes surveyed were new when purchased by their present owners, and one-third had been bought used, either from a previous resident in Idle Haven or from the lot of a dealer. Of the new mobile homes, 95 per cent cost more than $6,000 and 65 per cent cost more than the median price; whereas of the used mobile homes 56 per cent had cost their present owners less than $6,000 and 75 per cent had cost less than the median.

The difference in price between new and used mobile homes

is probably even more marked than these figures indicate, since many people who gave the price of their new mobile home did not include "extras" such as awnings, porches, steps, and skirting (the metal or wood facing that hides the wheels from view), which can add as much as $2,000 to the basic cost. On the other hand, the price of a used mobile home already set up in a park usually includes these extras. People who financed their mobile homes also probably underestimated the total cost, since they usually quoted the original sale price without including the interest they had paid or were paying. Such interest can add considerably to the cost of a mobile home, since most mobile homes are financed just like automobiles, by banks and finance companies utilizing "add-on" interest charges. (That is, interest at the stated rate is computed on the entire principal rather than on the declining balance.) In 1970, for example, the Bank of America was making mobile-home loans at a stated interest rate of 6.25 per cent. This meant that on a typical ten-year loan of $10,000 one ended up paying a total of $6,250 interest, an actual annual interest rate of 10.59 per cent. Some people in Idle Haven who were paying off such loans said they would not have bought a mobile home had they realized how much interest they would have to pay.

The low cost of mobile homes is one feature that makes them attractive to certain groups of people, but it does not explain why some and not others decide to buy a mobile home. For example, why are they not more popular with low-income ghetto families? The national mobile-home survey found that less than 2 per cent of the residents were black—a fact which it attributed to the high interest charged on mobile home loans and the attendant difficulties in meeting payments (HUD, 1968:92). Such an assumption, however, ignores many more salient factors that mitigate against Negroes' buying mobile homes, which we shall turn to in the following chapter.

In this chapter we have singled out some of the sociological characteristics of today's mobile-home residents. They tend to belong to the working and lower-middle classes; in California they tend to be elderly and retired and they tend to have fewer surviving children than the population as a whole. It is not impossible that at some future time the characteristics of mobile-home residents will change and that both the reasons for buying a mobile home and the resultant social structure in parks will also change. Already there are certain groups of people—for example, servicemen and their families living in mobile-home parks near a base, or construction workers and their families living in mobile homes at a remote construction site—who have formed highly specialized communities of mobile-home residents that will not be considered in this study. The particular group described in this study also possesses certain special characteristics, but it is a growing segment of the mobile-home population and the residents' choice of mobile-home parks has important implications for life in urban centers. Let us therefore look more closely at the reasons why they, and not others, have chosen this way of life and at how effectively a place like Idle Haven meets their needs.

3. The Search for Community

It has long been an article of liberal faith in our supposedly classless society that people should live in mixed urban neighborhoods where various ethnic groups, age groups, and income groups can mingle freely to their mutual interest and advantage. Thus Jane Jacobs (1961) has argued that Greenwich Village is a prototype of the mixed urban usage that city planners ought to encourage, with light industry, shops, cheap walk-ups, and expensive town-houses all existing cheek-by-jowl to produce a lively, egalitarian urban scene. Others have argued that the ghetto is purely a product of racism on the part of whites and poverty on the part of blacks, and that it will and should disappear when these two causative factors have been eradicated. Still others maintain that the flight to the suburbs by middle-class whites is a racist reaction likely to backfire on the whites, who will find such one-class communities boring, status conscious enclaves.

In 1962, Raymond Vernon challenged some of these assumptions by suggesting that most urban residents have always lived in segregated housing and that the flight to the suburbs by middle-class whites and their replacement in the central city by poor blacks is not a new process but only one that has vastly expanded during the past two decades. Among the causes he cites for this increased population shift are the post-World War II Negro migration from the countryside into the cities and the pervasive presence of the automobile, which has greatly facilitated the outward movement of whites. Vernon also argues that many jobs have followed the middle class into the suburbs and that therefore the average suburbanite has little to lure him back to the central city:

> "What they want out of life is to have access to their job, which for the most part has shifted outward, too; access to the bridge club, which is no unique institution and is not located in the central business district; access to the American Legion Post, of which there are many, not one" (1962: 61).

The only people who are seriously disturbed by the decline of the central city, Vernon argues, are cosmopolites who enjoy some of its unique institutions—such as opera performances, symphony concerts and art galleries, and businessmen such as bankers and stockbrokers who need to operate in a face-to-face environment. For these people the central city is a powerful magnet. But for the middle-income groups now living comfortably in the suburbs, the only development that might draw them back would be a kind of "golden ghetto" neighborhood, large enough to decontaminate it from the surrounding slums, in which these groups could feel secure in their property values and life styles.

Lest this assessment seem unnecessarily cruel to middle-class values, it should be borne in mind that other groups in America have also preferred to live in segregated neighborhoods. As Herbert Gans (1962) has demonstrated, ethnic ties may lead individuals to remain in a homogeneous neighborhood that other groups have branded a slum even when many of these individuals could afford to move elsewhere. It is possible that even if racial prejudice toward and poverty among blacks were to disappear completely, a substantial number of them would continue to live in homogeneous communities. In this connection, Bennett Berger has noted:

> "Even after discrimination on the basis of race disappears, . . . we have no evidence to suggest that segregation will ever disappear. If the experience of other ethnic groups is any guide (and I know of no better guide), many Negroes will choose to live among their own 'kind' even after they have formally free choice of housing. However 'kind' may be defined in the future, there is no reason *not* to expect social class and ethnicity to continue to play an important role—although it is quite conceivable that color may eventually not have much to do with ethnicity" (1966:90).

In situations where ethnicity does not provide the overriding bond, socioeconomic status usually does. As Eichler and Kaplan discovered when they investigated how "planned" communities were being received by the buying public:

> "From the buyers' viewpoint . . . one basic purpose of 'planning' in a new community is to minimize the insecurity that surrounds such a venture. . . . 'Planning' to these residents was a guarantee against the introduction of 'undesirable' elements close to one's house and immediate surroundings. Not surprisingly, the most undesirable were lower-priced homes inhabited by lower-income people" (1967:114–16).

Carl Werthman, who conducted the interviews on which Eichler and Kaplan based part of their study, has argued elsewhere that:

> "The meaning of 'planning' to most middle-class suburbanites is thus completely clear. It is defined as the process of maximizing the symbolic status of a community class image and the profit potential of homes; its purpose is the simultaneous protection of class image and financial investment; and the sources of emotional attachment to this definition and purpose are mobility aspirations and fear" (1968:127).

Even in a virtually uni-priced development like Levittown, Pennsylvania (where, in 1958, there were only three basic house types costing from $11,500 to $14,500), Gans found that new residents rapidly segregated themselves on the basis of socioeconomic class as defined by occupation and education and along religious and ethnic lines. Thus within a very short time various civic groups and clubs were organized which functioned primarily as sorting devices: working-class men tended to join the Veterans of Foreign Wars or the volunteer fire brigade; lower-middle-class men joined the Lions, Kiwanis, and Junior Chamber of Commerce; upper-middle-class men interested themselves in school and civic groups. Churches sprang up that divided people along religious and, often, ethnic lines.

Gans concludes that such sorting into homogeneous groups is a natural and desirable process in any community, and he even recommends that homogeneous blocks be deliberately formed—e.g., blocks on which everyone is working-class—because they make for friendlier relations among neighbors. It is interesting, therefore, that these sociological insights fail him completely when it comes to the issue of the racial integration of Levittown, which he supports even if it means wrecking the social structure of the community:

> "The criteria on which the advocacy of block homogeneity and community heterogeneity is based cannot justify racial homogeneity at either level. . . . homogeneity is only one value among many, and if any person chooses to move among people who differ in race—or age, income, religion, or any other background characteristic—he has the right to do so and the right to governmental support in his behalf. That such a move might wreak havoc with a block's social life or the community's consensus is of lower priority than the maintenance of such values as freedom of choice and equality" (1969:173–74).

This may be a ringing statement of belief, but Gans's own research would suggest that even where such *de facto* integration occurs it still does not lead to much actual social integration.

Just as suburban communities have been derided for their racially segregated, single class, age-homogeneous populations, so dire predictions were made when the first retirement communities were built. Elderly people needed to have younger and more active neighbors, it was argued; they needed to see and be around children. Yet retirement communities have proved to be popular with the people for whom they were designed, and a recent study of elderly individuals living in a large city has demonstrated that even in a heterogeneous urban setting, elderly people in age-homogeneous neighborhoods (defined as neighborhoods in which 50 per cent of the households included a man 65 or older or a woman 62 or older) have more friends among their neighbors than elderly people living in age-heterogeneous neighborhoods (Rosow, 1967). The study also found that socioeconomic class was an important variable and that middle-class elderly individuals were less likely to form friendships with their neighbors—and therefore less likely to benefit from homogeneous neighborhoods—than were working-class individuals.

Age, ethnicity, religion, socioeconomic status—all of these are social characteristics on the basis of which people may form groups that meet at a particular place and time or groups that are physically anchored to a neighborhood or enclave. Thus one may be elderly and belong to a Senior Citizens Club that meets once a week at the local YMCA, or one may choose to live in a retirement community. One may be of Italian descent and belong to an Italo-American Club, or one may live in an Italian neighborhood. Socioeconomic status cuts across social characteristics such as ethnicity and age to produce further subgroups. Elderly people of working-class backgrounds are likely to live in different retirement communities (or belong to different clubs) than elderly people who held professional white-collar jobs during their working days, and elderly working-class Jews are likely to choose still different clubs and neighborhoods. (Idle Haven, for example, contains no Jews and is 78 per cent Protestant.)

There was a time when it was more fashionable to recognize these facts of American social organization, and when, in fact, sociologists seemed to glory in the existence of different urban enclaves. The "Chicago school" of sociology that flourished at the University of Chicago during the 1920s and 1930s produced dozens of studies that testified to the social diversity of the city—a diversity that could be so clearly mapped in terms of neighborhoods that many sociologists ended up attributing causality to the ecological variable. Thus Faris and Dunham (1939) not only determined the rates of mental disorder for various parts of the city but also suggested that the high rates in the central city could be explained by the "social disorganization" of the district itself rather than by the socioeconomic, ethnic, age, or other characteristics of the people who live there. Similarly, Louis Wirth argued that as Jews moved away from the ghetto they would lose their ethnic identity, thereby attributing causality to the enclave that was itself a product of ethnic ties. As Amitai Etzioni has argued with regard to Wirth's book:

> "Wirth sees the geographical criterion as essential. Follow-
> ing Park he assumes that a group which is not concentrated
> in one area disappears, i.e., assimilates. . . . We would like
> to suggest that a group can maintain its cultural and social
> integration and identity, without having an ecological basis.
> . . . [However,] by stating that a group is non-ecological, it
> is not implied that the group is completely randomly dis-
> tributed in space. Most ethnic groups are relatively con-
> centrated on certain levels of stratification. The stratification
> structure uses space as one way of segregating groups and
> symbolizing distance and prestige" (1959:257–58).

The use of space to symbolize distance and prestige is certainly not unique to American society, but it may be more highly valued among Americans than elsewhere. Carl Werthman has argued that:

> "Since Americans do not explicitly acknowledge the exis-
> tence of a social stratification system based on differences
> in class and ethnic culture, the great majority of middle-class
> people have a strong tendency to translate the symbols of
> social superiority directly into reality, and thus any threat
> to these symbols is simultaneously a threat to personal
> identity. . . . [They] in effect rely on the appearance of their
> homes and the conduct of their families to demonstrate their
> membership in the middle class—a reliance on respectability
> that often makes them panic at the first sight of long hair
> on a teenager or weeds on a nearby neighbor's lawn" (1968:
> 152, 153).

As Werthman goes on to point out, one of the problems with tying one's class image to the appearance of one's home and lawn is that the desired image actually depends on the condition of the entire block or neighborhood, so that one "lazy guy" or one slovenly family that just "doesn't give a damn" can seriously undermine all of one's personal efforts. Moreover, the individuals who have the most to lose by not keeping up their homes and lawns—that is, the working class, for whom the next lower rung on the status ladder is the lower lower class, or "poor white trash"—are also the individuals who have the least money and the least energy to expend on such efforts. Many middle-class families solve the problem of lawn upkeep by hiring a gardener, and among those who do not, yard work is often considered a healthy form of weekend exercise for the husband who sits behind a desk all day. But for the working-class husband who cannot afford a gardener and who comes home dog-tired from a long shift as a railroad engineer or a machinist, mowing and weeding the lawn, or painting the house during his vacation, may be an impossible demand on his energy.

This working-class dilemma—the strong desire to "keep up" one's home and lawn on the one hand, and the physical and financial difficulties of doing so on the other hand—explains why many of the residents in Idle Haven cited ease of maintenance as a major reason why they had bought a mobile home. The exteriors of modern mobile homes are made of painted aluminum that requires only occasional hosing down with water and perhaps a yearly coat of wax (similar to that used on cars) to maintain its appearance. By contrast, one middle-aged not-yet-retired resident of Idle Haven said that he had painted the entire exterior of his former tract home three times in the seven years he had lived there. Exterior and interior maintenance of a home becomes even more problematic for widows—particularly those who have older homes seriously in need of repairs—and for older men who are in poor health, although these people tended to cite maintenance problems as a reason for buying a mobile home no more frequently than couples who were still healthy and employed but who had simply tired of the effort involved.[1]

---

[1] It has also been suggested that the popularity of mobile homes with working-class families reflects their insecurity about proper interior decorating: better to buy a fully furnished, color-coordinated "unit" than to risk making a wrong choice (Kendall, 1971:105–6). However, I found little evidence for this view in Idle Haven. To begin with, many of the new mobile homes are only partially furnished by dealers, and almost none of the used ones (sold either by dealers or by private individuals) comes furnished. Those who had bought fully furnished mobile homes had usually done so because they had no furniture of their own and it was cheaper than buying pieces individually. Many of these people went on to say that the furniture that came with their mobile home was shoddy and they had gradually replaced most of it. Residents who had moved into Idle Haven after selling their homes had almost always bought an unfurnished mobile home in order to use at least some of their own furniture. One widow reported that she had searched for over a year for a used mobile home with wood panelling that would match her prized antiques. On the other hand, the option of "starting over" with brand-new, matched furniture obviously appealed to some people who had spent a lifetime with hand-me-down odds

Gardening and its burdens also loomed large among the reasons why residents of Idle Haven said they had bought mobile homes. As often as not they did not dislike gardening as such but rather the enormity of the task they faced—particularly with regard to lawns. In Idle Haven most of them dispensed with lawns altogether—instead filling their small plots with colored rocks or redwood shavings—but many saved enough space to plant elaborate flower gardens. One retired man devoted a triangle of land behind his mobile home to twenty-four carefully-tended tomato plants, and an extremely old lady who could barely see or walk nevertheless kept an immaculate flower bed full of roses, fuschias, and dahlias. Even people whose gardens were entirely given over to rocks and plastic plants had usually spent considerable time and money in "decorating" their spot, but it was a single effort instead of a continuing concern.

The desire to have a garden that is status-enhancing but not bothersome was illustrated by the removal of a beautiful stand of eucalyptus trees in Idle Haven. About twenty of these trees ran along one side of the park, screening a section of railroad track only a few feet behind it. People who lived near the trees were always complaining about how messy they were and one autumn day a strong wind left their corner of the park ankle-deep in leaves. When I returned about a week later I found that, much to my dismay, all of the trees had been sawed down. However, the residents, some of whom were now only ten unobstructed feet from the railroad track, were pleased with the improvement.

Another gardening problem that Werthman points to—the question of how to keep one's neighbor from diminishing one's own status—is solved in mobile-home parks. Modern mobile-home parks have regulations that require tenants to keep their spaces neat and attractive and some, like Idle Haven, specify that "if a space is neglected, the management reserves the right to take over its care and bill the tenant for the actual cost of maintenance." Park residents are also protected from other practices that may have annoyed them in the working-class neighborhoods from which most of them came. One mobile-home resident and GSMOL official summarized some of the advantages of mobile-home living as follows:

---

and ends. One widow who clearly would have liked a decorator-styled interior pointed to her own rather pleasant if shabby collection of furniture and said to me, "I call this style 'Early Halloween.' "

"Controlled 5–10 mile per hour traffic allowing bicycle exercises and walking . . .

"No John-come-lately backyard or unpicked fruit and vegetables with the ever-present gnats.

"More rock landscaping, resulting in fewer rodents, moles and moths . . .

"No unsightly street parking nor lawn parking and dripping oil from cars.

"No open garage doors exposing garage clutter to the street.

"No clothesline displays.

"No street ball-games and litter.

"No neighbor building-line encroachments.

"No Jerry-built buildings.

"No unsightly utilities. [Modern parks have underground telephone and electrical wires.]

"No unsightly automobile repairing" (WMN, Oct. 23, 1967).

It is interesting, with regard to such park regulations and the general approval of them expressed by residents, that two of the couples interviewed in Idle Haven manifested strong compulsive tendencies—tendencies so pronounced in one case that even other residents had noted the mania for order and cleanliness. Both of these couples were childless, probably by choice. In one case they had moved into a mobile home because the maintenance of their large ("and beautiful") home and garden had become too much work for them; in the other case they had sold an equally immaculate home because, according to the wife who was alone a good deal, burglars were always trying to break in. In both cases the move to small, spotlessly kept mobile homes had seemed to ease, or at least render manageable, the problem of maintaining order in a messy, unpredictable world. Even so, one wife seemed to spend most of her days washing her plastic plants and cleaning the inside of her mobile home, into which no one (not even guests or interviewers) was allowed unless he took off his shoes; and the other lady spent much of her time washing clothes, since she and her husband could only wear things once before they needed to be cleaned. These cases were, of course, unusual; but they may reveal one personality type strongly attracted to the orderliness and security of mobile-home parks.

The regulations in mobile-home parks not only ensure that one's neighbors will maintain their lawns; they also ensure that one's neighbors will behave themselves and maintain proper standards of decorum. As one mobile-home resident and publicist has noted:

> "Modern mobile-home parks have regulations which insure that neighbors will not strew the landscape with debris or cleave the atmosphere with hi-fi sound at midnight. A visit to any expensive subdevelopment will show the advantages of such a semi-controlled environment" (WMN, Oct. 23, 1967:4).

One of the problems raised by attempts to control the behavior of individuals is the question of where one draws the line between acceptable and unacceptable behavior. When I asked the manager of Idle Haven how she solved this problem, she said that anything done in the privacy of one's own mobile home was none of her business but that creating a public nuisance in the park could be grounds for eviction. Thus, although there were several reputed alcoholics living in Idle Haven, only one man had been evicted for alcoholism because he "bothered the ladies" and "went around ringing doorbells" when drunk. However, there are many occasions when the distinction between public and private may be hard to draw. One day the manager pointed to a local newspaper item concerning an Idle Haven resident's teenage son, who had reportedly been arrested for stealing a car, and said to me "If I were smart, I'd evict the lot of them, but fast." The car was not stolen from the park, and she did not, in fact, evict the boy's family, although she clearly felt that the boy's arrest reflected adversely on the park's public image. Similarly, a number of residents would have liked to have seen her evict the parents of a boy who had allowed his hair to grow out to shoulder length and whose hippy appearance they considered to be a disgrace to the park.

Most residents view park regulations and the threat of eviction for noncompliance as valuable protection against the possibility of undesirable neighbors and claim to have no fears that the regulations will ever be turned against them personally. As one resident said, "If you behave yourself, you've got nothing to worry about." The most poignant exception was a widow whose husband had committed suicide while living in Idle Haven. Aside from coping with the gossip this incident had generated in the park, she said that she had been seriously worried about being evicted because of her husband's social delict. In Chapter 6 we shall return to the issue of eviction as it relates to the resolution of personal conflicts within the park, and in Chapter 8 we shall describe some more wide-spread eviction threats due to the financial gain involved to park owners and managers. However, for the present it should be noted that park regulations and the use of eviction, although they constitute a two-edged sword, are perceived by most mobile-home residents as working to their advantage.

Perhaps the chief advantage that mobile-home residents perceive in park regulations is their covert exclusion of Negroes. There is little doubt that racial discrimination by mobile-home park owners and managers is virtually universal and that this is the main reason why less than 2 per cent of the national mobile-home population is black (HUD, 1968:73). There is also little doubt that such discriminatory practices are extremely popular with mobile-home park residents and that racial fears are a major reason why some people move into mobile-home parks. As Werthman and others have noted, Negroes constitute a severe status threat to working-class whites, both in their neighborhoods and in their unions; but this is to put the issue too abstractly.

Many of the residents in Idle Haven had lived for many years in Oakland—a city which by 1983 is expected to have a population more than 50 per cent Negro. Since the residents of Idle Haven are both elderly and of the working class, they usually tended to live in older, less affluent neighborhoods which, during the last few years, have become solidly black enclaves. Their homes were usually small, inexpensive (ranging from $10,000 to $15,000), and fully paid for by the time they had retired. One retired teamster said he had always expected to live in his Oakland home for the rest of his life. However, as white neighbors had moved out and black neighbors moved in, he had become an alien in hostile territory. His wife had been spat at and jostled off the sidewalk by young bloods until she was afraid to go shopping alone or on foot. Their house had been twice burglarized while they were out bowling, and acid had been poured on their lawn. Finally, they had decided to sell their home, but considering its price and the fact that the husband was by now fully retired and living on social security payments plus a small pension, they could not afford to buy another house in a safe, respectable neighborhood. Then they had heard about mobile-home parks . . . .

This story, with minor variations, was repeated to me many

times during my interviews in Idle Haven. An elderly bachelor who had been living in an apartment in Oakland was mugged and robbed one evening, leading him to decide to buy a mobile home. Several women who had lived in mixed neighborhoods had become afraid, particularly because their husbands worked at night and they were left at home alone. Others said matter-of-factly that all their local friends had moved and that the neighborhood had "gone black." The pervasive tone of these remarks was one of fear—not so much an abstract fear of losing status or of being "contaminated" by contact with Negroes as the naked fear of being physically harmed or robbed.[2]

In many respects the problems of elderly, working-class whites who live in central cities are not so different from those of the black families who are supplanting them. Both groups are poor, with little prospect of increasing their incomes. Members of both groups are often at the mercy of government agencies, not only with regard to income supplements but also because their homes may be in the path of urban renewal projects or freeways. Several residents of Idle Haven who had not specifically moved because of the racial composition of their old neighborhoods said they had had to move because a freeway had "taken" their former home. Finally, like many ghetto families that are trying to run a business or raise children in a dangerous and demoralized environment, elderly white working-class individuals are trying to solve the problem of how to be respectable and safe although poor.

It is somewhat ironical that in their search for respectability and safety they have hit upon an institution that was not noteworthy for either immediately after World War II. Trailer camps used to be (and occasionally still are) regarded as encampments for transients with few ties and low morals. The insistence on strong regulations in modern mobile-home parks is probably in part an attempt to separate them from their carefree, lackadaisical ancestors. To the same end, many of the newer and better parks fine their residents a

---

[2] Some people who expressed these fears came to Idle Haven by a more devious route which beautifully illustrates the desires of people to seek out "their own kind." A retail store owner, who had moved out of a racially mixed neighborhood ten years earlier, had first invested in a rather expensive house in an upper-middle-class neighborhood. However, he soon felt acutely uncomfortable in such posh surroundings and declared the neighborhood to be "like a cemetery: you never saw anybody on the streets." This, in turn, had led him to buy a mobile home and move into Idle Haven.

quarter every time they use the word "trailer" instead of "mobile home." Yet symbolic attachment to mobile-home parks per se does not seem to be well developed among residents today (as distinct from the mobile-home industry, which worries a good deal about the "image" of its product). Most residents are perfectly willing to admit that there are good and bad mobile-home parks even today and they simply want their own park to be "nice."

More interestingly, they do not feel particularly threatened by the possibility of mobile homes being used in ghetto-renewal projects. When I asked several Idle Haven residents what they would think of such a development, they merely shrugged and said, "Why not? It seems like a good idea." Apparently so long as Negroes are not admitted to their own particular park, they see no potential threat to their status in having mobile-home parks for Negroes—that is, the focus of their attachment is the park as a community and not necessarily the mobile-home unit. This is an important point because I imagine that an enterprising Negro businessman who built a mobile-home park *for Negroes* would meet with little resistance on the part of the present mobile-home population and might develop an entirely new market for mobile homes. It would also be interesting to see whether a mobile-home park in a ghetto area might, through a residents' organization similar to those found in other parks, develop a community structure that could provide leadership experiences and other benefits for its residents. For example, since ghetto parks would have to cater to families with children rather than just adults, they might be able to provide for their residents a children's playground and the potential for organizing a communal day-nursery.

Given the homogeneous social characteristics and community ties of mobile-home residents today, any attempts to force the racial integration of mobile-home parks would seriously disrupt the social fabric. Several park managers have said to me that if they were forced to accept Negro residents many of their other residents would move at the first opportunity: "They wouldn't stand for it because we live too close together in a park." Even if such estimates should prove to be exaggerated (and many people would not move simply because they could not afford to), guarded comments by some Idle Haven residents suggest that while they might have to accept racially integrated parks, they could not be forced to associate with such "undesirable" neighbors any more than necessary. The implication is that either they would try to discourage the new tenants from participating fully in the park's community activities or they would cease participating themselves. In very large parks a process similar to that described by Gans for Levittown would no doubt occur, and the community would merely sort itself into homogeneous groups.

Even if mobile-home parks were forced to integrate racially, the sort of subtle discrimination practiced by many of them would not be easy to eradicate. In southern California, for example, some park residents' associations are fully chartered as private clubs that claim the right to vote on whether an "applicant" may become a member and, thereby, a resident in the park. Thus the manager in such a park can genuinely claim that while he may want to rent a space to someone, the residents' association has the final say.

In northern California, and no doubt elsewhere, different tactics are used which involve a close working relationship among mobile-home dealers and park owners and managers. There is, at the present time, a great shortage of mobile-home parks, compared to the rate at which mobile homes are being produced and buyers are willing to buy them. Mobile-home dealers must therefore be able to offer the potential buyer a place to put his mobile home in order to make a sale. Dealers do this by renting empty spaces in parks with an eye toward future use. Even new parks have relatively few spaces that the individual who already owns a mobile home (either new or used) can rent, because most of the spaces are spoken for (i.e., are being rented, whether occupied or not) by mobile-home dealers. Idle Haven had a working arrangement with two dealers, and each of these dealers was probably working with two or three different parks. This explains why 19 per cent of the residents interviewed in Idle Haven, when asked why they had chosen this particular park, merely said, "Well, it was the only one in which Eddie [or some other local dealer] had a space available."

Most mobile-home parks are thus full, regardless of whether they appear to have vacancies, because dealers are paying rent on the empty spaces. This arrangement obviously gives dealers an important role in screening prospective tenants—a role they must fulfill reasonably well in order not to antagonize the parks they work with. Therefore dealers, while they do not refuse to sell mobile homes to Negroes, merely neglect to offer them a place in a park and tell Negro customers that they will have to find one on their own. And this, as any customer—Negro or white—would soon discover, is virtually impossible. Most park managers, in addition to being tied to dealers, also have waiting lists of private individuals who would like to move into the park—for example, people living in another park who want to change location for one reason or another—so that they can turn away undesirable prospective tenants with a clear conscience.

The desire to protect oneself from unwanted neighbors is so strong among Idle Haven residents that it overpowers other strong desires, such as wanting to own a piece of land, or not having to pay rent to anyone. Many of the people interviewed said they would not live in a mobile-home park in which everyone owned his own lot because of the lack of control by management over resales. "What if you had a nice neighbor but he sold his space to someone you didn't like? You couldn't just up and move out because you'd own your lot, and you might even have trouble selling it." Some residents had also heard of "own-your-own-lot" parks where management lacked control over the maintenance and use of the communal facilities. Apparently in one such northern California park, lot owners were supposed to contribute a small yearly sum toward the maintenance of the swimming pool, but several residents who never used the pool had refused to pay their share and in the ensuing dispute the pool had remained empty of water for a year.[3]

In rental-type mobile-home parks, it is argued, one can always move out if an undesirable neighbor moves in. Moreover, the chances of getting an undesirable neighbor in such parks are sharply reduced because of the restrictive sales and rental practices by mobile-home parks and park managers and because rental spaces cannot be transferred privately without the permission of the management. Thus in a rental park someone who wants to sell or sublet his mobile home cannot do so unless management approves of the new tenant. Some managers do not allow tenants to mention the name of the park in advertising their mobile homes for sale (so that management is never implicated in a sale or obligated to allow a new buyer to remain), whereas others forbid tenants to advertise their mobile homes at all. In the latter case, the manager of the park becomes the agent for any used mobile home for sale in his park,

---

[3] Other Idle Haven residents were under the impression that in most "own-your-own-lot" parks, management did control resales, but they objected to buying such a lot on these grounds: "It's not really like owning a house on a lot because you can't do what you want with your property. You even have to sell it back to management at a fixed price and then they resell it and make all the profit."

and he often collects an additional fee from the seller for rendering this service.

Altogether, only half of the individuals interviewed in Idle Haven responded favorably to the idea of owning a lot on which to put their mobile homes, but of these two-thirds had in mind not a lot in a mobile home park but a lot—usually ranging in size from ¼-acre to 3 acres—in a recreation area. Of those who wanted to own such a piece of land, half had already bought one, where they planned to move their mobile homes as soon as they retired.

Extremely elderly people usually gave different reasons for not wanting to own land on which to put their mobile homes—either in a park or in the countryside. Some returned to the difficulties of upkeep and said they did not want all the troubles of owning land: if a water main broke they wanted to be able simply to call the manager. Others said they could not afford to own a piece of land, citing, in particular, high property taxes.

We shall return to the problems of taxation and costs in Chapter 8; however, it should be noted here that arguments to the effect that mobile-home residents pay a great deal less property tax than ordinary home owners are somewhat misleading. In California, mobile-home residents begin by paying a 5 per cent sales tax on the full retail price of their mobile home when they purchase it. Next they pay a yearly state license fee, similar to that paid on cars, of $11.00 per "unit," with the owner of a double-wide thus paying $22.00. In addition, California mobile-home residents pay a yearly "in-lieu" tax (that is, in lieu of a property tax) which is graduated according to the age and original cost of the mobile home. In 1969, typical in-lieu fees in Idle Haven ranged from approximately $18.00 (for a 10-year-old, 10 x 50 foot coach that had originally cost $4,000) to as much as $272.00 (for a 1-year-old 20 x 60 foot unit that had originally cost $16,000). California park residents also pay property tax indirectly through their rent, since the park owners pay a property tax on the entire park. In 1969, the owner of Idle Haven paid a property tax of $20,000, or $100 per mobile-home space. By comparison, the owner of a tract home across the street from Idle Haven paid a property tax of $460, but this tax was based on a lot 50 x 110 feet, large enough to hold almost three mobile homes, and it included the home itself. Thus mobile-home residents generally pay *proportionately* as much tax as ordinary home owners; they have merely found a way to buy a much less expensive roof over their heads and to park it on a much smaller parcel of land.

People gave other reasons for not wanting to own the piece of
land that their mobile home occupied. The main reason for not
wanting to own a lot in a mobile-home park was the lack of control
this gave one over the choice of one's neighbors, but many who
were then asked whether they would like to have their mobile
homes on lots *not* in a park said such a thing would be contrary to
the mobile home "way of life." "Why, I can't imagine it," one lady
spluttered. "One reason I live in a mobile home is because I want to
enjoy the activities in the park." This was a great-grandmother in
her 70s who had buried two husbands and was happily married for
the third time. She and her most recent husband had lived in an
apartment in Oakland for a while but they had found this too
lonely and confining. "Every morning we used to lie in bed and ask
ourselves, 'What shall we do today?' And everything took so much
effort—going to the Senior Citizens' Center [where they had met
each other], or visiting friends, or attending a club meeting. Here
we have the recreation hall and a lot of good friends within walking distance, and there's always something going on." This couple
not only took an active part in many of the park's planned activities
—cards, bingo, luncheons, breakfasts, dinners—but they also took
much pleasure in the more informal network of gossip, joint shopping trips, and neighboring.

The "friendliness" of mobile-home parks is often cited by residents as a major reason why they chose mobile-home life. Some
long-time Bay Area residents said that Idle Haven was no different
from their former neighborhoods (where some of them had lived
for 20 or 30 years) in this respect, but many who had been living
in racially mixed neighborhoods or in apartment buildings commented with delight on the helpfulness and openness of their Idle
Haven neighbors. Part of this style of friendliness in mobile-home
parks is a result of the parks' physical layout. As was noted earlier,
unlike most neighborhoods, parks are fenced, self-enclosed units.
Everyone belongs either on the outside or on the inside, and the
sense of belonging inside is heightened by the fact that people
attend social events together as well as being neighbors. This gives
the park something of the character of a club as well as a community. Residence in the park becomes a social attribute that enables
people to trust one another—much as one might trust a fellow Mason
or a fellow church member—regardless of more personal information. Thus a normally cautious widow said she had once accepted a

lift on a busy downtown street from a man who said he recognized
her because they both lived in Idle Haven, even though they did
not actually know one another.

The enclosed nature of mobile-home parks and the strong sense
of insider-versus-outsider this condition engenders among residents
makes them very safe from vandals and burglars. Since people in
the park know who "belongs" there and who doesn't, and since they
feel a sense of community with their fellow park residents, they
are quick to spot trespassers and to report them to the manager.
Also, since the mobile homes are placed so close together, neighbors
are apt to see or hear anything unusual in their immediate vicinity.
Many widows and women whose husbands worked at night reported that they felt a great deal safer from burglars in Idle Haven
than in an ordinary neighborhood. They were also not afraid to walk
home alone at night from the recreation hall—something few would
have ventured to do along city streets. Retired couples who enjoyed
travelling for a month or more at a time (and this included in particular couples who owned travel trailers) said that they never
worried about leaving their mobile home unattended: they notified
the manager and their immediate neighbors (who frequently took in
their mail and watered their plants) and their mobile home was
thereby placed under regular, if informal, surveillance.

As mobile-home parks grow in size—at this writing several 700-
and 1,000-space parks are being built—some of the benefits of
mutual surveillance will doubtless disappear or be replaced by
formal mechanisms (e.g., a gate keeper or a night watchman). As
soon as it becomes physically impossible for residents to know
everyone in the park, either personally or by reputation, caution and
suspicion are likely to return to some degree and people may become less apt to trust one another for no other reason than their
common residence in the park. Mutual aid and surveillance among
adjacent neighbors are not so likely to disappear because mobile
homes continue to be placed very close to each other, making eye-
contact and mutual acquaintance virtually unavoidable.

The importance of eye-contact to the style of life in mobile-
home parks explains in part why apartment buildings, in which
individuals live even closer together than they do in mobile-home
parks, do not develop the same sort of camaraderie and mutual aid.
Corridors, elevators, and lobbies that are used only in transit do not
encourage conversation or casual encounters. A widow in Idle

Haven, who had lived in an apartment for several months after being widowed, said that she used to feel immured in her apartment. "I'd come home from work, open my door and go inside, and there I'd be—alone, without a soul to talk to or even nod to—unless I went out and made a special effort." This was a lively, intelligent woman who worked during the day and who saw a great deal of her three children, all of them married and living in the Bay Area, on the weekends. She did not participate in any of the planned activities of the park; yet she felt strongly that the park was somehow "friendlier" than her apartment building had been and she was less lonely and afraid as a result. Much of this seemed to be due to the casual contacts she had with people as she watered her patch of lawn, took her laundry to the laundry room, or gathered her mail from her mailbox. All of these activities brought her into visual— and, often, verbal—contact with her neighbors or with passers-by who might be walking or bicycling around the park. (I myself approached her for an interview one Sunday as she was hosing off her porch.)

Of course, part of the style of apartment-house life derives not from the physical layout but from the social structure (or lack of it). In a situation where people live in close proximity but do not mix socially and have no formal social structure, coldness and formality are used to keep neighbors at arm's length, since one never knows who may be living next door. By contrast, in an apartment complex that *does* have a homogeneous clientele and a formal social structure—for example, a retirement tower—the complaints are often not of coldness but of a lack of sufficient privacy. In Victoria Plaza —a multistory retirement home in San Antonio, Texas—many residents were unhappy about the lobby, which also served as a Senior Citizens' Center and recreation hall, because whenever they entered or left the building they felt exposed to the stares and comments of a few "gossips" who made the lobby their outpost. Residents also complained about the corridors, which in this case were not socially functionless but ran along the outside of the building and also served as balcony space for each apartment. Again, those walking to their own apartments felt exposed to the stares of the "porch-watchers"; while those inside their apartments felt that their entire livingroom was exposed to the gaze of everyone who passed by (Carp, 1966:101, 111). Despite the corridors-cum-porches, however, there was not a great deal of interaction among neighbors or people on the same floor:

"One might suspect that the process of one person's becoming acquainted with other residents would spread out from his apartment, and that the probability of his ever getting to know another resident would be inversely proportional to the distance between the two apartments. But the expected did not occur. Though there was more social interaction with the person next door than with one at the other end of the hall, the majority of social contacts were with people on different floors of the building. This was true not only for selection of best friends, but also for visiting and eating together" (Carp, 1966:160).

As we shall see in the next chapter, this was not the case in Idle Haven, where neighbors were most frequently cited as best friends.

Regardless of whether one accords primacy to the ecological variable or the sociological variable, it seems safe to predict that vertical mobile-home parks will have a rather different social impact on their residents than today's mobile-home parks. Proposals for vertical mobile-home parks—a kind of "do-it-yourself" apartment building—envision a steel and concrete framework, much like a multistory parking garage, into which mobile homes will be lifted by crane. A prototype "apartmobile," as its developer has dubbed it, calls for a garage and a swimming pool at ground level, recreational facilities on the roof, and a central core elevator plus outside stairways (WMN, Aug. 25, 1969). Undoubtedly, such structures will be built within the the next few years, and they may prove to be an inexpensive way to prefabricate an apartment building. However, it seems unlikely that the mobile units, once installed, could ever be moved, both because of the expense involved and because mobile homes of different sizes and makes will not be as readily interchangeable in a multi-story façade as they are on the ground. Today's mobile-home residents who want to retain at least the option (or the illusion) of mobility will not like vertical parks for this reason, and elderly individuals who live in mobile-home parks rather than apartments because of the greater quiet or because they can no longer climb stairs will also find them inappropriate. And many current mobile-home residents will avoid high-rise parks because they will surmise, with some accuracy, that such parks will not perpetuate what they have come to like about the "mobile-home way of life."

The community formed by the residents of a mobile-home park is thus not created at will or out of whole cloth: it is the product of a number of factors, including the physical layout of the park itself, the formal social structure established by the residents, and the various sociological characteristics that residents have in common with one another—such as their age, income, and class background. But there are still other things that contribute to the creation of a tightly knit community. One of the chief ones is the fact that many people who move into a mobile-home park already know someone or are related to someone in that park. In Idle Haven, in addition to twelve extended families with members of the family living in the same mobile home,[4] there were eleven sets of relatives living in separate mobile homes within the park. These included six cases of widowed mothers and their married sons or daughters, three sets of cousins, and two sets of brothers and sisters. Thus thirty-four of the households in Idle Haven could count one or more relatives living in the park. Aside from these relationships, another fourteen of the residents interviewed indicated that they had moved into Idle Haven because they already had a friend or acquaintance living there. Thus another twenty-eight households in Idle Haven had a friendship in the park that predated their residence. All together, counting both friends and relatives, almost a third of the households in Idle Haven *knew someone* in the park regardless of any further friendships they might make.

These networks of friends and relatives are extremely important not only within a single park but also among mobile-home inhabitants generally. For example, not counting extended families or those households that had relatives living in separate mobile homes within the park, one-third of the households interviewed in Idle Haven had one or more relatives living in mobile homes elsewhere. Another third said they had relatives (brothers, sisters, children, nieces and nephews) who were planning to move into a mobile home at some time in the future. Although similarities in class background may explain some of this tendency for mobile-home residents to have relatives who also live in mobile homes, it seems probable that word-of-mouth and mutual visiting account for the extremely high incidence. Many residents specifically acknowledged that they had gotten the idea of buying a mobile home after seeing one owned by a relative or a close friend.

---

[4] This includes the nine extended families interviewed and three others who were not part of the sample. It does not include any households with teenage children, which would be counted as nuclear families.

The fact that so many mobile-home residents have friends and relatives who live in other parks helps to explain why moves from one park to another are not considered traumatic. A widow in Idle Haven, two of whose sisters lived in another park, was looking forward to the time when all three of them would be living in the same park. A couple now living in Idle Haven planned to retire to Clear Lake, where they and six other members of their family had already bought adjoining lots on which to put their mobile homes. Two couples who moved out of Idle Haven during the course of this study moved to the same park in northern California; and another couple, who moved only a short distance from Idle Haven to become the managers of a new mobile-home park, took two other Idle Haven households with them.

These kinds of interlocking relationships create a sort of supra-community embracing all mobile-home parks and have led to the often expressed feeling among mobile-home residents that they have created a new way of life. Even a move to a new park where one has no friends and relatives entails no great adjustments because one finds oneself among the same kind of people one already knows and because casual social patterns and the formal social structure in different parks are likely to vary only in detail and not in broad outline. It may be that in a geographically mobile society such as that found in the United States, duplicate and highly integrated communities are one way to create an instantaneous sense of belonging that nevertheless is rather easily transferable. For it is one of the features of mobile-home parks that while they are genuine communities, with strong in-group feelings, even important members can leave without creating a ripple.

The ease with which mobile-home parks accept new residents and forget departed ones probably dates back to the days when they were full of construction workers and other migrant laborers, who made friends quickly and easily because they were never long in the same place. Today studies show that the average mobile-home resident moves only once in 5 years—a record every bit as good as that of regular home dwellers (Construction Industries Research, 1967:15). Nor do mobile-home residents, at least in California, include a disproportionate number of recent immigrants into the state. Only 22.5 per cent of the Idle Haven residents interviewed were native-born Californians, but this is not a surprising percentage when one considers that according to the 1960 census only 40 per cent of all Californians were born in the state and that this latter

figure includes a large number of young children whereas the Idle
Haven population does not. Of the 145 households in Idle Haven
on which there is data concerning length of local residence, 17.9
per cent had spent all of their lives in the Bay Area. Another 27.6 per
cent had come to the Bay Area during the 1920s and 1930s, and
30.3 per cent had come during the 1940s and 1950s. Another 24.1
per cent had arrived during the 1960s.

Length of residence in the Bay Area becomes important in a
consideration of the extent to which Idle Haven residents have ties
with the larger community in which they live. One of the possible
results of having enclaves such as mobile-home parks within cities
is that residents will feel little social responsibility toward their
urban surroundings. Communities which have opposed the building
of mobile-home parks within their confines have frequently argued
that irresponsible residents of such parks would vote for school
taxes and other municipal bonds for which the home owner would
then have to pay. They have also argued that mobile-home parks
would "flood" the community with school-age children and require
city services for which they would not pay their fair share. These
are clearly biased and irrational assumptions which are not at all
borne out by the data. Most mobile-home parks being built today
are, like Idle Haven, adult parks catering to retired or nearly-retired
individuals. Not only do they not burden the school system, but
their streets are privately built and maintained by the owner of the
park and are thus not the responsibility of the city, as streets in an
ordinary subdivision would be. Finally, few residents in mobile-
home parks make any claims on city services such as the police or
the fire department, unless it is the occasional call for a resuscitator.

The real danger of enclaves such as mobile-home parks is that
they are so self-sufficient that residents in effect lose interest in and
control over their less immediate environment. Almost no one in
Idle Haven voted in local elections, and so few even knew the name
of their local Congressman (about four people in the entire park!)
that the question could not be used to differentiate between those
with and those without strong community ties.[5] Another question—
asking the name of the community's mayor—produced more interesting results (Table V). Knowledge of the mayor's name was strongly

---

[5] With regard to national politics, of the 122 households who indicated
their political affiliation, 48.4 per cent said they were Democrats, 34.4 per cent
said they were Republicans, 5.7 per cent said they were Independents, and 11.4

TABLE V

Knowledge of the Mayor's name in 145 Idle Haven Households

A. *By length of residence in the Bay Area:*

	Does know	Doesn't know	No infor-mation	Total N
	(per cent)	(per cent)		
All of life	9 (45.0)	11 (55.0)	6	26
1920s, 1930s	9 (25.7)	26 (74.3)	5	40
1940s, 1950s	8 (18.6)	35 (81.4)	1	44
1960s	5 (16.1)	26 (83.9)	4	35

B. *By subscription to newspaper:*

	Does know	Doesn't know	Total N
Local newspaper	22 (41.1)	31 (58.9)	53
Oakland Tribune	5 (11.1)	40 (88.9)	45
San Francisco Chronicle or Examiner	0	8 (100.0)	8
No newspaper	1 (6.3)	15 (93.7)	16
No data on newspaper subscription	3	20	23

related to length of residence in the Bay Area. It was also strongly related to being a subscriber to the local newspaper; however, there was a good deal of overlap between the two factors. Of the eighteen households that knew the name of the local mayor and had resided in the Bay Area all of their lives or since the 1920s and 1930s, fourteen also subscribed to the local newspaper. Among the thirteen more recent Bay Area residents who knew the name of the local mayor, eight subscribed to the local newspaper.

per cent said they were not registered. However, in the 1964 and 1968 national elections, Idle Haven residents did not vote significantly differently from the nation as a whole. Idle Haven voted as follows:

	Per cent of Total Vote	Democrat	Independent	Republican
Humphrey	44.4	69.5	42.9	9.5
Nixon	50.0	23.7	57.1	88.1
Wallace	4.6	6.7	0.0	2.4
Johnson	72.1	96.6	71.4	35.9
Goldwater	27.9	3.4	18.6	64.1

Given the sizeable number of people who subscribed to the local newspaper and yet didn't know the name of the mayor (which was, incidentally, a very common one) it seems likely that length of residence is the crucial factor producing ties—at any rate, political ties—with the community. This seemed to be especially true of those individuals who had spent most of their lives not merely in the Bay Area but also in the community where Idle Haven was located. Some of the people who had lived all of their lives in the Bay Area had lived in Oakland or San Francisco until their move to Idle Haven, and their ties with these communities (bolstered by subscriptions to the Oakland or San Francisco newspapers) remained much stronger than their new local ties. The typical response of such people, and of others who had come from further afield, to the question, "Do you happen to know the name of the mayor of ——?" was, "Well, I could tell you the name of the mayor of —— [the town in which they had spent most of their lives] but I'm afraid I don't know who is mayor around here." By contrast, people who had lived all or most of their lives in the community where Idle Haven is located, would answer, "You mean old So-and-so? Why, my kids went to school with him."

Many of the long-time residents subscribed to the local newspaper just to keep up with social events and people they knew. Among the more recent arrivals, some took the local newspaper because of a genuine desire to learn more about local affairs, and in a few of these cases the newspaper obviously made an impact. But for the majority it was merely a convenient way to keep informed of sales in local stores and a useful liner for the garbage pail.

Knowledge of the mayor's name is only one possible indicator of community ties and perhaps not even a very good one. However, it is difficult to assess local ties on the basis of participation in voluntary associations because, as many sociologists have demonstrated (e.g., Rainwater, et al., 1962; Komarovsky, 1962; Berger, 1960), working-class individuals are much less likely to belong to such organizations than those of the middle class. In Idle Haven the majority of people, when asked whether they had ever or still belonged to any clubs or associations, said, "No, we were never joiners."

Among those few who were joiners, the two groups most frequently mentioned were the Masons and Eastern Star. Twenty-two per cent of the men interviewed were Masons and half of these were still active in the organization. Fourteen per cent of the women were members of Eastern Star, and slightly over half of them were still active. The next most frequently mentioned group was the women's auxiliary of the Veterans of Foreign Wars, with nine women (6 per cent) claiming membership and two-thirds of them still active. Five people cited membership in the Neighbors of Woodcraft; four men had been Eagles (all of them now inactive); and four men were members of the American Legion. All other organizations mentioned had only one or two members in the park. They included other fraternal organizations, such as Eagles, Moose, Elks, and Oddfellows, and activity or hobby groups such as social-dance and square-dance clubs, a weight-reducing club, the Rod and Gun Club, and travel trailer and motorcycle clubs.

All together, only 21 per cent of the men and 20 per cent of the women interviewed were currently active in any sort of club or association outside of the park.[6] Another 25 per cent of the men and 18 per cent of the women had been active at some time in the past. Some of these formerly active individuals had had their club memberships severed by the move to Idle Haven or by a much earlier move to California. Some had belonged to associations in the midwest and let their memberships lapse altogether. Others continued to maintain memberships in San Francisco or in Oakland but no longer went to meetings because of the distances involved. However, an equal number of men no longer went to meetings due to age or illness, or because they had to work swing shift. A number of formerly active widows had quit participating in clubs when their husbands had died.

Nevertheless, for those who were active, club functions often played an important part in their lives. Several widows belonged to three or four clubs and attended a meeting of one or another of them nearly every week. And several couples who held important chairs in the Masons and Eastern Star and who obviously had some real leadership ability, exercised this primarily in their clubs and only sporadically within the park.[7] For all of these people ties outside the park were very important and were a major reason for remaining in the general area. On the other hand, some park residents —such as the six widows who attended meetings of the Veterans of Foreign Wars auxiliary—had no particular ties to their local chapter

---

[6] These percentages are strikingly similar to those found by Berger in his working-class suburb (1960:58–62).

[7] Some of the park activities of these people will be discussed in Chapter 6.

or to the people they had met there. The six widows usually went together to VFW meetings, and the activity merely seemed to reinforce their friendship within the park and give them an occasional outing.

Church membership was also explored as evidence of community ties, and in the case of people who had moved to Idle Haven from another community an effort was made to find out whether this move had lessened or otherwise affected their church attendance. However, only 21 per cent of the households interviewed went to church regularly—meaning once a week or several times a month—and another 11 per cent went occasionally—meaning several times a year (Table VI). The remainder went to church perhaps once a

TABLE VI
Religious Affiliation of Idle Haven Residents
(N=132 households)

	Per cent of total	Per cent active	Per cent occasional	Per cent inactive
Protestant	73.5 (97)	16.5 (16)	11.3 (11)	72.2 (70)
Catholic	18.2 (24)	50.0 (12)	12.5 (3)	37.5 (9)
Mixed Cath./				
Protestant	4.5 (6)	0.0	0.0	100.0 (6)
Mormon	2.2 (3)	0.0	0.0	100.0 (3)
Christian				
Science	1.5 (2)	0.0	0.0	100.0 (2)

year or not at all. These percentages are a good deal lower than those for the nation as a whole,[8] but this is not surprising considering that blue-collar individuals generally have a lower church attendance than white-collar workers and also considering the advanced age of some of the Idle Haven residents. Most of the people who did not go to church had never done so or had not done so for years, or they had quit going to church because they were too ill or frail rather than because their move to Idle Haven had severed their ties with a church they were accustomed to.

However, fifteen (11 per cent) of the households interviewed reported that their church attendance had been affected by the

---

[8] A 1969 Gallup poll showed that 42 per cent of the nation's adults attended church during a typical week; for Protestants the percentage was 37 and for Catholics 63. *New York Times,* December 28, 1969.

move to Idle Haven. One-third of these people had moved from regular attendance to occasional attendance, and two-thirds had changed from occasional attendance to becoming wholly inactive. Among the former were several individuals who continued to drive to their former church—now a considerable distance away—and who therefore went less frequently. There were also a few who had joined a local church but had simply not found it as congenial as their former one, and several women who used to walk to a church but now found themselves too far away to walk and did not like asking others for rides. (Of the 146 households interviewed, fifteen did not own an automobile. Of these, twelve were widows, who either did not know how to drive or could not afford to own a car; two were couples, and one was a bachelor.)

Considering the predominance of those who went from occasional to non-attendance, it seems probable that many of those whose church ties were disrupted did not have very strong ties to begin with. It is interesting, for example, that of the entire group of fifteen whose church attendance had changed there was not a single Catholic. Those Catholics who were accustomed to going to church regularly evidently experienced little difficulty in switching to one of two local parishes. There were also a number of extremely devout Protestants in the park who had not only switched their membership to a local church upon moving to Idle Haven, but who were also deeply involved in various church activities—the choir, the building committee, the men's club, etc.[9]

However, some of the Protestants whose church attendance was affected by the move to Idle Haven may have had strong ties to their former church and merely lacked the social skills or the energy to re-establish them in a new setting. There was, for example, an extremely old lady who had managed to walk to church when she lived in Alameda, where the church was only a block away. Since coming to Idle Haven she had seldom ventured outside her door, let alone outside the park itself. It is difficult, in such a case, to separate the impact of the move from her deteriorating physical condition, but it is generally true that the people in Idle Haven who were most socially isolated—not only with respect to the rest of the

---

[9] As Bennett Berger noted with respect to his working-class suburb, "There is a marked tendency for the figures [on church attendance] to bunch at the extremes. Apparently people go to church hardly ever or else very often, with relatively few in between" (1960:46).

community but also within the park—were also the least able to muster any initiative on their own. It is, in social terms, the equivalent of the rich getting richer and the poor getting poorer. This is a problem to which we shall return in the following chapters, in connection with friendships and mutual aid.

If formal indicators, such as political knowledge, membership in clubs and associations, and church attendance reveal that few residents in Idle Haven have strong ties to the external community, do they care at all about where the park is located? Oddly enough, the answer is an emphatic yes. As we noted earlier, 19 per cent of the households interviewed indicated they had had no choice in moving into this particular park—a dealer had offered them the space. (Many more households than this 19 per cent had acquired their spaces through a dealer, but they had decided on the park first and had then been steered to one of the dealers with whom the park had "an arrangement.") Of the remaining households, all of whom had actively chosen Idle Haven, 10 per cent had done so because they wanted a newer park—that is, they had moved from another, older mobile-home park in the immediate area in order to enjoy better facilities *within* the park. However, 15 per cent of the households had moved to Idle Haven because they already had relatives or friends living there, and another 48 per cent had chosen Idle Haven because it was close to their former neighborhood, family, friends, doctor or job. (Another 8 per cent chose Idle Haven for miscellaneous reasons, e.g., because "it looked like a nice park," or, in one case, because the construction worker husband had helped to build the park.) Thus, at least 63 per cent of the households had strong personal reasons for wanting to live in this particular park or in this particular part of the Bay Area.

It is these personal ties, rather than any abstract ties to a city, that govern the lives of Idle Haven residents. Within a large, diffuse, urban environment where roles are highly differentiated and secondary relationships abound, they have attempted to create a small, face-to-face community. Their social world revolves around their relatives, close friends, and neighbors within this small community—the mobile-home park—and around a network of friends and relatives in the surrounding metropolis. The urban scene itself —the hodge-podge of freeways, neighborhoods, and civic centers— is something they use without deep feelings of involvement or attachment. Perhaps it is increasingly hard to feel a part of any particular city within a metropolitan area where the end of one town and the beginning of another is signalled by nothing more than a sign or a change in street numbers. Mobile-home parks may, in one sense represent a kind of futuristic solution to problems of local government, social control, and anomie in an urban environment. In such a futuristic solution, community structure would be brought very close to the individual in the form of a small, self-governing enclave, on the one hand, and there would be integration at the metropolitan, areal level on the other hand.[10] The level that would be eliminated in such a dual system would be the level presently ignored by mobile-home residents—the cities themselves as they now exist within metropolitan areas.

In the next two chapters we shall explore in greater detail the social relationships within Idle Haven and how these intertwine with the network of relatives outside the park, and in Chapter 7 we shall look more closely at the formal social structure within the park in order better to assess both the strengths and shortcomings of this new form of community.

---

[10] Perhaps it is not so futuristic. Such a system would bear a strong resemblance to the Chinese *pao-chia* system, dating back to the middle of the Sung dynasty (960–1279 A.D.), in which every ten neighboring households were organized into a *chia* and every ten *chia* formed a *pao*, with federated *pao* under the *hsien*, or county, government. The head of each *pao* was elected by the members of the *chia*. "The duties of the *pao* and *chia* were defined as follows: (1) maintaining peace and order in the district, (2) taking the local census, and (3) encouraging good morals and good conduct" (Johnson, 1962:62).

4. Families and Friends

It should no longer come as a surprise to anyone that family ties play an important role in the lives of most urban dwellers. Ever since Louis Wirth described "The distinctive features of the urban mode of life . . . as consisting of the substitution of secondary for primary contacts, the weakening of bonds of kinship, and the declining social significance of the family," a host of sociologists have sought to modify if not overturn his assertions. Particularly within the working class it was found that relationships between parents and their grown children—especially mothers and daughters—involved residential proximity, mutual aid, and a great deal of visiting and casual socializing (Young & Willmott, 1962; Komarovsky, 1962). Such ties exist within white-collar and professional families as well, and although such families tend to live further apart geographically, modern means of communication (particularly the airplane and the telephone) and higher incomes enable their members also to keep in touch and to assist one another in times of need. Among upper middle-class families mutual assistance is more likely to be rendered financially than in terms of personal services such as baby sitting or home nursing, and financial aid is more likely to flow from parents to children than from children to their aging parents, as it often does in the working and lower middle classes. However, neither distance nor urban life seems to have destroyed extended-family obligations and affections.

Even social mobility, while it has an impact on extended-family relationships, seems to be less alienating than was once thought (Litwak, 1960a, 1960b; Adams, 1968). Bert Adams demonstrates, for example, that socially mobile sons tend to draw their parents partly into their new social world and that parental pride in their sons' achievements and feelings of responsibility and gratitude on the part of the sons create strong and affectionate ties between the two generations. Only downwardly mobile children seem often to be alienated from their parents and also from their more successful siblings.

Other studies have shown that while American kinship networks tend to be shallow both vertically and horizontally—that is, acquaintance with one's relatives seldom extends beyond one's parents, grandparents, aunts and uncles, and first cousins—they are unusually adaptable. Thus childless couples or single individuals often compensate for their lack of lineal descendants by maintaining close relationships with their own brothers and sisters and with their siblings' offspring (nieces and nephews). The lengthening of the lifespan and the reduction of the childbearing period have led to an increase in the number of four-generation families, which is also producing interesting role adjustments. For example, some young couples in their 20s are now exchanging services with their grand-parents (e.g., driving them to the doctor and the grocery store in return for baby-sitting) that in previous years would have involved their parents. Such adaptations of traditional family patterns accurately reflect the changing needs of various members at the same time that they attest to the continuing strength of the family as a source of mutual affection and aid.

Finally, a number of studies have testified to the important role played by the family in the lives of old people (most notably, Townsend's *The Family Life of Old People*). Even Cumming and

Henry (1961), who put forward the theory of disengagement, according to which disengagement from others is a natural process that occurs with aging and that does not necessarily lead to a lowered morale, found that some of their own data tended to dispute their assertions. Thus they argued that disengagement could be broken down into four stages and that morale declined in the intermediate stages (2 and 3) but reached or surpassed the morale of stage 1 (full engagement) once stage 4 (full disengagement) had been achieved. However, their data indicated that "the exceptions to the pattern of decreasing morale in the second and third stages and increasing morale in the fourth stage of disengagement are those men and women who have no siblings or children living in the same geographic area and those women who have both types of kin easily accessible" (Cumming & Henry, 1961:136). The former had a low morale even in stage 4, and the latter had a high morale even in stages 2 and 3. Thus close family ties have an important bearing on the well-being of elderly people.

It should not come as a surprise, therefore, that among the residents of Idle Haven who had at least one surviving child, 83 per cent had a child living in the Bay Area. This included 9 per cent who had a grown child living in the same dwelling and 4 per cent who had a child living separately but within the same park. Of the 17 per cent who did not have a child living in the Bay Area, 5 per cent had at least one child living in the northern part of the state (generally no farther than 3 or 4 hours by car from Idle Haven) and another 4 per cent had a child in southern California, about 6 to 8 hours by car and less than an hour by plane (Table VII). The table also reveals a slight tendency for daughters to live closer to their parents than sons. This becomes somewhat more pronounced when one takes into account all of the children of Idle Haven residents: then one finds that whereas 22 per cent of all sons live out of the state, only 12 per cent of the daughters do so; and that 59 per cent of *all* daughters live in the Bay Area as compared with 51 per cent of the sons.

All of the residents who had a child living in the Bay Area talked on the telephone with him or her at least once a week and some talked to each other daily. If it involved a toll call parents sometimes relied on their children to call them in order not to run up their own phone bill, but one woman who talked every Sunday to her recently divorced daughter in Fresno (about 200 miles away) confessed somewhat ruefully "my telephone bill looks like the national debt!"

TABLE VII
Proximity of Children to Idle Haven Resident Parents

	Nearest Child (N = 114)			All Children (N = 156)		
	Sons	Daughters	Total	Sons	Daughters	Total
		per cent			*per cent*	
Same dwelling	10 (5)	8 (5)	9 (10)	4 (5)	4 (5)	4 (10)
In the park	4 (2)	5 (3)	4 (5)	2 (3)	2 (3)	2 (6)
In Bay Area	70 (36)	70 (44)	70 (80)	51 (69)	59 (72)	55 (141)
In No. Calif.	2 (1)	8 (5)	5 (6)	13 (17)	13 (16)	13 (33)
In So. Calif.	2 (1)	4.5 (3)	4 (4)	8 (11)	9 (11)	8 (22)
Out of state	12 (6)	4.5 (3)	8 (9)	22 (29)	12 (15)	17 (44)
TOTALS	100 (51)	100 (63)	100 (114)	100 (134)	99 (122)	99 (156)

The mere fact that many older parents have at least one child living nearby does not indicate, of course, who moved closer to whom. It has sometimes been suggested that one reason why older people choose "mobile" homes is that it enables them to follow their geographically mobile children. It should be recalled, however, that 45.5 per cent of the households in Idle Haven had either lived all of their lives in the Bay Area or had come there during the 1920s or 1930s. The majority of households had raised their families in the Bay Area and still had one or more children living nearby. For these people the specific choice of Idle Haven as opposed to some other park was often influenced by where a child lived, but the initial decision to move into a mobile home was prompted by other considerations.

Only among the households who came to the Bay Area during the 1960s were there a substantial number who had moved long distances in order to be near their children or another relative. Twelve households—less than 10 per cent of the total number of households interviewed but a third of those who had moved during the 1960s—had come to be near a relative.[1] Most of these were recently retired individuals who had been forced to spend their working lives elsewhere—in the coal fields of West Virginia or travelling up and down the West Coast as travelling salesmen—and only retirement had enabled them to join a son or daughter, or a brother or sister, in the Bay Area. Even so, the choice of a mobile home was usually dictated by their low income or by the desire to own something smaller than an entire house, rather than by the anticipation that they would have to move again.

One of the advantages of a mobile-home park for older couples and widows who move away from lifelong friends and neighbors in order to be near their children is that the park serves as a ready-made source of new friends. Thus such uprooted parents do not become wholly dependent on their children for companionship and entertainment. One couple in Idle Haven who had spent their entire lives prior to their move to the Bay Area in New York City—and who acknowledged that they still wrote long letters every week to

---

[1] There were also two instances where the parental households had moved to the Bay Area first and had been followed by the households of grown children. The children, in both cases, were daughters—in one instance an unmarried daughter and in the other instance a divorced daughter with two children of her own.

old friends there—had nevertheless made numerous new friends in the park and took a very active part in all of the dinners, luncheons, and other occasions.

For most of the residents of Idle Haven the interplay of family and park friends is complex and various. Activities with children or other members of the family are generally assigned a higher priority than park activities. For example, although the park holds a Thanksgiving dinner and a Christmas party, these always precede the actual holidays by about a week because it is assumed that most people want to spend Christmas Day and Thanksgiving Day with their families.[2] Indeed, the park is very quiet on holiday weekends because the older residents are generally visiting relatives and many of the younger, still employed residents are taking advantage of a few days off to go fishing or camping. The sole exceptions to the familistic treatment of holidays are Easter and—surprisingly enough —Mother's and Father's Day. All three of these occasions fall on a Sunday and the park always holds its regular monthly breakfast (usually scheduled for the first Sunday of every month) on these particular holidays. Attendance at each of these three breakfasts includes about a third of the total park population—nearly twice that of the normal monthly breakfast. Among the attractions of the Easter breakfast are the specially flower-decorated tables with vases, made by the park's ceramics class, in the shapes of bunnies, chickens, and Easter eggs. The park's church-goers attend Easter breakfast early and then go on to church, but for many of the residents the breakfast itself seems to represent a sort of semi-religious occasion when they are especially gracious to other park residents, dress up in their best spring outfits, and then perhaps celebrate the rest of the day by going out for a drive or to a movie.

At Mother's and Father's Day breakfasts the atmosphere is less decorous and more jocular. On Mother's Day all the women who are members of the park's association can attend the breakfast for free (usually there is a nominal charge of 65 cents per person) and the men do all the cooking and serving. On Father's Day, of course, this practice is reversed. Occasionally mothers or fathers who are also being feted by their children will bring them (and the grandchil-

---

[2] But park acquaintances serve as a substitute for those who have no families. In addition to the Thanksgiving dinner for everyone in the park, four childless couples got together on Thanksgiving Day and cooked a turkey in the recreation hall's kitchen and had dinner together.

dren) to the breakfast. Thus a very young couple of grandparents
(in their early 40s) came to the Mother's Day breakfast with their
daughter, son-in-law, and two grandchildren; and the grandmother
announced that on this particular Mother's Day she was getting
them for breakfast and the other grandmother was getting them for
dinner. A widow who had been estranged from her daughter for
many years and who had only effected some sort of reconciliation
the previous year, at her husband's funeral, came to the Mother's
Day breakfast proudly showing off a huge orchid that her daughter
had sent her. In instances such as these the park celebration serves
partly as a public confirmation of family solidarity. But for most
elderly residents, whose children are themselves mothers and fathers
and who are therefore caught up in family celebrations of their
own, the Mother's and Father's Day breakfasts are primarily park
celebrations to be enjoyed in the company of one's peers, among
whom one can reminisce and take credit for having done one's duty
toward society.

   There are many other formal and informal occasions when a
resident's family and park friends are brought into contact, either
directly or indirectly. The guiding principle seems to be that one's
family (having "good" children and beautiful or accomplished
grandchildren) enhances one's status within the park, and that one's
status within the park can be used to enhance one's position vis-à-vis
children and grandchildren. With regard to the first alternative, for
example, there is always a great deal of gossip and bragging around
the recreation hall about one's family. Pictures of a daughter's new
house are circulated and a new grandchild, particularly if he lives
in the area, is bound to show up at a monthly luncheon where he
can be admired by the other grandmothers.[3] The monthly mimeographed park newsletter also contains a great many items about
the families of residents. Some typical examples (quoted verbatim
except for changed names) are:

   Alma Mark's granddaughter is apparently coming along
   fine after her last operation. Poor little tyke, she sure has

_____

   [3] Another example of status-building within the park occurred one evening
while approximately eighty people were gathered in the recreation hall to play
bingo. A young man, seated next to a couple who were residents in the park, was
announced to the group as "Sergeant ————, the son of Mr. and Mrs. ————,
who is just back from Vietnam." He received a huge ovation.

had a rough go of it. She will have to go back for another one too. Keep your fingers crossed for this little one who is fighting so hard to live.

Any volunteers for sewing on buttons? Well, someone is needed at the Jones residence. Betty Jones's family really believe in propagating the race. Her daughter Suzie presented them with a baby boy named William. Her son, who lives in Fresno, Calif., also presented them with a boy, named John, and her nephew who just recently returned from Vietnam last summer had a baby boy also named Billy. How about that one for the books? Betty has busted all her buttons off. Can't blame her can you?

Al and Marie Whitsun announced the wedding of another granddaughter on June 18. She graduates from high school and celebrates her 18th birthday and becomes a bride all in 10 days time.

Grace Mallory is very proud of her daughters and son-in-law. Grace attended three graduations. Ellen from San Francisco State and her husband George from University of California Medical School (he received his Doctor of Pharmacy degree) and Nancy graduating from San Jose State. You can see by this that not all students are rioting. Some really want to go to college to study. I am sure that we of this park join Grace in her pride of her kids.

Condolences go to Rose O'Riley who just lost her beloved sister. Many of you will remember her sister who was a frequent visitor to the park. That gal sure has really had her share of sorrow.

The use of the park to enhance one's status within the family can be illustrated in a number of ways. Most of the park's functions —such as its monthly breakfasts, dinners, dances, and bingo nights— can be attended by friends and relatives of the residents. They usually involve a small fee for both guests and residents, but for many residents a $1.00-per-person spaghetti feed in the recreation hall is an easy and popular way to entertain their children and grandchildren. At the monthly dances (further discussed in the following chapter) many of the park residents who attend invite friends and relatives who live outside the park and form a "table" by themselves. One of the park's merrier widows once told me that she had fourteen relatives at the most recent dance.

In the summertime the park is also extremely popular with residents' grandchildren because it has a swimming pool. Out of the residents interviewed, only 9 per cent said that they themselves used the pool regularly, and another 19 per cent had used it once or twice; however, many who never used the pool themselves could be observed sitting beside it watching a grandchild splash about. The recreation hall is also available to residents of the park who want to book it for a private party. Thus a number of wedding receptions for children and grandchildren have taken place there at no extra cost to the family. Others have used the recreation hall for family reunions too large to be held in their own mobile homes, or for their children's baby showers. Perhaps the most spectacular exploitation of the park (and its residents) on behalf of one's own family was a bridal shower given in the recreation hall for the manager's daughter. In addition to a few school friends of the bride-to-be and a few female relatives of the groom, most of the fifty or so ladies who attended were residents of the park. The bride-to-be received an incredible number of gifts—a few of them modest, often hand-made, items such as embroidered dishtowels or crocheted pothold-ers, but many of them rather expensive and some of these from residents who lived on welfare checks. A few women in the park who were invited but could not attend nevertheless also sent pres-ents. This event was obviously somewhat unusual in that the man-ager of the park wielded considerable power over people's lives and few who were invited felt they could afford to antagonize her (myself included).

The members of a park resident's family and other residents in the park interacted and complemented each other in a variety of ways. The first person turned to in times of serious illness was al-ways a relative—usually a child—if available. But neighbors in the park were sometimes the first on the scene in a serious accident or illness, and therefore to call a doctor or an ambulance, and they were also helpful in relieving relatives of the burden of care in prolonged convalescence. For example, a widow who had had a serious operation spent the first two weeks after being released from the hospital at her son's home, but thereafter—although still weak—she returned to the park, where neighbors did her shopping and some of her cooking and cleaning. A neighbor had also looked after her plants and canary while she was away. Another widow broke her leg while coming down her front steps and was driven to the hospital by a neighbor. Thereafter she followed the same pattern as the other widow—first staying with her daughter and then returning to the park, still semi-invalided but under the watchful eye of neighbors and friends.

Some residents were also sensitive to the fact that neighbors or friends of theirs in the park had children who neglected them and tried to compensate for some of this neglect. One widow who was on bad terms with her son and who had broken her shoulder and several ribs in a severe fall had a neighbor (in this case a close friend dating from many years preceding their residence in the park) who brought her a hot dinner every evening for 6 weeks. Other widows who could not drive and whose children seldom visited them or drove them anywhere were often invited along by other women or couples when they went shopping. The manager of the park also occasionally telephoned the children of residents whom she believed were not being looked after properly.

As we noted earlier, 83 per cent of the households interviewed who had children had one or more of these children living in the Bay Area and most of these were on extremely good terms with them. However, the few who were estranged from their children, or —more commonly—from one child, seemed to have lost contact completely; there seemed to be no such thing, in Idle Haven, as a strained but civil parent-child relationship. One man who was married for the second time said he had two sons by a previous marriage but he had not seen them for seventeen years and he had no idea where they were living or what sort of jobs they had. Another said one of his wife's sons by a former marriage had "dropped out of sight" 10 years ago. These few cases in which parents and children had totally lost touch always involved severely disrupted families: usually the parent (that is, the resident of Idle Haven) had been divorced and remarried, but occasionally it was the child who had been married several times and had drifted from area to area until the parent no longer knew where he or she lived.

Another occasional cause of estrangement between parents and children was social mobility on the part of the child. There were two virtually identical cases in Idle Haven of widows estranged from their sons: both women were pleasant but uneducated, and both sons had Ph.D.'s and were professors. One woman had not seen her son for 11 years and depended on her four daughters, all of whom lived in the Bay Area and were married to working-class men. The

other woman, whose son lived in the Bay Area, saw him occasionally; she largely blamed the son's wife for the fact that she was
never invited to their home and that her neighbor in the park had
had to look after her when she broke her shoulder.

There were also some residents who were unable to rely on
their children because their children were virtually as old—and in
some cases in much worse health—as they were. An 82-year-old
widow whom I visited one rainy February afternoon told me that
she had not left her mobile home or seen a live human being in
over a month. Her daughter, in her 60s, who usually came to see
her about once a week, had been ill and so they had only talked on
the telephone. When I asked this woman how she did her grocery
shopping, she proudly led me into the kitchen and showed me a
huge upright freezer that her daughter had bought for her sometime
before. It was filled not only with frozen vegetables and meats, but
also with frozen bread, fruit juices, and various deserts, so that it
seemed possible that this woman could be virtually self-sustaining
for about a month, as she claimed she was. What surprised me more,
however, was that she seemed not at all disoriented or depressed
in her isolated state. Although she had not been expecting me, she
was neatly dressed in a housedress and stockings; and when I asked
how she spent her time she showed me a stack of some 80 pillow-
cases (bought at a January "white sale") that she was in the process of embroidering as gifts for various relatives for their future
birthdays, possible weddings, and the following Christmas. Thus,
although physically isolated, this woman still felt herself very much
a part of an extensive family network.

Of the men and women who were childless, about half were
close to one or more of their siblings. One childless divorcée, for
example, had moved away from southern California upon her retirement specifically in order to be close to a married sister. This
sister, a long-time resident of the Bay Area, had included her in a
number of her own clubs and friendship groups so that the divorcée
relied mostly on these new friends and very little upon the people
she had met in Idle Haven. Another woman—a childless widow who
had married late in life and most of whose family lived in the Bay
Area—said that her brothers and sisters and their families kept her
so busy that she really "didn't feel like a widow."

Several other men and women who were themselves childless
were married to someone who had had children by a previous marriage, and as a consequence they had a good deal of contact with

the children and grandchildren of their spouses. Unfortunately, such relationships were generally severed by the death of the spouse whose children they were. One widow who had helped to raise her late husband's two sons had lost all contact with the sons after her husband's death. But whereas stepchild (as well as in-law) ties seem to be easily severed by the death of the connecting relative, sibling ties are not only substituted for ties with children, but they are often extended downward one generation upon the death of a sibling. Thus there were two childless widows and one childless widower in Idle Haven whose closest relative turned out to be a nephew.

One Idle Haven case that illustrates several ways in which relatives were substituted for each other involved an 82-year-old woman who had been widowed at the age of 61. She had subsequently sold her home and lived for about 15 years with her unmarried daughter (her only child, another child having died in infancy), until the daughter had died at the age of 54. She had then gone to live with her widowed older sister, and together these two had moved into Idle Haven—partly because the sister's home had become too ramshackle to repair and partly because the sister could no longer negotiate the steps leading up to the house. Two years after moving into Idle Haven the older sister had died, leaving most of her possessions—including the mobile home—to her son but subject to the sister's use during her lifetime. This son, himself in his 60s, paid the park's rent and utility bills for his aunt and took her grocery shopping every Sunday. He had also sold his mother's car and with the proceeds bought his aunt a splendid color TV set, and he had bought her a new stereo record player when her old one broke down.

In addition to her nephew, however, this elderly widow could also call on friends in the park and on a close neighbor. The friends were a married couple nearly her own age whom she had known for many years and who had been instrumental in getting her and her sister to move into Idle Haven. The husband occasionally ran errands for her during the week—such as going to the bank—which her nephew could not attend to because he was at work then. The husband also did some heavy housecleaning for her, such as washing the windows and—once a year—the outside of the mobile home. She paid him a little for this because he needed the money, but it was also clear that he would not have performed the jobs or accepted the money unless they had been close friends. Similarly, there was a neighbor who "looked in" on this widow at least once a day and who did some light housecleaning (vacuuming, dusting, changing the linens) for her once a week, also partly out of friendship and partly for the money. The neighbor was an attractive middle-aged Mexican woman (the only one in the park) who had had no children and who desperately missed her own mother and brothers and sisters in Mexico. The relationship between her and her 82-year-old neighbor was clearly one of mutual benefit: the younger woman had gained a substitute mother and the elderly woman a substitute daughter.

In order to gain a fuller picture of the extent and nature of friendships and neighboring among residents in Idle Haven a number of interview questions (see the Appendix, questions 30–35) were devoted to this topic. For example, everyone was asked to name his three best friends in the park, and these sociometric choices were then analyzed to determine the percentage of friends who were also neighbors, the percentage of reciprocal choices, the existence of cliques, the most frequently named residents, the most isolated residents, and the possible influence of people's location within the park on their friendships and degree of social participation.

Contrary to the residents of Victoria Plaza (Carp, 1966:156–58), among whom such sociometric questioning produced a great deal of "politicking" and pressure to "vote for" certain candidates, residents of Idle Haven took the questions very matter-of-factly and, almost without exception, enjoyed answering them. Out of the 131 households who were asked, only five refused to answer. Of these two were households who deliberately "kept themselves to themselves" and did not participate in any park activities; two were women who maintained friends among many disparate (and sometimes feuding) groups in the park and who said they could not possibly single out their three *best* friends; and one was the assistant manager in the park, who subsequently became the manager and who, conscious of her formal role, said she was "friendly with everyone, but friends with no one."

There were obviously vast differences in the way given individuals construed the word "friend." Some people said they had no really close *friends* in the park and would answer the question only when it was rephrased in terms of residents with whom they were *friendly*. Others responded with alacrity even though they were obviously naming the only three people in the park whom they knew at all. Interestingly enough, the latter often named their two immediate neighbors (one on either side) and the *manager* of the park as their best friends. The manager, who received the greatest number of choices (17), was mentioned either by very socially active residents who were genuine members of her friendship group[4] or by very socially isolated residents who probably considered her a friend because she was someone they felt they could call on in the event of a genuine crisis. While these two interpretations of friendship may differ, however, it would be difficult to argue that one has more substance than the other.

Altogether, a total of 399 friends were named by the 126 residents who answered the question. Of these 399 choices, 214 (53.6 per cent) were "neighbors"—here defined as individuals living on either side of, or directly opposite, or on either side with one mobile home separating them from the respondent. Among the 399 friends named there were seventy-one reciprocal friendships (that is, in 142 instances people named someone who also named them), and of these seventy-one reciprocal relationships, forty-two (59.2 per cent) were again with neighbors. Thus, regardless of whether one considers all of the "friends" named or singles out only the reciprocal relationships as the more likely to be genuine, it would appear that slightly more than half the friendships in Idle Haven were with neighbors.

One could argue that the tendency to choose neighbors—including the reciprocal choices—does not reflect genuine friendship so much as it is an artifact of the questionnaire, but observation would indicate otherwise. Mobile homes are placed so close together that one can scarcely avoid meeting one's neighbors and talking to them from time to time, and these casual encounters produce a kind of knowledge about one another that often leads to mutual responsibility if not necessarily to deep affection. For example, one middle-aged but frail-looking woman professed not to be active in the park and not to know anyone very well; however, she named her three

---

[4] The manager, in this instance, is the original manager who admitted me to the park and not the assistant manager who replaced her midway through the study. The original manager very definitely had a friendship group that wielded considerable power within the park, and some residents criticized her sharply for "playing favorites." This criticism no doubt contributed to the assistant manager's desire to be even-handed and her unwillingness to name her three best friends in the park. For a discussion of power-plays within the park and the circumstances surrounding the original manager's departure, see Chapter 6.

immediate neighbors as the people whom she knew best and when asked whether she had ever exchanged any "favors" with them she thought a moment and then said, "Well, a few months ago Lucile Snow across the street felt another heart attack coming on and discovered she was out of nitro[glycerine] pills. So, knowing I also have heart trouble, she came over and borrowed some of mine." Another woman—a frosty widow who had not gone out of her way to make friends in the park and who never attended park functions because she was allergic to cigarette smoke—nevertheless mentioned that she had gotten to know one of her neighbors rather well. She then explained that this neighbor's husband had died shortly after they had moved into the park and that she had made a special effort to befriend her because "I know what she's been going through." These two ladies frequently went shopping or out to lunch together and they had visited each other on two occasions when each had been briefly confined to the hospital.

Other services routinely exchanged by neighbors in the park included watering each other's plants, taking in mail, and feeding goldfish and parakeets when people were ill and hospitalized or on vacation. Residents also fed and cared for each other's dogs and cats on occasion, but this was generally a favor exchanged only with a really close park friend who might or might not be a neighbor. Neighbors also brought each other homemade cakes, cookies, custards, and other delicacies—particularly when they knew someone was ill. One bachelor even recalled that a neighboring lady had brought him some cough medicine because she had heard him coughing late one night.

Most of the neighboring just described was done by women, but men were also involved in neighborly exchanges. For example, men often borrowed tools from each other, whereas women generally preferred not to borrow things. Men with mechanical aptitude were often asked by neighboring widows to unstop a sink or to fix a balky window. One woman called on a neighbor's husband to come and break down her bathroom door when she heard her husband collapse in the bathroom and found the door locked. Another frightened widow phoned her neighbor in the middle of the night and asked the husband to check the security of her mobile home because she was sure she heard someone walking on the roof (it was a cat).

All of these casual (and sometimes intimate) relationships depended upon the basic trust engendered by the social homogeneity of the park. This is not to say, however, that relationships among neighbors were always cordial. People were reluctant to air specific complaints, but it was clear that living so close together also produced tensions. The chief offense appeared to be undue noise. Several residents, at one time or another, complained either to me or to the park's manager about a neighbor's dog that barked too much. One poor woman, made very nervous by her own dog's barking but also hypersensitive to what neighbors might say, kept her dog quiet by feeding him tranquilizers. Another source of tension was neighbors who drank too much and who argued or shouted when they were drunk. In almost all cases the park's alcoholics were pointed out to me by their immediate neighbors, whose attitudes ranged from mild amusement to exasperation. When such cases became too bothersome, neighbors usually notified the manager, who then either warned or evicted the tenant.

It was clear, however, that neighbors overlooked a good deal of bizarre behavior in each other. One widow whose late husband had been an alcoholic complained bitterly that neighbors in the park had, in fact, helped cater to his alcoholism by giving him an occasional drink or loaning him the money with which to buy a bottle. (A male neighbor confirmed this by saying that Harry had been a nice guy who drank a little but who had good cause because his wife kept him on such a short leash.) Neighbors also tended to tolerate noisy family quarrels on the grounds that such strained relationships would resolve themselves without recourse to eviction. When I once expressed surprise that a couple I had interviewed some months earlier had since separated and moved out of the park, a neighbor of theirs assured me that it had been "in the cards" for a long time and that she hadn't been in the least surprised. Another very pious former widow described to me how she had come to marry her second husband: "He and his wife were living next door to me in another park, but I knew things weren't going right between them. I could hear them arguing all the time, and I used to pray to God to give them help." She acknowledged that God had answered her prayers in a most unusual way.

If more than 50 per cent of the residents' park friendships were with neighbors, then one's exact location within the park obviously had an important impact on whom one met and got to know. I occasionally interviewed people whom I thought would have something in common with someone else in the park, but because they lived at opposite ends of the park from each other and did not attend park social functions very often they had never met. However, neighborly relationships did not have to be based on identical interests or close similarities in age in order to be successful. There were a number of widows who had befriended neighbors who were also widows, but there were just as many widows who had befriended a somewhat younger neighboring couple with whom they had a surrogate maternal relationship. Many residents, in talking about their relations with neighbors, commented that they were especially lucky to be living in such a friendly part of the park; but these comments occurred at random and were not, in fact, restricted to a particular part of the park. Almost no one, moreover, said that given a choice he would prefer living in another part of the park, and the few who did express such a preference did so for physical reasons (they wanted a larger space, or one farther from the railroad track) rather than for social ones.

When the park was first opened, some of the residents had chosen their spaces on the basis of anticipated social roles. For example, among those who chose spots at the very back of the park, at the farthest possible remove from the recreation hall, were a number of couples who wanted no part of the park's planned activities or any "togetherness"; whereas several extremely gregarious couples who were interested in leadership roles chose spots that clustered around the recreational hall and the manager's unit. After the park had filled up, however, and some of the original residents had moved away, new activity-oriented residents sometimes entered the park in spots far distant from the recreation hall while non-activists came to occupy certain centrally located positions.

The passage of time also altered the behavior of some of the original residents. Many of the couples who had deliberately chosen a spot as far distant as possible from the recreation hall had, over the years, become good friends with all of their immediate neighbors. On the other hand, a couple who had rented one of the most prominent spots in the park—directly opposite the recreation hall and diagonally across from the manager's space—had had a radical change of heart. The husband had been the park association's first president and he and his wife together had organized most of the park's activities. But about a year after the park was opened they had had a serious quarrel with a rival group of park leaders and, as a result, had withdrawn completely from all park activities and even neighborly relationships.[5] Toward the end of my study they

---

[5] The wife was still so bitter four years after this event that in response to my mimeographed letter indicating that I hoped to interview everyone in the

moved to another, brand-new park, and when I asked whether they were planning to live close to the recreation hall again the husband vehemently shook his head and said he had chosen a space as far away from the new hall as possible.

Thus while a new park may begin by having certain enclaves of active and inactive residents, or a "widow's row," these differences are usually dissolved by the passage of time and events. Some people move, others get angry or decide to be friendlier, and still others experience a change in status—e.g., they are widowed, or remarry, or become seriously disabled—so that no part of the park is lacking in the general social material for a variety of neighborly relationships. One may ask whether, regardless of the social characteristics of the residents, certain ecological spots in the park lead to individuals' having fewer or more friends. For example, does it make a difference whether one lives at the end of a street, in a cul-de-sac, or directly opposite the recreation hall? One famous study (Festinger, *et al.*, 1967) has argued that in a homogeneous community—in this case an enclave of married college students—physical location has an important bearing on how many friends one makes, how popular one becomes within the community, and how soon one hears a rumor. Idle Haven revealed no such ecological patterning. The twelve most popular residents, each of whom were mentioned between nine and six times by other residents, were scattered throughout the park—in the middle of long streets, on corner locations, at the front of the park (with no facing neighbors), and at the back of the park. Their popularity and range of friendships in all cases depended upon their personalities and other social characteristics.

The differences between popular and unpopular residents—between those who had many friends and those who had none—and between neighbor and non-neighbor friends are complex. It is, for example, too simple to say that friendships formed with non-neighbors are closer and more "real" than neighborly friendships. As has already been noted, the manager of Idle Haven was frequently named as a friend by people whose only tie to her was a vague belief that they could depend on her in time of need. Conversely,

---

park she sent me a postcard saying: "Dear Mrs. Johnson, Regarding your mimeographed letter . . . . Please do not contact us as we have nothing good to say and are only here as there isn't another park we could move to . . ." She steadfastly refused to be interviewed and I ultimately had to settle for a brief, clandestine talk with her husband one day while she was out.

some of the neighborly relationships were very close and genuine, even though the individuals had not met before they had moved into Idle Haven. In general, however, it was true that while neighbors could be close friends they were more likely to be casual acquaintances, whereas non-neighboring friends could be casual acquaintances but were more likely to be close friends. Some of the reasons for this become apparent when one looks at how people acquired non-neighboring friends within the park.

One common explanation for a non-neighboring friendship was that it predated the resident's move to Idle Haven. As was noted in the previous chapter, fourteen of the households interviewed said they had moved to Idle Haven partly because they already knew someone who lived there. Inevitably these friends were mentioned among the three park residents whom people knew best, and in only one instance were such old friends also neighbors. (Similarly, in only one instance did relatives in separate mobile homes live adjacent to one another. This was largely a result of the time that people moved into the park. Once Idle Haven was full, people who wanted to join friends or relatives took any suitable vacancy rather than waiting for a specific spot to fall vacant.) Other park residents discovered after they had moved to Idle Haven that somone they used to know (in another park or neighborhood, on a former job, or through a club in which they used to be active) also lived in the park, and this often led to renewed friendships. Still other residents who had not known one another discovered that they worked for the same company or store and began exchanging rides to and from work, which led to friendships and—in one instance in Idle Haven—to marriage. There were also two marriages between residents in Idle Haven which led to friendships between the in-laws of the married couples, all of whom also happened to live in the park.[6]

---

[6] Over a 5-year period three marriages took place between Idle Haven residents. One of these was between two of the young people who had entered the park as teenagers. As a result of this marriage, both sets of parents became good friends. Another marriage occurred between a widower and a divorcée who, although both lived in the park, did not know each other until a meeting was arranged by another park couple who knew them both. The third marriage took place between a middle-aged widower and a young woman who had been living in the park with her grandparents. In this case the widower discovered at work that there was a young woman in his plant who also lived in Idle Haven, and as a result he looked her up and suggested they start driving to

Perhaps the most common way that non-neighbor friendships developed, however, was as a result of the social activities sponsored by the park. Although neighborly relationships developed between residents who had only the most general social characteristics in common—that is, the fact that they were white, working-class, and middle-aged or elderly—non-neighbor friendships were more likely to be based on specific shared interests, often ones that residents had discovered in each other as a result of some park activity. In the course of the 5 years that Idle Haven had existed, a large number of clubs had been started by various interested residents: a bowling team, a golf club, a ceramics class, a photography club, a gardening club, a handicraft class, a Spanish class, an exercise class, bridge and canasta clubs, square-dance and ballroom dancing clubs, an Eastern Star and Masonic "Joiners" group (for men and women in the park who belonged to these two lodges), and a Bible class. Some of these groups had had only a brief existence and then failed because the participants lost interest; others were abandoned when dissension within the group developed.[7] Other groups, such as the bowling team, had an intermittent existence depending upon the number of men in the park interested in participating. Even when such groups failed, however, friendships made as a result of them often persisted. Men who had participated in a defunct golf club still golfed together, and couples who had discovered they shared a passion for dancing still went out dancing together.

Activities engaged in by park friends thus ranged well beyond the strictly park-sponsored occasions. Women went shopping and out to lunch together; couples who knew each other well sometimes went fishing and hunting together, or they went to Reno for a weekend of gambling and drinking. There were also various kinds of assistance for which people were more likely to call on a close

---

work together. The widower's mother, who also lived in Idle Haven, and the girl's grandparents became friends as a result of the marriage.

[7] As Ronald Frankenberg demonstrated in *Village on the Border* (1957), in face-to-face communities where open hostility causes grave disruption, group projects are repeatedly launched and then abandoned in the face of conflict, only to be relaunched later in some slightly different form. Another common practice in such communities is to arrive at all decisions by consensus rather than forcing issues to a vote; and when unpopular decisions must be made, to place in positions of leadership an outsider or a newcomer, who has few ties to established factions and who can also serve as a scapegoat. See also Arthur J. Vidich and Joseph Bensman, *Small Town in Mass Society* (1968), especially Chapters 5 and 6; and Chapter 6 below.

park friend, who could be but often was not a neighbor. For example, three residents of Idle Haven went on vacations and in each instance left their dog or cat in the care of a non-neighboring friend. Close friends also felt free to make heavier demands on each other than they did on neighbors. It was not at all uncommon for a neighbor to drive someone to the hospital, but when the husband of a woman who could not drive was confined to the hospital for six weeks, she turned to non-neighboring park friends for *daily* rides.

When it came to asking park friends over for dinner or a cocktail, however, most residents in Idle Haven conformed to the working-class stereotype of seldom having friends into their homes.[8] Many said that their mobile homes were too small (as, indeed, some of them were), although these same people often entertained vast numbers of relatives in them. The only residents who gave dinner parties for friends were white-collar families. However, even these dinner parties usually had a specific purpose: for example, a group of about five couples who were close friends celebrated each other's birthdays and wedding anniversaries. But there were no dinner parties of the sort where a host or hostess invites a group of congenial friends to dinner a week, or two weeks, hence. One of the two engineers in the park, who was clearly used to a more upper middle-class type of entertaining, replied, when I asked whether he had ever had anyone from the park over for dinner: "We used to, but we quit because nobody ever returned the invitations."

Some couples occasionally played cards with each other in their mobile homes, but these couples were usually the same ones who also had dinner together. Working-class residents who wanted to play cards tended to drift into the recreation hall to see if they could get a game started there. The canasta club—a closed group of twelve women—used to meet once a week in each other's mobile homes with the hostess of the week providing sandwiches and coffee, but it was moved to a cardroom in the recreation hall because some of the women's livingrooms were too small to hold three card tables.[9]

---

[8] Compare Berger, 1960: 64–72; and Komarovsky, 1962:311–20.

[9] The canasta club (actually, two tables of canasta and one of pinochle) was started in direct opposition to the Tuesday and Thursday afternoon card group (here usually referred to as the bridge club). This original card group, which in recent times has consisted of between three and four tables of bridge

No one in the park claimed he had ever had a friend over to watch television—probably because everyone in the park had at least one television set, and 50 per cent had color sets. Nevertheless, when the Oakland Raiders and the Kansas City Chiefs played in Oakland for the championship of the AFL, there was a great exodus of men to those few mobile homes in the park that had rotating antennas. (The game was not being televised locally, but those with rotating antennas could bring in Sacramento or Salinas stations.) Similarly, very few residents said they had ever had friends in for coffee or tea, but this was in fact a rather common occurrence. Most people only meant that they had no formal tea parties, but friends and neighbors (and anthropologists) who dropped in casually were usually offered a cup of coffee or tea. It was also not uncommon to see two neighboring men standing outside their mobile homes on a hot day having a beer together.

Thus, while there may not have been much formal visiting among park friends, there was a good deal of informal coming and going. Not everyone in the park was equally receptive to casual visits, however, and there was a variety of devices used by people to guard their privacy. Some residents complained that one of the drawbacks of mobile-home living was that people could always tell when you were home because they could see your car in the driveway. (Mobile homes typically have a carport but not a garage.)[10] Thus many people who are at home and who hear an unwelcome visitor at their door are forced to play possum. Some are more skillful at this than others—retreating out of sight and not making any noise—so that they can later claim to have been napping or in the bathtub. But I have rung a number of doorbells and heard the sounds of television or of cooking without getting an answer. (Of course, perhaps some of these people genuinely didn't hear me.)

There is also an unwritten rule in most mobile-home parks that anyone who has the curtain pulled across his glass door does not want to be disturbed. Many older mobile homes have such glass doors and this device does, indeed, seem to work very well. When

---

players, was at one time dominated by a rather unpleasant woman (since evicted from the park as a "troublemaker") who did her best to drive out non-bridge players. One of the non-bridge players decided that she would start a canasta club which one could join only by invitation, and that she would invite some of the women who had been insulted by the bridge-playing group.

[10] Long before this was pointed out to me, I was unconsciously checking for cars as I approached the home of someone I wanted to interview.

the curtain is not pulled one can see almost the entire livingroom and one assumes that the occupants (who can often be seen inside, watching television, or ironing, or sewing) are not averse to company. Many of the newer mobile homes, however, have ordinary wooden doors and for them this signaling device no longer works. It is widely assumed that residents of such mobile homes are indicating their desire for privacy when they shut their livingroom drapes, but this may not always be the case. One woman who said she kept her drapes pulled to protect her furniture from the sun added mournfully, "I guess I should keep them open; I'd get more visitors."

A more unusual device for protecting one's privacy in a mobile-home park is the widespread lack of doorbells. It is hard to say to what extent the omission of doorbells is intentional, but it is so common that it must serve a useful purpose or at least not be detrimental to mobile-home life. Many older mobile homes apparently came without doorbells and people never bothered to install one. Many newer mobile homes have doorbells to begin with, but the addition of screened porches or extra rooms makes the doorbells inaccessible to visitors. It is, of course, possible to argue that the lack of doorbells is simply a sign of how "friendly" and "ingroup" most mobile-home parks are: strangers seldom call and anyone else is welcome just to walk in. There is another omission, however, that clearly does have an anti-social purpose, and that is the lack of a name-plate on the front of one's mobile home. Most mobile homes have large and handsome name-plates affixed to their fronts announcing who lives inside—sometimes only the last name, e.g., "The Jewetts," but more commonly both first and last names, e.g., "Judy and Ted Harkness," or just first names, e.g., "Bill and Ida." The omission of such a name-plate effectively prevents most park residents (other than immediate neighbors) from finding out who lives in such an unidentified mobile home and it tends to discourage casual visiting. Another way to ward off unwelcome callers is to erect a sign on the front of one's mobile home proclaiming the resident to be a "Day Sleeper."

One might suppose that such safeguards against overfamiliarity mean that almost everyone in a mobile-home park has more social contacts than he can use or wants—but such is not the case. As Irving Rosow has noted with regard to retirement communities and their rounds of social activities:

"It seems likely that the residents [of these communities] . . . tend to be socially skilled and active persons who take full advantage of the social opportunities around them. Conceivably, the socially inept are among those who do not fit into the social pattern of these communities. They may need more help to become integrated than they are receiving" (HEW, 1968:134).

There were a number of residents in Idle Haven who were quite isolated and who would have benefitted greatly from having someone visit them on a regular basis. Often these people were very old and could not get about much so that no one in the park outside their immediate neighbors even knew they lived there. Many of these neighbors made genuine efforts to be kind and sociable toward such isolates, but the relationships were usually too one sided to be activated frequently. "I should go see her more often," one woman said to me of another woman in the park, "but I get so tired of listening to her complain about all her ailments." Other individuals in the park who had trouble making friends were people who tended to be depressed, or "nervous," or shy. Again, there were usually neighbors and friends who were willing to make the effort now and then, but these were more acts of charity than genuine friendships.

It was also clear that women who entered the park as widows had a much harder time making friends and were a great deal less active in park activities than married women or women who had been widowed after moving to Idle Haven. This may, in part, reflect what Zena Smith Blau (1961) has called the structural constraints on friendship in old age. There are more couples than widows in Idle Haven and therefore couples tend to set the dominant social tone in the park and to seek their friends among other couples.[11] Another contributing factor is that women, regardless of whether they are widowed or married, do not like to come to park activities alone. Several women whose husbands worked at night said that they did not attend park dinners or bingo because they did not want to come alone. Widows also gave this as a reason for not participating more. However, women who were widowed after

---

[11] It would be interesting to see whether, in a park where widows outnumbered couples, widows played a more prominent role in planned activities and were more frequently named as friends. Some evidence from a high-rise retirement complex in the Bay Area would suggest that this may be so; however, class may be the more important variable. Most of the residents in this apartment complex are upper middle or upper class and such single and widowed women are used to running club meetings and doing things on their own.

having lived in Idle Haven for some time usually had a circle of friends to draw on, and they were more likely to continue the activity patterns they had established before the death of their spouses.

Residents who were active in the planned activities of the park were more likely to make non-neighbor friends; however, unless residents had a friend or a neighbor with whom to attend park functions they were much less likely to come. Just as in high school a student feels lonely entering a cafeteria by himself and may, in fact, have trouble finding a place to sit because various tables are staked out by cliques of friends, so in Idle Haven residents tended to come to the park dinners in groups. Some groups of friends even brought their plates and silverware to the hall in mid-afternoon in order to lay claim to a table. Dinners and dances, in particular, were occasions when few people came alone or even with just their spouses. Breakfasts, luncheons, and bingo evenings were more fluid, and although residents often sought out a friend to sit by they would come to these events alone. One shy woman, however, had not even dared to come to the handicraft class—a very *ad hoc* and fluctuating group of women—until she had found a neighbor willing to accompany her.

Such cliquishness—whether real or imagined on the part of the outsider—tends to discourage the newcomer to an already established community. In Idle Haven, neighbors or the park association's president usually invited and accompanied new residents to their first monthly dinner or breakfast, but unless the new residents made friends easily and rapidly, they were likely to feel ill at ease coming alone to subsequent gatherings. One Idle Haven couple was particularly upset about a dance they had attended at which they had more or less sat by themselves all evening and had danced only with each other while at other tables groups of couples were sitting together and exchanging partners. It is difficult to say, however, whether this couple's feelings of being left out—which led to their leaving the park after two years' residence—was caused by group indifference to them or by their own lack of assertiveness and awkwardness in making new friends.

It was certainly not impossible for new arrivals to the park to make friends and become solidly established in the park's social life. Of the twelve names mentioned most frequently as friends, only five had lived in Idle Haven since its inception, whereas the others had entered the park after its social structure was well developed.

It is true that all of the twelve households who were frequently named as friends were active in park activities; that is, they had a somewhat higher visibility than individuals who merely befriended their neighbors. Seven had been officers of the park's association at one time or another, and all participated in at least one of the park's formal activities. Interestingly enough, and supporting the earlier argument that widows in the park tended to be more retiring, all of the twelve names frequently mentioned were those of married couples. It could be argued that a couple, consisting of two separate individuals, is twice as likely to make friends as a single person, but among only half of the twelve couples was the husband active *in any way* within the park. In almost all cases it was the woman—or the couple as a unit—that was being cited as a friend.

Park friendships and neighborly relations, and their interaction with relatives in and outside of the park, are thus complex and various. Much depends upon an individual's personality and gregariousness, but much also depends upon whether one is married or alone, and upon one's age and general health.[12] The interplay among some of these variables, as well as an important function of park friendships, is illustrated by the response of residents to a death in their midst. A few of the residents in Idle Haven felt that one of the drawbacks of living in a form of retirement community was the number of deaths that occurred. Such deaths seemed to depress them and they generally avoided attending the funerals. However, many other residents pointed out that there were actually not so many deaths in the park but that one tended to hear about them simply because the park was a small community. They also perceived that one concomitant of hearing about deaths in the park and knowing the individuals involved was the social support residents could give the survivor.

During the year that I was studying Idle Haven, six residents died. Five of these deaths went unremarked except for a notice in the monthly park bulletin and a sympathy card sent by the park association's "Sunshine Girl" to the surviving relatives. The reason

---

[12] Frances Carp found that people with more "friendship votes" tended to be younger (1966:164). In Idle Haven, eight of the twelve most popular couples were in their 60s; three were in their 50s; and only one was in their 70s. However, it is my impression that good physical health is a far better guide to activity levels (which, in turn, are related to popularity) than chronological age. Idle Haven residents in their 50s and 60s who were in poor health were just as socially and physically inactive as some residents in their 80s.

for this lack of park involvement, however, was that in four cases
the dead resident was a widow or widower and the surviving relatives did not live in the park, nor were the funeral arrangements
always made locally. In the fifth case the surviving husband continued to live in the park, but even as a couple he and his wife
had made few friends, partly because his wife had spent so much
time prior to her death in the hospital. However, the sixth death
involved a couple who, while they had only lived in Idle Haven for
six months prior to the death of the husband, had been drawn into
the friendship circle of their married middle-aged daughter, an active park resident for five years. The 77-year-old father had entered
the park with terminal cancer, and his daughter had told friends
that her chief concern had been to get her parents "settled" near
her before his death. The father nevertheless had had some good
days in the park when he had joined his wife and daughter at
bridge, or bingo, or a potluck dinner. He died quite suddenly one
night, less than a week after I had seen him cheerfully playing
bingo.

The funeral was held locally, and over the weekend that his
body lay in state at the mortuary, half a dozen couples from Idle
Haven went to pay their last respects and to sign the guest book.
At the funeral service, aside from members of the family, who sat
in a separate room, there were about twenty mourners, eighteen of
them residents of Idle Haven. Most of the bridge club, the assistant
manager of the park, several neighbors, and several close friends of
the daughter and her husband were in attendance. Moreover, the
service itself was conducted by a young resident of Idle Haven who
was planning on studying for the ministry and who had been a park
neighbor of the dead man and his widow. Although this young man
knew little and said nothing about the personality or the life of the
dead man and instead delivered a rather stiff-necked sermon about
whether we living were fully prepared to meet our Maker (had we
been in the dead man's shoes), the widow and her daughter were
clearly touched by the service. The widow later said to me that she
was also pleased to have given the boy an opportunity to "get some
experience."

After the service all of the mourners returned to the Idle Haven
recreation hall, where about four long tables had been set up and
covered with white paper cloths. Several of the women were serving
coffee and cakes they had baked for the occasion. The atmosphere
was at once less solemn and sadder. People laughed and joked (and

ate a great deal of cake) but also reminisced about the dead man. The widow said she could not, in all conscience, wish him back with all the pain he had had; the daughter cried copiously and was embraced and consoled by her women friends. It struck me as a fine community send-off for a 77-year-old man who had only lived in the park for six months and who had either outlived or moved away from most of his former neighbors and friends. It was also a great source of emotional support for his widow and daughter, who, I was pleased to note, were back at the bridge table the following week.

5. Aid and Trade

The patterns of mutual aid that exist in a mobile-home park such as
Idle Haven contribute greatly to the residents' sense of community.
In fact, as Alvin Gouldner has argued, the norm of reciprocity
functions in any social system to stabilize and maintain human relationships. In general, this norm demands that "(1) people should
help those who have helped them, and (2) people should not injure
those who have helped them" (Gouldner, 1960:171). One of the
ways reciprocity functions to maintain relationships is through the
mechanism of rough equivalence. Thus a ride to the grocery store
may elicit a plate of cookies in return, but while both participants
will understand these to be reciprocal gestures, neither will be sure
at the end of the exchange which one of them is "one up." And so
the exchange pattern will continue.

We have also noted, however, that some residents in Idle Haven were in a poor position to engage in reciprocal relationships. As Gouldner acknowledges, the norm of reciprocity has its dysfunctional side and may induce tensions and changes into social systems as well as contributing to their stability. For example:

> "The norm may lead individuals to establish relations only or primarily with those who can reciprocate, thus inducing neglect of the needs of those unable to do so. Clearly the norm of reciprocity cannot apply with full force in relations with children, old people, or with those who are mentally or physically handicapped, and it is theoretically inferable that other, fundamentally different kinds of normative orientations will develop in moral codes" (Gouldner, 1960:178).

Some of the Idle Haven residents who could not reciprocate neighborly gestures would have benefitted from gestures rendered in response to a different normative orientation: for example, regular visits by a practical nurse. It goes without saying, of course, that were mobile-home parks to be filled exclusively with extremely aged, indigent, and otherwise socially incapable individuals, all social relationships would have to be based on norms such as those of service and the result would be a caretaker institution rather than a community.

There was actually a large area of discretion in Idle Haven within which reciprocity among friends and neighbors could be negotiated. Perhaps the most typical pattern involved equivalent services—a plate of cookies in exchange for a ride to the hospital or the store; some repairs by a man around a widow's house or on her car in exchange for her services as a babysitter with a pet or some plants. But individuals who, because of age or ill health, felt they could not return favors and individuals who had to make heavy and repeated demands on others found it easier to shift from payments in kind to payments in cash. The elderly widow who had such a close maternal relationship with her Mexican neighbor also paid her about $5 week for housecleaning and other services rendered. There were several other women in Idle Haven who "worked" for someone in the park on this basis.

The interesting thing about these work arrangements was that they were so clearly based on friendship and reciprocity rather than on the impersonal criteria of the job market. One sturdy widow in her seventies was paid $5 a week by a younger but very frail widow who also lived in the park. For this amount, the older woman "visited" the younger one every other day or so and performed a variety of minor services: on some days she merely "picked up" the livingroom and did a little grocery shopping; on other days she took some clothes to the laundry room and put them through the washer and dryer. But mainly the arrangement gave each woman someone to talk to, and it was not incidental that each cited the other as a close friend. The older woman (who, like the younger one, received old-age assistance payments from the state) had also tried doing housework for a bachelor in the park, but this relationship had foundered precisely because the bachelor had insisted on treating her as a paid employee. He felt she did not work hard enough for the money, and she had found him rude and "unfriendly."

The use of money as a medium of exchange in relationships based on friendship and neighborliness also caused problems for people. Where it was regularized, as in the case of the two widows, it seemed to work out very well; but in instances where money was offered on an *ad hoc* basis it was very often refused and this made repayment a growing burden for some people. One elderly childless couple, neither of whom could drive or walk very far because of age and illness, were entirely dependent upon park neighbors and friends for rides to the doctor, stores, and church. They had a variety of neighbors who very willingly met these needs; and the elderly couple, who were fairly well off financially, regularly offered their benefactors a dollar for gas or for their trouble. But of course many people refused these dollars and the elderly couple came to feel increasingly burdened with obligations they could not discharge. After 5 years in Idle Haven, where they were extremely happy in all respects except this one, they finally moved to an apartment that was located across the street from a grocery store and on a major bus line. The obverse of the situation just described could also be found in Idle Haven. There were some widows, for example, who were without cars but who seldom accepted rides because they knew they would be obligated to reciprocate financially—something they either could not afford or did not want to do. "I'd rather walk two blocks and take the bus," one of them said. "It's cheaper and less trouble."

Residents of Idle Haven were clearly torn between their feelings that the park was "one large, happy family" where the normal rules of the market place did not apply and their suspicions that "everyone is out to make a buck" regardless of the circumstances. This ambivalence produced some epic disputes within the park and it was also responsible for the great emphasis on "equity" or fairness that pervaded most park endeavors. Just like peasants in a backward society whose lives are guided by an "image of limited good"—a belief that if one of them prospers it must necessarily be at someone else's expense—and who therefore endeavor by means of gossip and rituals of exchange to equalize their positions, the residents of Idle Haven zealously guarded their rights vis-à-vis everyone else. Windfalls and achievements outside the park were, of course, exempt from this kind of envy: someone who got a raise, or bought a new travel trailer, or went on a trip, might be called a lucky fellow but no effort was made to call him to account because he had gotten something others did not have.[1] By contrast, within the park there was a serious debate among officers of the residents' association (whose total 1969 membership, at $1 per person per year, consisted of about 200 out of the 360 residents) as to whether the association should send "get-well" cards to everyone in the park who was ill or only to association members. The officers opted for the latter alternative because "people shouldn't get something for nothing." Similarly, great concern was often expressed at officers' meetings over residents who, at park dinners, managed to get two desserts or, at park breakfasts, wrapped up some toast or a piece of sweetroll to take home.

The two clearest illustrations of the concern for equity within the park were situations in which I myself played a minor role: in one instance by providing an acceptable solution and in the other by unwittingly creating a major problem for some of the association's officers. The first case was launched at a board meeting of the park association's officers, who were discussing the problem of how to increase attendance at the monthly park association meetings. Several officers acknowledged that the meetings were often dull and suggested that interesting speakers should be obtained—for example, a speaker from the social security office, or a speaker on mutual

---

[1] George Foster, who coined the phrase "the image of limited good," notes that in peasant societies also, achievements wholly removed from the community are not subject to envy. Thus, in Mexico, a peasant may find it hard to get ahead in his own village but he is not censured for making a lot of money as a migrant worker in California (1967:315–17).

funds, or someone from the police department. (I was asked to speak but declined on the grounds that my research was not yet complete. However, I later used the speaker format—and my husband—to conduct a small sociological experiment, discussed in Chapter 7.) Several officers also suggested that some form of entertainment might draw more members to the meetings. Various alternatives were discussed. Slide showings and 16 mm. movies were rejected, in part because of difficulties in obtaining and setting up the necessary equipment and in part because the majority felt that such amateurish efforts simply could not compete with the attractions of television. One officer, however, suggested that her brother, who was a professional magician, might be willing to put on a magic show at one of the association's regular monthly meetings, and this proposal was greeted with a great deal of enthusiasm.

The woman who made the suggestion was urged to contact her brother (who lived in the Bay Area but not in the park) to work out the details. She warned the other officers that her brother's fee would be approximately $50 for a half-hour show, but this did not seem to worry anyone since the association's treasury, at that point, contained several hundred dollars. At the board meeting in the following month she reported that her brother would be delighted to put on a show for $50 and suggested several dates when he would be available. This produced a lengthy discussion about which date would be the most desirable from the standpoint of drawing a large attendance. It was decided that the summer months, just then beginning, would not be a good time because many park residents would be away on vacations. The September association meeting was finally selected. As the discussion drew to a close one of the officers sighed and said, "I suppose we'll be criticized for using $50 out of the treasury for something like this." Someone else responded that people who wanted an excuse to criticize the officers could always find one and that this was no reason not to go ahead with the plan.

Nevertheless, at the next board meeting the entire issue of the magician and his fee was raised again for discussion. There seemed to be a great fear that some residents unable to attend the association's meeting or not interested in magic tricks would claim the association's funds were not being used for the benefit of everyone, and none of the officers seemed willing to take responsibility for such a potentially dangerous decision. Although the meeting ended on an inconclusive note, most of the officers were clearly looking for a way out. The solution to this impasse was apparently found later that same evening. A few of the officers knew that I wanted to do something for the people of the park upon completing my research, as a way of thanking everyone for their cooperation. I had asked several officers for suggestions and advice about the form this thanks might take, and—for reasons discussed further below, which also involved the concern for equity in the park—I had had some trouble finding an appropriate gesture. The day after the inconclusive board meeting, however, I was approached by one of the association officers, who suggested to me that perhaps I might like to sponsor the magician. In this way I could let the board off the hook financially and morally, at the same time that I would be expressing my thanks to residents of the park. I agreed that it was an ingenious solution, and as a result the September association meeting featured a magic show—complete with two live rabbits and somewhat longer and more expensive than originally planned—courtesy of the park's anthropologist.[2]

The following month, once again at the officers' board meeting, a different problem arose. There was a long discussion about plans for the park Christmas party—an annual event featuring a dinner, the exchange of small presents, a Santa Claus, and entertainment provided by a local dance studio. This party was the only wholly free event on the park calendar—free, that is, to all association members—and it drained the treasury of the several hundred dollars that it had amassed during the year in the form of $1 memberships and the proceeds of a white elephant sale. Because the party was in some respects a reward for loyal park association members, great stress was placed on not admitting "free-loaders." The membership roll was even declared closed during the month of December so

---

[2] The magic show produced one further complication—namely, the question of whether residents' grandchildren would be allowed to attend. The association's officers referred this decision to me, arguing that it was now "my show." I was surprised to find myself using some of the same evasive tactics I had previously seen others in the park use in order to avoid offending anyone. It was rumored that some residents intended to bring their grandchildren without asking for permission, and it would therefore have been unfair to refuse permission to those who were considerate enough to ask. At the same time, I was warned, it would be unwise to issue an open invitation to all grandchildren of park residents, since this would produce a deluge. I concluded that the best course of action was to say nothing and to avoid all direct inquiries. Fortunately, this solution was greatly simplified by my decision to take a two weeks' vacation just before the magic show.

that no one could join the association just in order to attend the Christmas party. In the midst of a thorough airing of all these issues there was an awkward silence, suddenly, as several officers turned to look at me. Did I want to attend the Christmas party? I naturally said I would very much like to attend and offered to pay the association dues. Several officers objected to this, however, on grounds that only residents of Idle Haven could belong to the association and I did not live in the park. I suggested that perhaps I could be made an honorary member of the association, but the board feared that by allowing a non-resident to join the association it would invite criticism and set a bad precedent for residents' children and grandchildren, and former residents who still had ties to the park, who might also want to become honorary members. Several board members argued that I ought to be allowed to attend as a non-member because of my special role within the park; however, others pointed out that this would create a precedent for residents who might have relatives wanting to attend the party. Someone then pointed out that a bona fide houseguest of a park resident could be allowed to attend the Christmas party, and several people promptly offered to put me up overnight so that I could attend the party legally. I suggested jokingly that perhaps the problem could be solved just as easily by my buying a mobile home or marrying one of the bachelors in the park.

The issue was not a joking matter for the officers, however, and it preoccupied them for nearly an hour. Their concern with precedent and equity made it impossible for them either to admit me as a member or to allow me to attend as a non-member. Finally, on the assumption that one of the chief stumbling blocks was their concern that no one should get something for nothing, I suggested that I be allowed to attend the party as an "observer" rather than as a guest. Specifically, I asked to come after the dinner was over, merely in order to watch how the park celebrated Christmas. This proposal was greeted with an audible sigh of relief and accepted with no further argument. Accordingly, I arrived at the Christmas party an hour late, just as dinner was drawing to a close, and although I was graciously offered a cup of coffee and some dessert, I noticed that several officers (the only ones privy to our agreement) looked somewhat relieved when I refused.

These two incidents illustrate the great concern of the park association's officers not only to be "fair" to everyone in the park but also to protect the enclave of the park against outsiders (including residents' relatives) and, on occasion, to protect a special enclave—the association's members—from the incursions of non-association members who were nevertheless park residents. This type of balancing act is not at all uncommon in other small communities, and it produces a distinctive leadership style—including a great reluctance to become an officer, avoidance of clear-cut decisions, attempts to achieve unanimity rather than to vote on matters, and a reliance on irregular channels of communication, particularly gossip. Some of these features of park life will be discussed more fully in the next chapter, which deals with the formal social structure of Idle Haven.

There was, however, another facet to the problem of maintaining equity—or balance—within the park that caused a great deal of trouble. This involved the question of whether and how people should be allowed to practice their trade within the park. Most of the residents of Idle Haven were blue-collar workers, and many of them practiced trades that were potentially useful to other residents: for example, auto repair, carpet laying, electrical appliance repair, plumbing, carpentry, and so forth. Were such skilled workers obligated by the unwritten rules of neighborliness and friendship to render their services for free (or for a token exchange), or could they charge full price for their work or products and even exploit the park as a closed market within which to drum up trade?[3]

There were, for example, a number of men and women in the park who worked for others or who had businesses upon which their livelihood depended and who could not therefore offer their services or products at a discount. Such individuals often posted notices advertising their businesses on the bulletin board in the recreation hall, but they expected to deal with park residents as customers rather than as friends. For example, there were notices posted by one woman in the park who sold cemetery plots, by another who sold mobile-home lots in a recreation area north of San Francisco, by a third who sold Avon products, and by still another who prepared income tax returns. Several of the men in the park merely advertised their places of business—e.g., a large department store, a small appliance repair shop, or a concern that erected mobile-home awnings. Such individuals hoped to cultivate some customers

---

[3] The problem exists within the middle class as well, particularly for highly paid professionals such as doctors and lawyers, who may find themselves being pumped for free advice at social gatherings and the homes of friends.

within the park but, with the exception of the Avon lady, they did not depend exclusively upon the park for business.

There was a much larger number of residents, however, who had developed a small sideline, usually unadvertised, which they practiced only within the park. There were, for example, several women who sold greeting cards, or stationery, or spices, out of their mobile homes, or who held Tupperware or lingerie or wig parties in the recreation hall. There were also three retired men of whom one repaired typewriters and small machines, another gardened for several people in the park, and still another made some extra money by weatherproofing people's mobile-home roofs. There were also several women who had hobbies that brought them a financial return. One woman and her husband collected rocks and semi-precious stones out of which they made very attractive pieces of jewelry that they sold around the park. Several women would sell some of the ceramics they made in the park's ceramics class, and others would knit sweaters or sew dresses for a price. Buying something of this nature within the park was never a straightforward affair. A woman might come into the recreation hall with a catalogue displaying various kinds of stationery and say casually to those assembled, "I'm going to order some of this for myself; is there anyone else who would like some?" The unspoken understanding was that, as at a Tupperware party, if the hostess or amateur saleslady did get someone else to buy something she would get hers for free.

In the course of my interviewing I took advantage of such unspoken conventions by buying things from people as a way of recompensing them for their time and trouble. (I was also, of course, buying their good will toward me and my project.) Thus, I acquired a great many interesting pieces of handiwork, ranging from crocheted pot-holders to plastic flowers, ceramic trivets, and a toilet-paper cover in the shape of a doll wearing a hoop skirt. My most instructive encounter in the realm of park sales, however, was with an old lady who knitted extremely colorful lap robes out of scrap wool that her son bought for her from a nearby carpet factory. She had made herself a kind of primitive loom out of a length of wood and some large nails and she usually had several different pieces of work in progress since she tried to use the wool scraps in interesting color combinations. Her livingroom floor and most of her furniture were covered with the completed throws. After having finished the interview and having complimented her work I asked whether she would consider selling me one. She seemed to be very surprised and said she had never sold her work before,[4] but when I pressed her a little she finally said, "Well, how much would you offer me?" I made a hasty mental estimate of both the amount of work involved and the amount of money I carried in my purse, and said, "I would think such a beautiful lap robe would be worth at least $10." Whereupon, without a moment's hesitation, she replied, "I really couldn't take a penny less than $15." I was not sure at first whether I had $15 with me (as it turned out, I did), so I offered her a check, which she refused out of the mistaken notion that a check might be traceable by the "welfare people." And so we finally settled our affair in cash.

Undoubtedly one reason for the conspiratorial nature of these transactions was that the income was not reported to either the internal revenue service or the state's old age assistance program. The sums of money involved were not very large, however, and they were used either as pin-money by women whose husbands were still employed or as supplements to the meager budgets of retired couples or widows. The small sums involved and the face-to-face nature of the sales situation probably account for the fact that no one in the park objected to these small enterprises. In fact, many people benefitted from them at one time or another—either as buyer or as seller—and they contributed to the park's image as a self-sufficient, tightly knit community. It was only when personal profits were surmised to be large that envy became rampant and that residents began to insist upon a distinction between the park as a friendly community and the marketplace mentality assumed to exist outside of it.

Three cases may serve to illustrate the problems created by what some residents deemed to be "money-grabbing" within the park. Two of these involved residents who wanted to practice their professions in Idle Haven and the third involved a resident who tried to run the park's bingo games along more-or-less business lines.

The first case centered about a park couple who, together with a third non-resident, made their living as a small dance combo. Although in their 60s and semi-retired (that is to say, they no longer played six evenings a week in supper clubs or bars), they still played frequently at Elks' Club dances and other group occasions. When

---

[4] As a matter of fact, I don't think she ever sold the laprobes in the park but instead took them to a weekend flea market—or perhaps her son sold them there.

they were first considering selling their home and moving into Idle Haven the manageress was so pleased at the thought of having such a couple (and their talents) in the park that she "held open" a space for them for several months while they sold their house. Not long after they had moved to Idle Haven they played in the recreation hall several Sunday afternoons in an effort to start some "tea dancing," but only about six couples actually came to dance and others either sat and listened or continued with their card-playing. The trio therefore abandoned this particular attempt to interest park residents in their services.

Less than a year after entering the park, however, the husband allowed himself to be elected president of the residents' association and, as a result of interest expressed by several residents, he tried to initiate monthly Saturday-night dances to be held in the recreation hall and sponsored by the association just as monthly breakfasts, dinners, and bingo were. Sponsorship by the association implies not that a small fee will not be charged but that the association's treasury will make up any deficit and that the association's insurance policy covers anyone present at the event.[5] In the case of the dances, tickets were sold at $1.25 per person and attendance was limited to approximately 200 people (or 100 couples). The $250 in proceeds went to cover the fees of the three musicians ($75 each per evening) with $25 to cover the cost of paper cups, coffee and doughnuts (liquor and "set-ups" were furnished by the guests themselves).

These dances caused an enormous amount of backbiting and dissension within the park. The president of the association was charged with using the power of his office to fatten his own wallet; after all, hadn't he performed free of charge on several previous occasions and was it not customary for talented park residents to contribute their services free of charge? The president argued (belatedly) that as members of the musicians' union he and his wife and partner could not perform without a standard union fee—not a very powerful argument in a community where nearly everyone belonged to a union of some sort. He also maintained that many residents had requested that dances be held. Others argued that since not everyone in the park wanted to dance the activity should not be

---

[5] The matter of insurance may seem to be a minor issue, but I attended one association-sponsored event at which an old lady, a guest of a park resident, slipped and broke her wrist. In this case the association's insurance policy paid her doctor bills.

sponsored by the association, whose treasury was potentially liable for any deficit incurred. In fact, the players did not run the risk of incurring a deficit because they sold some of their tickets in two other nearby mobile-home parks (whose residents were only too pleased to come because their managers did not allow dances in their recreation halls); but this practice produced still further criticism within Idle Haven. Why should the park's association sponsor an activity attended primarily by outsiders?

In the face of such criticisms, the dances were abandoned. They were revived, however, a year later with the encouragement of the Idle Haven manageress, who liked to dance and who seemed to be of the opinion that so long as people had a good time it didn't matter who made a little extra money. This time the dances were sponsored not by the park association but by a special "Dance Club" headed by a close park friend of the combo-playing couple. Otherwise, the format was the same as before. Of 200 dancers, about a third were residents of Idle Haven or their relatives and guests, and the remainder came from the two nearby parks or from the ranks of local Elks and others acquainted with the trio. This solution dampened much of the overt criticism, but there was still a good deal of grumbling from non-dancing residents who lived near the hall (the noise bothered them and several times a none-too-sober departing guest backed his car into someone's rock-garden or front porch) and from residents who felt the facilities of the park were being exploited for private profit. In some ways the detractors were right, of course, although they tended to overlook the advantages for park residents in having such entertainment available on their premises.

A somewhat more muted but equally vexed case concerned the status (and pay) of the park's resident cook. Many mobile-home parks have monthly potluck suppers, which are sometimes poorly attended because everyone who comes must bring a prepared dish sufficient to feed four people and many residents find it simpler (and cheaper) to eat at home.[6] Idle Haven, during the course of its 5 years of existence, had been blessed with two "professional" cooks as residents—both of them men, one of whom had been a cook in the army and the other a cook in a large public institution (name-

---

[6] In Idle Haven a potluck supper (on nights when the cook was busy) drew between thirty and forty residents, as compared to the ninety to a hundred who attended the fully prepared dinners.

ly, a jail). Given the social composition of mobile-home parks today, the presence of such talents among the residents is probably
not at all uncommon (just as one is liable to find plumbers, carpenters, and electricians); and I shall therefore describe in some detail
the saga of the two cooks.

The first cook (long retired from the army and working as a
warehouseman) apparently volunteered his services shortly after
the park opened simply because he liked to cook. He began by
making pancakes at the monthly breakfasts and soon branched out
into main dishes for what became semi-potluck suppers. He also
persuaded the park's owner to enlarge the recreation hall's kitchen
and have it fitted with a professional range and griddle. As soon as
this was accomplished he bought the park some large professional
cooking utensils, which he obtained from restaurant-supply houses
at wholesale prices. These purchases, as well as purchases of food,
for which he submitted itemized bills to the park association's officers, created grave suspicions that he "must be making something
on the side, or else why would he do it." The officers made some
telephone inquiries to his suppliers, and although nothing was ever
proved against the poor man their suspicions probably contributed
to his decision to leave the park.

The second cook, who had entered the park about a year prior
to the first cook's departure, stepped into the empty slot. (It is worth
noting that he never interfered or offered his services so long as
the first cook was in charge, although he may have contributed to
the gossip about the first cook.) Since he was still employed as a
cook, this second man had the additional advantage of being able
to buy food for the park's breakfasts and dinners at wholesale prices.
The bills he submitted to the association's officers were always
eminently reasonable, and yet before long some residents were
certain that he, too, must be growing rich at the park's expense. In
one sense they were right that his motives in cooking for the park
were not wholly altruistic, since it netted him catering jobs for private park receptions, weddings, and the like. When I was searching
for a way to thank residents for having cooperated with my study, I
at one time contemplated asking the cook to cater a dinner for
everyone in the park at my expense. I abandoned this idea when I
discovered that people were more likely to interpret my gesture as
an effort to enrich the cook than as a treat for them. Even one of the
residents who knew the cook well responded rather cynically, when
I asked what he might charge me for such a dinner, "Well, he has
three different prices: one for people whom he doesn't know at all;

one for people he knows; and one for people he knows and likes." I cite all of these gibes because they illustrate some of the jealousies and suspicions aroused by financial ventures within the park and not because I necessarily believe them to be true. For example, the cook baked hundreds of cookies for the guests at the magic show and refused to charge me a penny for them.

Still a third instance of park censure involved a man who became so embittered as a result that although he continued to live in the park he no longer attended its functions, used its public facilities, or had anything to do with the other residents. A jovial, decisive salesman, he had entered the park about a year after it had opened and had obviously impressed people with his leadership abilities. Partly because of this and partly because he was a ham radio operator and owned several microphones and amplification equipment, he had been asked to take charge of the bingo evening that the park association sponsored once a month. Bingo, at the time, was a desultory affair which drew only about thirty-five people who contributed 50 cents for three cards and who played for cans of food and dime store trinkets bought with the previous month's proceeds.

The salesman newly in charge of bingo decided that by offering better prizes and getting more residents to participate it could be made into a "paying proposition." These are his words, but I suspect he meant a paying proposition for those playing bingo rather than for himself. He raised the cost of the cards to three for $1; and using his own money and some wholesale connections he began to buy things like clock radios, electric knives, patio chairs, hibachis, and the like. He would then advertise a certain number of these items as prizes in the monthly park newspaper and pay himself back as money accumulated from the bingo sessions. Of course, some months attendance might be low because of rainy weather, and he would have to give away some expensive items anyway because they had been advertised. He would make this up the following month by giving somewhat cheaper prizes. A neighboring lady kept books on all of these complicated transactions, and together they even kept some records to see which prizes really drew in the customers.

During the two years that bingo was run on this basis, attendance jumped to well over 100 participants per month, although it was not always clear whether all of these people were residents of Idle Haven. Demonstrating a considerable talent for hucksterism, the salesman had also made a large sign reading "BINGO TO-NIGHT," which was clearly visible from the street leading into the park and which was probably designed to be read not merely by residents driving into the park but also by non-residents merely driving past. Eventually a cabal of other park leaders protested such practices and accused him, also, of profiting from the enterprise. Again, the latter charge was doubtless untrue, since he left a surplus of $180 to the bingo game, but was probably motivated by the financial success of the venture.

It is difficult to assess the total impact of such suspiciousness on a mobile-home park community. As in the case of closed peasant communities with an "image of limited good," innovative behavior tends to be inhibited. Even the more imaginative leaders in Idle Haven occasionally remarked about their more cautious and critical compatriots that "just because they don't get any fun out of life, they don't want anyone else to have fun either." At the same time, a mobile-home park is not a self-sustaining economic entity and so the inhibiting of innovative behavior does not necessarily produce stagnation. In a community where many people are retired and living on very limited incomes it may, in fact, have the salutary effect of protecting them from being cheated or forced to "keep up with the Joneses." Thus mobile-home parks appear to have functional mechanisms not only for keeping out undesirable residents but also for controlling what are deemed to be undesirable tendencies among those who do get in. Backbiting and mutual suspiciousness should not, in any event, cause one to lose sight of the many valuable and mutually supportive patterns of aid and trade that do flourish in such a community. Just as the supportive and restrictive aspects of peasant life are usually considered two sides of the same coin, so the positive and negative aspects of life in a mobile-home park are not easily separable, either for the social analyst or for the resident.

To this point, social life in Idle Haven has been described largely in terms of informal patterns because they are the ones in which almost everyone in the park is involved. However, there is a formal social structure in the park without which most of these informal relationships would not exist, or at least not to the same extent. (It has already been noted, for example, that many non-neighbor friendships were first formed at scheduled park events.) It is to this formal social structure, and the complex relationships between formal and informal leadership roles, that this study now turns.

6. *Social Structure*

So far Idle Haven has been characterized as a small community because of the similar social statuses of the residents and because the social links, or networks, among them make it a community rather than a mere collection of urbanites such as one might find in a tract or an apartment complex. As Ronald Frankenberg has written:

> "Community implies having something in common. In the early use of the word it meant having goods in common. Those who live in a community have overriding economic interests which are the same or complementary. They work together and also play and pray together. Their common interest in things gives them a common interest in each other. They quarrel with each other but are never indifferent to each other. They form a group of people who meet

frequently face-to-face, although this may mean they end up back-to-back. That people in such an area of social life turn their backs on each other is not a matter of chance. In a community even conflict may be a form of cooperation" (1966:238).

This quotation says nothing about a formal social structure, and many mobile-home parks smaller than Idle Haven are genuine communities without a formal social structure (these are the parks wherein everyone is "just like a member of the family"). However, communities beyond a certain size generally must develop a formal structure in order to perform certain integrative functions that will maintain them as communities. It is not easy to imagine a park much larger than Idle Haven and lacking such a structure which would be anything but a collection of urbanites living in a mobile-home tract. Most parks the size of Idle Haven or larger have a formal social structure and a variety of leadership roles that have an important impact on the lives of residents.

Idle Haven, after it had been in existence for about 6 months and after most of its 200 spaces had been filled, created, with the blessings of the manageress, a residents' association, complete with by-laws and a charter. The elected officers of the association were to include a president, vice-president, secretary, and treasurer. In addition, there were to be five appointive positions filled by the president—a "Sunshine Girl," a social chairman, a membership chairman, a welcoming chairman, and a chairman in charge of "facilities and arrangements"—and these plus the elected officers, the immediate past president, and two appointed board members, were to constitute a governing board of twelve. The board was to meet once a month, usually on the last Monday of every month, in order to plan the following month's activities, which were to be announced and discussed at the general meeting of the association, usually held the first Wednesday of every month. Officers were to be elected for 6-month terms, with elections held every April and October; and the purposes of the association—as stated in the by-laws—were to be strictly social and not concerned with the management of the park. Association dues were set at $1 a year per resident and membership in the association was voluntary.

This was the formal structure created shortly after the park itself was established. Needless to say, the passage of 5 years' time has produced a number of intended as well as unintended changes in this structure; and it has also left behind a history of disputes, compromises, innovations, and failures. I shall describe some of these ups and downs in order to explore the nature and problems of leadership in such a community (e.g., the interaction between park leaders and management) and the differences between formal and informal leadership roles. By formal leadership roles, I mean those roles specifically created by the residents' association charter. By informal leadership roles, I mean both certain roles that individuals take upon themselves as instigators of small organized groups in the park and certain positions from which individuals try to exert leadership informally within the park as a whole. The role of the manager is discussed separately since it is pivotal in any park and in fact determines what sort of social structure will be allowed to develop.

At the time that this study was made, the formal leadership structure of Idle Haven had already undergone a number of changes. For example, the board was tacitly composed of ten rather than twelve individuals. The role of chairman of "facilities and arrangements" had been allowed to atrophy since most of its functions could be assumed by the social chairman (or, as we shall see later, by a number of informal leaders). The role of welcoming chairman had also been allowed to lapse after its last occupant, an extremely devout woman, had resigned after being severely criticized by some park residents for trying to convert new residents rather than merely welcoming them into the park. (Actually, she seems to have done little more than give out some information about local churches in addition to telling new residents about park activities.)

Two other appointive positions—those of "Sunshine Girl" and membership chairman—had become virtually the permanent property of two particular women and had thus taken on some of the characteristics of informal leadership roles. With the exception of a year-and-a-half interruption early in the history of the park, the "Sunshine Girl" of the association had always been a mild-mannered, slightly deaf woman who enjoyed "being in on things" but was too shy (and too handicapped by her deafness) to take a very active part. Encouraged by her friends, she had taken on the job of "Sunshine Girl," which required her to purchase (with association funds) and send out condolence and get-well cards to members of

the association who had been bereaved or who were ill or hospitalized.[1] Every month at the association meeting she would read
the list of cards she had sent during the previous month and she
would also read aloud any thank-you notes she had received. The
names of people ill or bereaved were furnished to her by hearsay or
by the manageress and were also frequently mentioned in the
park's monthly newsletter. Not merely the sending of cards but
particularly the reading aloud of the names at the association meetings greatly enhanced the solidarity among residents of the park,
since such dissemination of news about who was ill frequently led
individuals to extend personal condolences or to offer their services.
For example, an announcement about a resident who had required
numerous blood transfusions led several other residents who did not
know the ill man personally to donate blood in his name. The fact
that the "Sunshine Girl" was universally regarded as a sweet, warm-
hearted woman also probably contributed to the role's effectiveness.

The role of membership chairman had also become the personal
province of one individual, but in this case it was a very different
sort of woman who had made the job her own for very different
reasons. A dynamic 70-year-old widow who was very active in the
park before her husband's death and who remained so afterward,
the membership chairman was better known in the park as editor
of the monthly newsletter. Having had some experience editing a
hobby newsletter, she had volunteered to put out a park newsletter
shortly after the park had opened and, at the time of this study, had
done so without missing an issue (not even when her husband died)

---

[1] Occasionally a congratulatory card was sent when an association member got married, but most of the cards marked either illness or death. Wedding
anniversaries and birthdays, being too numerous, were not commemorated by
the association, with the exception of one tenant's ninety-fifth birthday and the
manageress's birthday. At one association meeting there was a discussion as to
whether a young tenant who had recently given birth to a baby should be sent
a card, but it was decided that since the park did not allow young children to
remain as tenants and since the new parents would therefore soon be forced to
leave, a congratulatory card would not be appropriate. There was also some
question as to whether the young parents were association members. In the
early years of the park, the "Sunshine Girl" had sent cards to everyone in the
park, regardless of whether they were or were not association members, and a
$5 flower "memorial" had been sent on behalf of the association for any resi-
dent who had died. However, a group of association officers (a "clique" in the
opinion of some residents) had abandoned this policy on the grounds that it
was becoming too expensive, although an unstated but probably more powerful

for over 5 years. The park's owner provided the mimeograph machine, paper, and ink, but she had bought her own electric typewriter and not only wrote the monthly four-page paper but also typed, mimeographed, and collated it. (Two retired male residents of the park distributed it to people's mailboxes.) She had, moreover, set up an elaborate file for items to be used in the newsletters: monthly announcements of coming events; news about illnesses in the park and items of interest about residents' travels, families, or new purchases; funny anecdotes of happenings within the park; and a variety of poems, jokes, and "inspirational" messages. Some of the news items about residents were furnished to her directly by residents but many more were simply items that she picked up in the course of casual conversations around the park. (She also acknowledged that she picked up many items of gossip that she would never dream of printing in her newsletter.)

By nature a gregarious, humorous, quick-witted woman who obviously relished being a part of all park activities, she nevertheless did not want to have either the responsibility of a leadership role or the anonymity of being just another participant. For this reason she tended to take upon herself informal roles which would permit her to remain an observer with a concrete task to perform. At all association breakfasts, dinners, and bingo evenings, for example, she served as ticket-taker, sitting by herself at a small table near the entrance to the hall. At many other events that she attended (e.g., dances), she made clear that she was there partly in order to cover the event for the newsletter. In the same spirit, she had always attended association board meetings—regardless of who the

---

motive was the concern for equity—the feeling that residents who were not association members should not get something for nothing.

Two other association members, both women with strong personalities and leadership ability but difficulties in working with others in the park, decided that the new policy was grossly unfair, and with $25 of their own money, they had constituted themselves as a non-association "Park Sunshine Committee." During their first year in operation they claimed to have sent several memorials and small presents to park residents in the hospital who would otherwise have been neglected. However, when they held a stationery and greeting-card sale in the recreation hall one evening in order to raise more money for their project, only six residents came to buy anything. The two women considered this a severe censure by the park's ruling clique, although rainy weather probably contributed to the poor turnout. However, it is true that anyone who wants to start a group independent of the association must have a nucleus of friends who will support his initial efforts or the support of the informal leaders.

officers happened to be—because she needed to find out for the newsletter what the monthly calendar of events would be. Since she was always at board meetings anyway, and since she doubtless recognized that without a formal position on the board her right to be there might someday be questioned, she had allowed herself to be appointed membership chairman and had turned the job into a more or less permanent assignment.

As membership chairman, she kept track of all association members in the park, collected annual dues from them, and visited or talked to all new residents in the park and invited them to join the association. Aspects of this job obviously meshed well with her role as newsletter editor. She was also methodical enough not only to keep accurate books but also to have compiled some rather extensive private statistics about the park—for example, a list of all deaths that had occurred in the park and an accurate list of all those who had moved out.[2] Although many park residents considered her a "spy" for the manager and a nosy, meddling woman, in her informal role as editor of the park's newsletter, she provided probably the single most important integrative mechanism in the park. Her formal role as membership chairman merely served to facilitate and legitimatize this much more valuable informal role.

The other formal leadership roles within the park—the elected ones of president, vice-president, secretary, and treasurer, plus the appointed one of social chairman—generally changed incumbents every 6 months as stipulated. There were, however, numerous exceptions. At the time of this study, both the social chairman and the secretary had served a year in office and the treasurer was entering her second year. There were good reasons why this should have been so. Neither the secretary nor the treasurer were, strictly speaking, leadership roles. They required some special aptitudes and a good deal of time, but their incumbents could be individuals who,

---

[2] My own statistics, however, came only indirectly from this source. Having been denied access to the park's records by the manageress, I borrowed from the membership chairman and newsletter editor all of the back issues of the newsletter, from which I extracted—among other things—the names of every resident ever mentioned and any subsequent information about them, such as whether they had died or moved out of the park. I knew that not all movings-out were reported in the newsletter, on grounds that it would make the park look unduly unstable, but I assumed that all deaths were reported. I also assumed that every new resident was likely to be mentioned at least once, since one could not predict at the outset whether a resident would prove to be

like the "Sunshine Girl," were willing but not necessarily self-assert-ive participants. The treasurer, for example, was always a man or a woman who had had some bookkeeping experience, and the secretary was always a woman with a better than average education (e.g., a retired teacher, a retired career secretary, a college-educated house-wife, or—early in the history of the park—one of the park's college-going teenagers).

The social chairman was always a woman, usually a friend (or, in one case, the wife) of the incumbent president, and often some-one with demonstrated organizational abilities who had been active in church or club social affairs. The chief tasks of this appointive role were to plan and drum up committees of assistants for the monthly breakfasts, luncheons and dinners. For this reason, the in-cumbent had to have not only a certain flair for organizing people but also a reservoir of activity-oriented friends in the park on whom she could call for assistance. The social chairman was always a "popular" individual or, at the very least, someone who had the strong backing of a clique. In order to function properly, the social chairman also had to be on good terms with the president and vice-president of the association, but this was not a difficult requirement since it was an appointive position and the president nearly always pressed a personal friend into serving as his or her social chairman. One president appointed his wife as social chairman on the grounds that since she would be helping him with all of the park's formal events anyway, she might as well get some credit for her work.

The president and vice-president, together with the social chairman, constituted the chief formal leadership roles within the park. This does not mean, however, that they were necessarily occu-pied by people who were also informal leaders. As has already been noted, one of the most important informal leaders in the park, the editor of the newsletter, held a rather minor formal position. The

---

active or inactive in future park activities, nor how long he would stay—assump-tions which proved to be remarkably accurate with reference to the then-current park population. Having thus compiled a roster of all the residents who had ever lived in the park, I then subtracted those who still lived there at the beginning of my study and those who had died, and I obtained the total number of people who had moved out. From this I computed a yearly move-out rate—which proved to be entirely accurate in predicting how many people would move out during the year when the study was made, as well as the following year. Not until my study was over, however, did I learn that I might have saved myself a good deal of work, since the membership chairman had also been keeping track of these statistics!

informal leaders derived their power—and their desire to use it covertly rather than overtly—from their close association with the manager. The manager in a mobile-home park plays a crucial role in its social organization and thereby distinguishes it from an open community where leadership groups may vie with each other but do not have to take into account the power of a manager who can evict residents from the community. Depending on the manager's choice, in fact, a mobile-home park can have one of several different types of social organization.

In many parks managers simply refuse to allow tenants to form any sort of association or formal groups on the grounds that these will create gossip, dissension, and challenges to management's authority. Such parks, unless they are very small, generally have a rather atomized population and lack both informal and formal leadership roles and any sort of communal activities. One park manager who marvelled at all the activities I had described to her going on in Idle Haven said to me that her tenants must, somehow, be different since they seldom used the recreation hall for any purpose. When I suggested that perhaps the problem lay not with the tenants but with the association's leadership, she replied, "Oh, I don't allow them to have an association or any sorts of clubs in the park. That just causes nothing but trouble."

In actual fact, preventing the formation of any sort of groups or leadership roles in a park does not lessen gossip and backbiting and may, ultimately, lead to a serious challenge of management's authority. Such centrally administered parks have very restricted communication channels between residents and management, and residents may come to resent certain park policies so deeply that they will organize in direct opposition to the manager. In several parks where residents were forbidden to organize chapters of the GSMOL (Golden State Mobilehome Owners League) clandestine chapters with a strong esprit de corps were promptly formed, and in one Bay Area park where residents were not given scope to express their collective dissatisfaction with the way the park was being maintained, a rent strike and a picket line were organized. In the latter case the park owner retaliated with a series of evictions, some of which residents fought in the courts, and many residents simply left the park because it had become an armed camp. The social fabric evidently degenerated to such an extent that a year and a half later the owner himself moved into the park in an effort to restore harmony. A newspaper article, written by one of the tenants, noted hopefully that: "[the owner's] purpose in moving here, already a pleasant and friendly park, was to bind the tenants into a cohesive, public-spirited community." The article goes on to describe the election of a new park association president whose

> "acceptance speech stressed the theme: 'Love Thy Neighbor.' 'Let's get together,' he said, 'and kindle a burning desire to change Shady Acres from a park to a closely-related family.' From a cluster of coaches, Shady Acres' new image is emerging into a neighborhood full of community spirit" (WMN, February 3, 1969).

An interesting alternative to allowing no organizations in a park might be called preemptive organizations, in which the manager allows no elective tenants' groups to form but organizes and runs all park activities himself or, in very large parks, hires a recreation director. It is worth noting that the Idle Haven combo-playing couple, who ran afoul other leadership groups in that park, subsequently left to become the managers of a new park in which they themselves intended to run the only park activities to be allowed. There are a number of consequences in creating such a form of social organization. As in the first-mentioned type of park, the channels of communication are restricted and the inevitable criticisms of planned activities (by residents who feel left out, or who find dances too noisy, or dinner menus too spicy) can have only one target—the park's management. Although there are no formal leaders (other than the management) such a park is not lacking in informal leaders because management must nevertheless rely on some residents for support and assistance (decorating committees, ticket sellers, cooks, clean-up helpers, and the like). Residents who take on these roles are likely to become powerful but feared: they will be in leadership positions because of their close association with the manager or recreation director, and this will mean that they will have some voice in what happens in the park. But they will also be a position to report damaging gossip to management, get people evicted, or simply get special favors for themselves, which will be noted and resented by others. If the informal leaders in such a park ever become controversial or discredited there are no alternative leadership groups to which management can turn, and it may have on its hands a seriously antagonistic, disrupted community.

The third alternative—and the one chosen by the manageress of Idle Haven—is to allow tenants to organize their own activities and choose their own formal leaders. This does not mean, however, that such a park will not also have informal leaders—friends of the manager who monitor and moderate the formal leaders and who provide a kind of parallel, or infrastructure, for the park. In Idle Haven the informal leaders seldom took any formal leadership roles, although some had held such roles early in their stay in the park and had come to know the manageress in this way. When formal leadership was in the hands of a strong clique not allied with the manageress, the informal leaders stayed in the background altogether and even the assisting committees were recruited by the formal leaders. However, when the formal leaders were relative newcomers to the park (as they often were) and included individuals who had no abiding interest in exercising leadership within the park, the informal infrastructure came into play—guiding and advising the new association officers, serving on their committees, supporting scheduled events, staying behind after dances and dinners to help clean up, and so forth. Some of the informal leaders had also taken on more or less permanent informal leadership roles—such as editing the newsletter, running the monthly bingo evening, or organizing a twice-yearly bus trip to Reno—which gave the park social structure a good deal of stability and continuity despite the twice-yearly changes of officers and occasionally bitter factional disputes.

The succession of formal leaders in Idle Haven illustrates the process of clique-formation in a small community. Once the initial stage of "pulling together" and "getting to know one another" is passed, and once several sets of incumbents have succeeded each other into office, invidious comparisons begin to be made, groups coalesce, and competition and hostility among various groups appear. As Frankenberg has described the process in the small Welsh village he called Pentrediwaith, there are several ways of coping with such hostility among leaders in a small, face-to-face community. One mechanism is to discontinue activities that become too controversial—that is to say, blaming the controversy on the activity rather than on disagreements among the planners—and to create new activities as a communal outlet, until these too are swamped by disagreements or old hostilities. Another mechanism, also noted by Vidich and Bensman (1968), is the tendency for small communities to fill their formal leadership roles with relative newcomers, who are both free from past controversies by virtue of ignorance and non-implication and who can be more readily sacrificed as scapegoats should they in turn become embroiled in controversy. In Idle Haven, as we shall see, both mechanisms were used.

When the park was newly organized, the first two men who served as president of the association were both out-going, organizationally able men who collected around them a willing group of helpers, although it was already evident that another group of residents was coalescing around the manageress and that this latter group intended to remain somewhat aloof from all in-office leaders. By the middle of the second year that Idle Haven had been in existence, still other alternatives to the initial formal leadership group had developed. One opposing group took the form of a clique which called itself "the North Forty Bunch"—a reference to a certain section of the park within which most of them lived, although affinities of age, education, and life style were more important than purely spatial factors in bringing them together. Consisting of about five or six couples who were somewhat younger, more sophisticated (that is to say, more middle than working class), and more affluent than the average Idle Haven resident, they decided one day to "liven the place up" and "show the others how things should be done." The day before the park's third routine election of officers— there was, as usual, only a single nominee for each elective position —the North Forty Bunch printed up a hand-bill offering an alternative slate (consisting entirely of its members) and a group of teenagers (primarily this group's children) staged a noisy campaign tour through the park. The result was that the North Forty slate won overwhelmingly, thereby humiliating the formally nominated candidates and causing a serious rift within the park.

This rift deepened and, for at least one couple, became permanent shortly after the new president took office. Known subsequently as the fruit-pie incident, it involved one of the early association presidents, who had tried to continue being "helpful" to the newly elected clique by buying on a special sale a great many frozen fruit pies for one of the monthly dinners. These pies were too numerous to store in various officers' freezers and so many of them had been placed in the recreation hall's refrigerator, where they had begun slowly to defrost. Someone—some say a member of the newly elected clique, others say a member of the informal leadership group around the manageress—began to spread a rumor that the pies would spoil and that everyone would be made ill from eating them. The former and current presidents tried to squelch these rumors by cooking

one of the pies and eating it themselves (with no ill effects), but
when the rumors continued the new president decided unilaterally
to end the speculation—and save the monthly dinner, which he
feared would otherwise be poorly attended—by throwing all the
pies away. The ex-president who had bought them was furious at
not having been consulted and henceforth would have nothing to do
with either the association, or its activities, or its officers. It was two
years before he could even bring himself to speak to the man who
had discarded his fruit pies.

After this first polarization had left both sides demoralized a
new set of leaders took the helm—in this case, the combo player and
his friends, who were both newcomers and anxious to initiate a new
activity, dancing, into the park. As has already been described in
the previous chapter, this group also generated fierce opposition,
which led to the temporary abandonment of the dances. Because
the counter-group that developed to this particular clique also had
the manageress as a target (among other faults, she liked to dance
and had encouraged the combo leader and his clique), this conflict
was eventually resolved by the eviction of one tenant and "strong
warnings"—which led to voluntary departures—to seven others.
However, the evicted clique had effectively destroyed the combo
player's ability and willingness to serve as a formal park leader,
and in the wake of this controversy the association nearly ceased to
function because no one would agree to serve as an officer. The
manageress eventually persuaded two members of the North Forty
clique to serve consecutive terms as president, and under their
leadership a modicum of peace and cooperation returned to park
activities. However, the next three presidents were residents who
had each lived in the park less than a year at the time they were
elected and who could therefore be expected to know nothing of
past controversies. These three presidents were also women, whereas all of the earlier presidents, with one exception, had been men.

The manageress of Idle Haven was obviously not neutral in
the park's factional disputes even when she was not openly intervening and evicting one of the contending groups. It was quite
evident that the most successful type of formal park leadership, from
her standpoint, was that which had evolved in the more recent
past: new (in terms of their length of residence in the park) and
relatively lackluster formal leaders who could be guided and controlled by the informal leadership structure. Nevertheless, formal
leadership by a strong clique not allied with the manageress could

sometimes be useful in harnessing otherwise dormant (and possibly hostile) energies on behalf of the park. It is significant, for example, that after the park's most serious factional conflict the manageress turned to a clique she basically disliked—the North Forty Bunch—rather than to any of the informal leaders in her own coterie. However, the importance of the informal leadership group should not be underestimated and is attested to by their behavior in the one situation that might have been expected seriously to threaten them: the departure of their patron, the manageress.

The first manageress of Idle Haven left in August of the sixth year that she had lived and worked in the park. Rumors of her impending departure began to circulate in mid-summer, when she told close park associates (including myself) that she was looking for a new job. The reasons given at the time were her desire for a better salary and a serious disagreement with the park owner about physical improvements that she felt should be made within the park. During the subsequent two months, one could sense among many residents a gradual readjustment of their loyalties. Many individuals who had privately disliked her or who had clashed with her as members (or leaders) of powerful cliques—such as the North Forty Bunch—acknowledged more or less openly that they would be pleased to see her go. Elderly residents who had relied on her as a friend and a protector were genuinely worried because she was leaving but were much relieved by the news that the assistant manager—a woman who had also lived in Idle Haven since its inception and who was well known to everyone—would become the new manageress. Informal leaders also expressed pleasure at the fact that they knew the new manageress and "could work with her," but they clearly felt that their implicit status within the park was somewhat insecure. Therefore, at the fall association elections immediately following the first manager's departure, almost the entire slate of candidates consisted of individuals who had previously played only informal leadership roles; and six months later this slate allowed itself to be reelected to a second consecutive term. Having reasserted their informal control within the park and established their rapport with the new manager, however, these leaders surrendered their formal roles and returned to less visible positions. The new association officers elected after this year-long interregnum were almost all unknown to me because they had entered the park in the year since I had completed my study.

Some of the less visible positions maintained by informal

leaders were actually quite visible to other park residents because of their durability: for example, the editor of the monthly news-letter, the married couple who ran the monthly bingo evening, the cook, the couple who organized a twice-yearly bus trip to Reno, and the two women who ran the ceramics room. However, the power that these informal leaders exercised within the park derived only in part from these long-term informal positions; much more important was the fact that they used their positions to remain in close personal touch with the manager and to exert a strong in-fluence over park events.

There were also a number of residents in Idle Haven who took on informal leadership roles without having any desire to exert leadership within the park as a whole. Such residents either had a special skill that they felt they could offer to others or they had become the informal leaders of small groups within the park that exerted no wider influence. Informal leaders of this sort included a retired handicraft teacher who held a handicraft class every Wednesday morning in the recreation hall for anyone who cared to attend and a very devout man who held an inter-faith Bible class in his mobile home every Tuesday evening.

The handicraft teacher was a buoyant, inventive woman who taught her pupils how to make a variety of ingenious, inexpensive items, such as hand dusters out of yarn and folded coat hangers, or knitting bags out of fabric scraps and half-gallon plastic Clorox bottles. She also taught more traditional crafts such as metal etching and leather working. Her steady circle consisted of about six rather shy women who enjoyed each other's company and who frequently did not participate in any of the specific class projects but simply brought along their own embroidery or knitting. The teacher did not seem to mind, nor did she seem to care that the "class" size fluctuated rather wildly from week to week. Her best-attended sessions were some special candlemaking classes held just before Christmas, which always drew between twenty and thirty women.

Similarly, the Bible class was offered by a rather care-worn, deeply religious man who made no attempt to generalize his leader-ship beyond this small group. Regular participants, in addition to the leader and his wife and one other married couple, consisted of approximately seven women—most of them devout and lonely widows. The group's leader, although not a minister, had trained for the ministry in his youth and intended to work as a lay preacher upon retirement from his job. Better educated than most of the residents in the park, he obviously enjoyed and had a genuine gift for teaching. He usually began his class with a reading of a chapter from the Bible, together with a detailed and fairly literal interpretation of its meaning. This was followed by questions and some discussion by those in attendance, and usually led into a more generalized discussion during which tea and cookies were served. One evening, for example, a reading of Chapter 5 of *Romans* led to a discussion of whether Adam's original sin had been rebellion, which in turn produced a lot of talk about rebellion among the younger generation, the situation in the schools, sex, dangerous drugs and so forth.

These two groups were created and led by talented non-power-oriented individuals who believed that they were merely offering a "service" to the park and who were not particularly interested in creating their own clique or enhancing their own prestige. Nevertheless, both groups depended for their continued existence on a small core of loyal followers, and these steady attenders were doubtless under a good deal of moral pressure to remain loyal. This type of pressure to be loyal to a group in a small community has been well described by Ronald Frankenberg:

"Participation in city recreations is for most of its inhabitants voluntary. Plays, films, dances, concerts, may be available, but they may be taken or left alone. If there was a play or concert in Glynceiriog Hall, villagers often felt obliged to go—'to put in an appearance.' The organizer of the play was not an impersonal businessman in an office elsewhere whom one had never met. He was a cousin, a fellow church or chapel member, a friend, or just a fellow villager. His efforts had to be supported because it was the norm, because one wished him well or had to appear to wish him well (or at least not to wish him ill). The following week one might oneself be organizing a function or wanting to borrow some tools. One good turn deserves another" (1966:239).

In Idle Haven, particularly the smaller groups involved personal commitments that some residents felt they could avoid only by not participating at all. One devout woman who might have been expected to be a participant in the Bible class, when asked why she had never attended it, said, "I always felt that if I went once and then didn't go the next time Mr. Bevin [the teacher] might be offended." Another resident who enjoyed playing bridge had quit attending the bridge club altogether because the other players had insisted he come at noon, whereas he wanted to eat his lunch and watch the television news until one. It has already been noted (pp. 90–91) that a former leader of the bridge club at one time antagonized a large contingent of card players by demanding that everyone play (or learn to play) bridge. This insistence on purity and loyalty within the bridge-playing group led another resident to form a canasta-and-pinocle group which, in order to maintain *its* integrity, restricted its membership to twelve and had a number of "alternates" who were asked to play only when one of the twelve was absent.

The most striking example of the pressures to maintain in-group loyalty involved the Idle Haven ceramics class, which was created soon after the park opened by a woman resident who knew how to glaze and fire ceramics. With the assistance of the park owner a sizeable room adjacent to one of the laundry-rooms was converted into a classroom, with shelves to hold paints, glazes, and pottery, and long tables and benches at which to work. The group required a joining fee of $20, and the original fees were used to buy two electric kilns. Subsequent fees have been used to buy paints and glazes to repair the kilns; participants pay for their own "green ware" and also pay a small amount for each piece that they complete. The group met every Monday and most of the women (there were only two male participants and neither of these was ever in evidence) spent their time painting and glazing a variety of vases, bowls, hanging wall plaques, garden figures, and figurines. Some of these they kept themselves and others they gave as Christmas and birthday gifts to relatives and friends. (A few of the women also made items which they would sell to other women in the park, although this was always done in an *ad hoc* fashion because it was supposed to be illegal under state law.) One of the most popular items made by almost everyone in the class was a ceramic Christmas tree, about a foot high and hollow, into which small plastic "candles" were inserted and which could then be lighted by placing a light-bulb inside.

The ceramics group was formally limited in size to thirty-five members, but at the time that Idle Haven was being studied only twenty-eight then-current park residents were signed up, and of these only about eight participated regularly. The remainder had fallen by the wayside as a result of a bitter disagreement between the original "teacher" of the class and a group of participants who had asked her to teach someone else to operate the kilns and to share some of her dictatorial powers within the group. This slight rebellion had so enraged the teacher that she had resigned from the group, bought her own kiln, and continued to hold counter-classes for her faction in her own mobile home. Eventually, even living in the park had proved too upsetting for her, and she had moved to a nearby neighborhood—where she continued to hold ceramics classes for her supporters in the park. She also continued to visit some of these supporters in their mobile homes to ensure that they did not backslide and join the opposition.

About a year after leaving Idle Haven, this embittered woman committed suicide, and her behavior vis-à-vis the ceramics class is now widely interpreted as evidence of mental instability. How-ever, in view of the behavior of several other scorned park leaders (e.g., the association president in the fruit pie incident, and the former bingo-organizer) her case seems to be only a somewhat more extreme example of a not uncommon situation. Moreover, the controversy also had a profound impact on many residents who still live in the park and who show no signs of being mentally unstable. Unable to resolve the problem of loyalty to the group as a whole and to its original leader, many women simply withdrew altogether and quit participating in ceramics classes of any sort. Some of these women went even further and quit participating in other park events, where the factional alignments had a way of reappearing, and most of them maintained their aloofness from park events even though the parties to the original conflict had long since left the park (or died). Like the association president whose fruit pies were destroyed (and who eventually left the park) they played a con-scious role of being "in" the park but no longer "of" it.

There were also a certain number of aloof residents who had withdrawn not because of group conflicts within Idle Haven but because they had had similar experiences in other parks and had vowed not to repeat them. Another couple, having watched a major blow-up in Idle Haven shortly after they had moved in, had con-cluded that their leadership abilities were best exercised in a context where they did not also have to live. Thus they had chosen to remain very active in their Masonic orders and, although often asked to take on formal leadership roles within the park, they had steadfastly declined to get involved. They had taken on an informal leadership role within the park, but it was not one that involved the creation of a small group or that required a frequently repeated effort. Once a year, during the fresh crab season, they organized a "crab feed" for anyone in the park who cared to participate (for a small fee). This dinner—the only monthly dinner not planned and executed by the incumbent association officers—had become this couple's carefully circumscribed venture into park participation.

As these examples should have served to illustrate, Idle Haven lies somewhere between the city, where attendance at public events is largely voluntary, and a village such as the one described by Frankenberg, where it involves all sorts of personal obligations. About a third of the residents in Idle Haven (about 120 individuals) treated park events as something that they felt no obligation to attend and seldom did. Many of these residents were only minimally involved in the park's social fabric, either by choice or because of extreme old age or ill health. However, this group also included those residents who had been very active at one time but who had fallen out with either a particular group or the park social structure as a whole—and for these residents non-attendance at park events was certainly not a matter of casual choice—they deliberately avoided any sort of involvement. For approximately two-thirds of the residents, however, some or all of the park events exerted a certain amount of obligation. Neighbors were apt to ask why one had not played bingo the previous evening, or friends might wonder why one had not attended the monthly dinner; and if one had promised to help set tables or clean up after dinner one might actually be chided for not having been there.

For association officers, in particular, attendance at all park functions during their term of office was virtually mandatory and took precedence over family or personal social engagements. Many ex-officers reported that during their terms of office they had had to pass up certain activities outside the park that they would otherwise have engaged in because their duties within the park came first. However, this scale of values only became operative once someone had accepted a formal leadership role; it was very common for nominees to decline nominations because they were planning on taking a long vacation during the period when they would be in office, or because of the demands of their job, family or health problems, or obligations to other organizations such as a church or a lodge.

Informal leaders were under somewhat less stringent obligations to attend all of the park's scheduled events regardless of whether or not they felt like it. However, those who played an informal leadership role in the park as a whole rather than in one small group, generally felt obliged to "show their support" by attending routine functions, such as association meetings, as well as any extraordinary functions planned by the formal leadership group. Thus, attendance at association meetings and monthly potluck luncheons averaged between twenty-five and thirty-five residents, almost all of them either formal or informal leaders, and the attendance at two special "fun nights"—evenings of adult games planned by the park's social chairman—drew an even more select group of twenty supporters. By contrast, the monthly breakfasts and dinners drew between seventy-five and a hundred residents (unless it was a potluck dinner, in which case attendance again fell to thirty-five to forty and consisted of primarily formal and informal park leaders), and bingo drew sixty to eighty participants. The Christmas party—the great social event of the year (and also entirely free)—was usually attended by some 200 residents.

These attendance figures reveal not only the approximate size of the leadership group (twenty to forty), as compared to the larger and more fluctuating group of approximately 200 residents who attended events from time to time; they also reveal what sorts of events draw residents spontaneously as opposed to events that become "chores" attended primarily by the leadership group. Prepared dinners and breakfasts, as well as bingo, were obviously popular. Dances had but a limited appeal and could survive in the park only because residents of several other parks as well as outsiders also participated. It was widely believed within the park that more people would attend the association meetings if somehow they were made more "interesting," but efforts to produce this result by bringing in speakers (e.g., myself, my husband, or an investment counselor) proved unsuccessful. The only increase in attendance at an association meeting occurred the month there was a free magic show, my farewell present to the park, which brought out about 100 residents. These tastes and trends in activities will be discussed further in the following chapter, which deals with leisure and life styles, and where we shall also explore in greater detail the differences in participation between men and women.

One further activity reveals the kind of semi-urban, semi-village atmosphere of Idle Haven, and that is gossip. Gossip has been a frequent topic of interest among anthropologists because in small, self-sufficient communities it may be the principal form of social control. Instead of legal procedures, suits, or formal complaints, gossip may be used to discourage certain activities or to punish those who nevertheless engage in them. Gossip is, of course, also a way of expressing hostility in an environment where most direct expressions of hostility cannot be allowed (because of the harm this would do to the small social group's cohesiveness) and where one cannot readily leave the group even if one's hostility is great. Some anthropologists have viewed witchcraft accusations, which occur in certain societies, as an "advanced" form of gossip that may be used to curb powerful leaders (Bohannan, 1958) or overly successful women traders (Nadel, 1952), or to perform the same generalized sorts of functions as gossip (Kluckhohn, 1944). Gossip is also a way of disseminating news rapidly; and it can be, for those who engage in it if not necessarily for its victims, a pleasurable social activity that promotes in-group solidarity (Gluckman, 1963).

It has been said that in a highly differentiated society, and more particularly in an urban environment, gossip loses its efficacy as a means of social control. One may still gossip about the man next door but the chances that this gossip will alter his behavior are slim. Gossip does, of course, continue to exist within groups whose members have some social claims on each other—for example, within families, professional associations, private clubs, and friendship groups—where its effect on an individual or individuals may be devastating. In a mass society, public gossip such as that found in newspapers and magazines may also serve as a form of social control over highly placed individuals, as well as helping to promote a generalized sense of solidarity among its consumers and reinforcing certain widely accepted standards of morality.

Despite such possibly salutary aspects, gossip (or, for that matter, witchcraft) is a difficult topic to study because the average layman regards it as a reprehensible activity, to be denied at all costs. Thus even if a researcher is convinced that gossip reinforces moral standards, promotes in-group solidarity, and permits the venting of hostilities, he will have a hard time finding anyone who will admit to gossiping or to having heard any gossip. Even researchers themselves have been somewhat ambivalent in their treatment of gossip in their writings. If it is basically a socially functional activity, then its partial disappearance in complex, highly differentiated societies ought to be regarded as a loss—or at least as something for which substitute mechanisms (legal sanctions, moral standards purveyed by mass media) must be found. And yet, very few researchers have regarded the lack of efficacious gossip in an urban context as a loss, and its putative reappearance in suburbia has been loudly decried. When some postwar suburban tracts full of couples of similar ages and backgrounds were found to indulge in kaffee-klatsching and a certain amount of "keeping up with the Joneses," sociologists began to warn of the evils of such mutual surveillance rather than looking for some of the functional aspects. They did not argue, for example, that in the absence of nearby relatives, many of these young couples may benefit from learning child-rearing practices and other behavioral standards (including, to be sure, consumption patterns) from each other.

It is important to bear in mind this ambivalence—both public and professional—toward gossip when looking at Idle Haven. One of the first women I interviewed said to me that a mobile-home park was just like an army camp: you could "hear just about anything." When I later tried to pursue this remark by asking about gossip, however, she hotly denied that there was much gossip in the park. I recalled her earlier remark and asked what she had meant by it, whereupon she said, "Well, the other day, for example, I heard that Mr. Sands had a bloodclot in his leg and that his wife was afraid they would have to amputate it, and some people said this was just gossip. But I talked to Mrs. Sands, and it turned out to be true!" For this woman, anything that could be verified was not gossip but news; and, as we noted earlier, news-bearing is also one of the accepted social science definitions of gossip.

This is not to say that people in the park were blind to what was morally creditable, discreditable, or neutral news. The editor of the monthly newsletter knew very well that she could publish the fact that one couple was leaving the park in order to move to Clear Lake but that she could not publish the fact that another couple was leaving because they were getting divorced. But in the context of conversations a great deal could be (and was) said with a minimum amount of censure being attached. Thus, while one might not wish to write that a suicide had occurred in the park, gossip about the event was by no means mean-spirited. Gossip about "drunks" in the park, while a little more acerbic, was more amused than morally outraged in tone, and most residents did not expect such gossip to change anyone's behavior. It did, however, serve to reinforce their own beliefs concerning what was proper and improper.

Yet there were types of gossip in Idle Haven that were designed to serve as forms of social control, although most of these were not effective in and of themselves: they derived their real power from the ability of the manageress to act on them. For example, there was a good deal of gossip about a long-haired "hippy" who lived with his parents in the park, but this gossip was aimed less at getting him (or his parents) to cut his hair than at getting the manageress to evict him. Similarly, some of the informal leaders were often called "gossips" by other residents in the park—not because they necessarily gossiped more than anyone else but because they carried their gossip to the manageress's ears.

A park manager is in a difficult position with regard to gossip and social control. On the one hand, he or she is a member of a small community and, as such, is personally subject to its stated and unstated conventions. Most park managers are very sensitive to this fact because they have come up from the ranks of ordinary mobile-home residents. Many of them have lived in mobile-home parks for some time before deciding to look for a managing job, and some have slowly worked into a manager's or an assistant manager's slot within the same park where they have long been living. Not being "professional" managers—and being, in fact, very similar in age and outlook to the people they supervise—gives them a healthy tolerance for "harmless" gossip about park situations that are best left alone. At the same time, in their roles as managers they acquire new responsibilities toward the social fabric of the park. Other residents expect a manager to maintain the moral tone of the park—e.g., to evict blatant disturbers of the peace or residents whose behavior offends a large contingent of fellow residents—and to see to it that the park's physical appearance does not deteriorate.

A mobile-home park manager is also responsible to the park's owner, who may see the park as little more than a profitable investment. Such an owner's view may be an enlightened one and entail the provision of all sorts of services for his tenants—for example, sauna baths, pool tables, shuffleboard courts, and so forth. However, tenants may demand things he is unwilling or unable to provide: free turkeys for the annual Christmas party, money in order to sponsor a park bowling team, money with which to hire a professional crafts teacher. And, of course, a major bone of contention between owner and residents in any park is periodic rent increases.

These conflicting desires and obligations must be mediated by a manager to the satisfaction of both owner and tenants. If a manager pleases only the owner, the tenants are likely to become restive; on the other hand, if a manager sides exclusively with the tenants he is likely to lose his job. The first manageress of Idle Haven alternated skillfully between pleading the desires of the tenants to the owner and explaining the owner's position (what he would and would not do) to the tenants. She herself had a clear understanding of her role as a broker. While in the recreation hall, she would often and loudly lament the niggardliness of the owner; however, when I once asked her whether, in view of her complaints, she would not find it easier to be an "owner-manager," managing her own park, she promptly said, "No, then there would be too much pressure from tenants to do this and do that. It's better to be able to say, 'I would like to give you such-and-such, but the owner won't hear of it.' "

Because a manager's job depends on his or her skill as an intermediary between the tenants and the owner of a park, most managers do not look with kindness upon attempts to circumvent their position—for example, by tenants attempting to communicate directly with the owner. In Idle Haven, the same group of residents that criticized the manageress for favoring park dances also tried to institute a park ombudsman who could take residents' complaints directly to the owner, and it was probably this line of attack on her authority that was chiefly responsible for their being evicted or declared *persona non grata*. This unhappy experience with direct political influence led the association officers, and particularly the park's informal leaders, to reassert with new vigor the principle that the association could only discuss social matters.[3] It was also, of course, what made the informal leaders so powerful and what made gossip such an important channel of communication. If one could be evicted for trying to change the park directly, by com-

---

[3] I did not realize the importance of this principle until I myself violated it one evening. I had arrived at the recreation hall somewhat early for an association meeting when an elderly female resident entered the hall with a badly bloodied knee and scratched hands. She had fallen just outside the hall, having tripped over a cement car-stop installed to keep cars from driving through the plate glass windows. Various residents commiserated with her and said that the car-stops should be painted with luminous paint. The meeting that evening was quite short so that when the president asked for new business and no one raised the issue of the car-stops, I ventured to ask, "What about Mrs. Sardo's knee?" Instantly, several of the more experienced residents turned to shush me and one of the informal park leaders rose to say that this was not an issue that could be discussed by the association. The fact that the manageress was not present at this meeting may have made it even more imperative to observe the taboo against overt criticism so that no one could be accused of talking behind her back.

municating with the owner or otherwise trying to subvert the manager, then the only way to be effective was *through* the manager,
by having her ear and persuading her either to have the owner do
certain things or to have certain tenants reprimanded or removed.

Although a manager stands at the apex of all park gossip chains
(at least, if his or her close acquaintances have been well chosen)
he or she is not therefore immune from being gossiped about, sometimes to devastating effect. Malicious gossip about the manager—
e.g., about his or her taking kickbacks from dealers, or exacting sales
commissions on mobile homes sold within the park—is standard fare
in most mobile-home parks. However, this sort of gossip can lead to
evictions, and so residents tend to be cautious about what they will
say to whom. Precisely because gossip concerning the actual operation of the park is dangerous for residents, gossip about a manager's
personal life tends to become a substitute and to be nastier than
usual. Of course, part of this is also due to the manager's high
visibility within the park and the general expectation that he or she
will set a good example for others. Thus it was not at all uncommon,
in Idle Haven, to hear residents say in an aggrieved tone, "She [the
manageress] is always telling *us* not to drive so fast in the park, but
she herself is the worst offender," or "You should have seen the
kind of condition *she* was in last night after the dance!"

It was ultimately an item of personal gossip (and the situation
being gossiped about) that contributed to the departure of the first
manageress of Idle Haven. Shortly after she had told various residents that she was looking for a better-paying job, the rumor spread
that in fact she was having an affair with the husband of another
woman in the park—and this while the other woman was lying in a
nearby hospital recovering from a heart attack. The rumor turned
out to be true. The husband of the manageress decamped and filed
for a divorce, and the owner of Idle Haven was upset because he
had been paying for the services of a couple (the wife to run the
office and keep the books, and the husband to do the maintenance
and heavy cleaning in the recreation hall and laundry rooms). Even
had the manageress been able to persuade the park owner to hire
her new friend, it seemed unlikely that the former wife, the husband, *and* the manageress could all have continued to inhabit the
same park. And so the manageress and her lover left amidst a storm
of gossip and speculation.

The first wife remained in Idle Haven, and her response to the
gossip was itself an interesting example of the strains and rewards

of living in a small community. During the first weeks after her husband and the manageress had both left the park, she was seldom seen around the recreation hall. Gossip about the whole affair took place in hushed tones and cryptic sentences and ceased at once whenever she appeared. After about a month of this, the wife decided to break through the awkward silence that developed whenever she appeared by making open references to what was obviously on everyone's mind. She not only began to berate her husband publicly for what he had done, but she volunteered detailed accounts of the separate maintenance hearings she was just then attending. Thus she in effect managed to turn the situation to her advantage by exchanging information that everyone wanted to hear for public sympathy and support for her position. When last seen, she was—if not exactly a gay divorcée—at least a reasonably happy, well-integrated member of the park community, and there were even some mild attempts under way to pair her off with one of the eligible men in the park or to introduce her to some of the unmarried or divorced work-mates or friends of other residents.

In this chapter some of the formal aspects of the social structure of Idle Haven have been outlined as distinct from the more informal patterns of neighboring, aid, and trade. This social structure generates conflict as well as cohesiveness, but even the conflict is an indication of the extent to which residents care about the community they have formed. Moreover, while residents may feud among themselves, they are united against the outside world—against attempts by city fathers to tax them as ordinary real estate owners, against opening the park to "undesirables" (not merely Negroes but anyone with young children or slovenly habits). They are, in short, a tightly knit, homogeneous community and they want to keep it that way.

7. Leisure and Life Style

Leisure, as many writers on the subject have had occasion to note, is a difficult concept. It is usually defined operationally as "free time," or "uncommitted time," and it is generally held in contrast with that time which is committed to productive labor. If one accepts this definition, however, can children and elderly, retired individuals—none of whom is engaged in productive labor—be said to possess leisure? Does the concept not lose its meaning when it is separated from its opposite—work—and, from the standpoint of the individual who has retired from work, is it not difficult to structure one's life in terms of something that is supposed to be, by definition, structureless? As Stephen Miller has noted:

> "The dilemma of the retired person engaging in leisure activity is that he must identify himself with and justify his participation in an activity which society has defined as

superfluous in character, or play as opposed to work" (1965: 79).

Taking a different tack, Bennett Berger (1962) has argued that leisure is not really unconstrained, or "free," time since it is, in fact, hedged about with many do's and don't's and other culturally-determined requirements. From the time of the Greeks, who thought of leisure as affording the opportunity for free men to cultivate the arts, philosophy, politics, and athletics, to the time of the industrial revolution, when Calvinist businessmen worried that their factory workers did not use their leisure to some "wholesome" end, the concept has always been subject to societal values. Nor is leisure in today's society free from such normative constraints; one has only to recall the numerous polemical articles arguing that "mass culture" or television is debasing public tastes to realize that all leisure pursuits are not regarded as equally worthwhile.

Leisure time is also constrained in the sense that there are many social occasions when an individual may feel he *has* to participate, and even those activities that he engages in on a purely voluntary basis may be invested with strong personal values. Thus, as Berger wryly notes, one may find it "emotionally more difficult to beg off (for phony reasons) from a previously accepted invitation to a party given by a friend, than to call the boss to say one's sick and not coming to work" (1962:38). This line of reasoning leads Berger to speculate that perhaps with the increasing alienation from work, the values attached to leisure pursuits may become paramount —not only subjectively but also in terms of the integration of the social system:

"As work loses its power to command the moral identifications and loyalties of men, as men look away from work to find moral experience, society loses an important source of normative integration. . . . In such a situation we may expect, if the functionalist view of society as a self-balancing system has any merit, the transfer of functions formerly performed by the institutions of work to the 'leisure institutions,' and this, it seems to me, is precisely the significance of the enormous increase in attention which the problem of leisure has received in recent years" (1962:44).

If new values are to be attached to leisure pursuits, can it be that the elderly will find themselves in the vanguard of a new leisure class devoted to self-expression and self-fulfillment? Irving

Rosow, for one, doubts it. He argues that the allocation of prestige in modern, industrial societies will continue to be based on one's socioeconomic role and that retired individuals will continue to have a relatively low status because they are no longer full-fledged members in this productive hierarchy.[1] This low social status of the elderly is not only the result of their no longer being employed but also a result of their generally declining incomes, which may produce downward adjustments in life style, and their generally poorer health, which may produce still further curtailments in role commitments. Thus the young are not just being gratuitously cruel when they regard the elderly as being "out of it"; to a large extent they are merely attaching an accurate label to the status accorded the elderly by the society as a whole.

Although the elderly may share a disvalued and rather low status in modern industrial societies, this is not to say that their previous status positions in the socioeconomic class structure become entirely irrelevant. A retired lawyer still has a somewhat higher status than a retired plumber. More important, the retired lawyer is likely to be able to validate this higher status with a higher retirement income, which will also enable him to perpetuate his previous life style. Even when health and income do not permit an elderly individual to do many of the things he used to do in his youth, his leisure tastes are likely to remain strongly conditioned by his formal education and pre-retirement socioeconomic status. A retired lawyer or professor is likely to enjoy reading and listening to classical music, whereas a retired steamfitter or plumber is likely to prefer watching the roller derby or listening to popular music.

In this chapter, we shall look at the use of leisure time as it is affected by four sociological variables. Age (and, more particularly, retirement) is the first of these. As we have already noted, leisure may pose problems of self-definition for the elderly, retired indi-

---

[1] Lecture before the Adult Development Research Seminar, January 24, 1969, entitled "Retirement, Leisure, and Social Status." Rosow implies that in traditional, preindustrial societies, the elderly may have a much higher status because they are the repositories of traditional wisdom and counsel. Cf. Margaret Mead (1970) who posits three different types of society—the postfigurative (traditional), the cofigurative (industrial), and the prefigurative (postindustrial). She argues that in the postfigurative society the young learn from the old (hence the elderly have a high status), whereas in the prefigurative society change is so rapid that the old must learn from the young (and the elderly consequently have a low status).

vidual; he must readjust his life and his identity in terms of activities that he previously regarded as "time off" from work, where his true social identity lay. Or he may simply have much more leisure time to fill than ever before, although Sebastian de Grazia has disputed this:

> ". . . The great gulf of free time into which older people, in particular the retired, are said to fall is not appreciable. . . . An hour and a half or so more free time a day is what seems to be the case. . . . It would seem, then, that after the age of 50 activities in and around the house are expanded or done more carefully or slowly so that the time gap left by work is easily filled" (Kleemeier, ed., 1961:128).

Even if too much free time is not a problem, age and its physical disabilities, or a reduced income, may prevent an individual from engaging in certain leisure activities that he used to enjoy: he may no longer be able to afford travel, and he may no longer be able to drive a car or play golf, or see well enough to read.

Pre-retirement socioeconomic status is a second variable affecting the use of leisure time. Reading, concert-going, golf, tennis, and travel abroad, as well as participation in voluntary associations, tend to be upper- and upper middle-class pursuits, whereas attending ball games, hunting and fishing, bowling, and camping tend to be lower middle- and working-class leisure activities. As we shall see, watching television is not a class-restricted activity, and aging brings to the fore certain new hobbies, such as gardening, which also crosscut socioeconomic statuses.

Still a third factor that has a significant impact on the use of leisure time is gender. Men and women tend to pursue somewhat different hobbies throughout their lifetimes and women generally have more leisure time in which to develop their hobbies. Women who have been housewives—or even women who have worked part of their lives (as distinct from having had careers)—do not face a retirement crisis in which they must relinquish jobs to which their identities are strongly bound. If they strongly identified with the mother-role, they may have experienced a severe crisis when their last child left home, but generally speaking women have had long years of practice in finding and gaining personal satisfaction from leisure pursuits. They have also had a great deal more practice than most men in structuring their own time. Men who are used to the rhythm of an office day may find it difficult to adjust to a freer schedule. Thus, it is not surprising that one hobby and recreation center for the aged found it had a better attendance of old men if it *required* them to attend from 9 a.m. to 5 p.m. (Cumming and Henry, 1961:152). Women also retain their jobs as housewives into old age, so that they are never entirely without chores around which to structure their leisure.

Gender interacts with socioeconomic status to produce some important differences in the extent to which men and women engage in leisure activities together. Most studies of working-class families (particularly Komarovsky, 1962; Young and Willmott, 1962; and Bott, 1957) have commented on the rather rigid role segregation that exists among husbands and wives. Men tend to take their night out with the "boys"—either playing poker, or drinking, or bowling— and they may even spend their vacations going hunting or fishing with male friends. Women have their own circle of women friends with whom they go bowling, or to a movie, or out shopping (although, as Mirra Komarovsky points out, young working-class wives with children at home may simply be housebound and quite isolated). As Elizabeth Bott has demonstrated, this pattern of role segregation tends to be strongest among couples who have a close-knit social network consisting of extended-family members and friends, whereas more isolated couples with loose-knit social networks tend to do more things together and to develop less highly segregated conjugal roles.

Close-knit social networks tend to be more common among working-class than among middle-class families; however, Idle Haven contained a number of couples—e.g., couples who had married late in life, or were childless, or had moved to California only recently, or came from very disrupted family backgrounds—who were quite socially isolated and who were consequently very close to each other. Another factor that may have been instrumental in the more egalitarian role relationships of these couples was their age. Several studies have demonstrated that sexual role differentiation tends to decrease with aging and retirement. Men tend to take on household chores that they formerly delegated to their wives, they tend to conceive of their marital roles more in terms of companionship than in terms of being a "provider" (Lipman, 1961), and they are more democratic and less authoritarian in their relationships with their wives (Reichard, 1962:42). Psychological studies reveal that older, retired men give more rein to their nurturant and affiliative impulses, whereas older women seem to become more tolerant of their own aggressive, egocentric impulses (Reichard, 1962; Neugarten and Guttman, 1958). All of these tendencies are likely to affect the life styles of individuals and how they spend their leisure time.

A final factor that affects the use of leisure time is the social setting. As both Robert Kleemeier (1961) and Irving Rosow (1967) have observed, elderly people who are physically isolated from their peers tend to participate in fewer activities and have fewer friends. Conversely, segregated settings—where everyone is roughly the same age—and congregated settings—where many people live closely together with little privacy—both tend to promote activity and social interaction among the aged. A third characteristic of special settings for the elderly—the degree to which they are institutions with social control over their residents—has an inverse relationship to social activity: the more institutional the setting the less spontaneous social activity there is likely to be. Kleemeier argues that all special settings for the aged can be described in terms of these three independent dimensions—congregate, segregate, and institutional (or control)—and that each of these setting characteristics has predictable effects upon the attitudes and behavior of their inhabitants (always taking into account certain individual attributes—such as energy level). As examples of special settings for the aged and their dimensions he cites:

> ". . . [T]he senile ward in a mental hospital would be high in all three characteristics, while a ward in a general hospital serving all age groups would be highly congregate, highly institutional, but low in age segregation. The frail or ill aged person living with his family but receiving various kinds of home medical and nursing services would be in an institutional setting which was neither congregate nor segregate. On the other hand, a residential hotel patronized exclusively by older people could be characterized as being highly segregate and congregate but not institutional" (1961: 286).

Applying these dimensions, Idle Haven clearly constitutes a setting that is segregate and congregate but not institutional. It maximizes friendships among its residents and it also provides an opportunity for residents to initiate organized activities, both of which, according to Kleemeier, are characteristic of segregate and congregate settings. Some individuals in the park devote much of their leisure time to formally planned activities, whereas others simply take advantage of the informal opportunities for joint activities—a casual game of golf, an evening of bridge, a shopping trip. The park setting itself also creates or makes feasible certain leisure pursuits that people might not otherwise engage in: for example, bicycling—not a hobby that one associates with the elderly—is popular in mobile-home parks because the streets are quiet and generally free of automobiles. "Sidewalk-superintending"—watching mobile homes being removed or installed—and helping to install and dismantle porches, awnings, and skirting are also popular activities with many Idle Haven men. In addition to providing such new leisure activities, a segregate and congregate setting such as Idle Haven also tends to foster their acceptance because participants mutually reinforce each other's behavior. As Irving Rosow has noted with regard to segregated housing for the aged:

> "The concentration of people with common status and problems, with similar life experience and perspectives, maximizes the opportunity for new friendships. . . . New group memberships afford new identifications and psychological support as well as mutual aid. . . . The reintegration of older people into new groups may facilitate their transition to a new aged role, especially when there has been confusion about this. Aged peers provide role models on which a person may pattern himself. The older group can also generate new activities which crystallize new role dimensions. By clarifying expectations and appropriate behavior, especially in dealing with the leisure of retirement, older people provide each other with new norms" (1962: 337).

Bearing in mind these four variables—age, socioeconomic status, gender, and social setting—let us look at some of the leisure pursuits of Idle Haven residents, beginning with one that is virtually ubiquitous in our society and therefore difficult to analyze in terms of any specific sociological trait: television viewing. According to Gary Steiner (1963), in 1960, 90 per cent of the households in the United States had television sets and used them an average of five to six hours a day! More surprising, Steiner found that the "viewing diet" is remarkably similar for people of all educational levels:

"With college education, people devote less of their viewing to action, and a trifle more to news, public affairs, and heavy drama. But the differences are not large, nor are they always progressive with education. The diet of the second highest group [3–4 years of college], for example, is virtually indistinguishable from that selected by the very lowest. On the whole, it is the high-school graduates who appear to have the 'lightest' tastes of all" (1963:168).

What does change with educational level is the attitude of the viewer: although the college-educated individual watches roughly the same types of programs as the non-college-educated viewer he is more likely to be ambivalent about the time he spends in front of his television set and less apt to characterize television as "a perfect way to relax." The college-educated viewer also watches fewer television programs than his non-college-educated counterpart. Thus, while the relative proportions of programs watched may remain similar for both groups, the actual number of programs seen range from an average of forty per week for grade school graduates to twenty-five per week for college graduates; and much of this decline, as education increases, occurs in the numbers of action (westerns, crime, adventure) and comedy and variety programs watched. As Steiner observes, it is difficult to say whether absolute or relative comparisons are the better indicator of program interest;[2] however, the absolute viewing time of college graduates would indicate that they are somewhat less interested in television per se than the less well educated.

Viewing tastes (as distinct from actual viewing habits) also differ with educational levels, although some of these differences are obscured when one considers only the broad categories, such as "action" programs. Action programs were mentioned as favorites by 28 per cent of Steiner's grade school respondents, 31 per cent

---

[2] "Is someone who watches fifteen newscasts and five movies more interested in televised information [i.e., news] than another viewer who sees thirty newscasts and twenty movies in the same period? Should a college graduate get credit for more interest in world affairs because he watches fewer westerns?" (Steiner, 1963:170). In other words, relatively speaking, the first viewer has a television diet of 75 per cent news and 25 per cent entertainment, whereas the second viewer has a diet of 60 per cent news and 40 per cent entertainment; however, in absolute terms, the second viewer watches twice as much news as the first viewer.

of his high school graduates, and 24 per cent of those with university educations. However, within this broad grouping of programs, westerns declined in popularity as education went up, whereas crime dramas, and police or detective programs actually increased in popularity among the better-educated groups. Steiner tends to be suspicious of measures of taste because he believes that many better-educated individuals are more selective in their responses than in their actual viewing habits. "If a professor and a blue-collar worker watch both *The Untouchables* and *Omnibus* regularly, the professor may be relatively more apt to cite *Omnibus* as an appropriate 'favorite'" (1963:128).

On the other hand, a listing of all the programs watched by an individual—even when it is in the form of an accurately kept diary—is not necessarily an infallible guide to what sorts of programs that person likes. Many people (particularly women) simply turn on the television set while they are doing something else, such as cooking, or ironing, or sewing, and pay only minimal attention to some of the programs. For example, many women in Idle Haven watched the afternoon movie on a local channel, not because they were particularly keen on movies (which ranked rather low in their listing of favorite programs) but because during the commercial breaks the station played "Dialing for Dollars." If a viewer was called and could answer a relatively simple question about the movie being shown he received anywhere from $5 to $25. Obviously this sort of viewing has rather little to do with program tastes as such.

On the whole, Steiner found more clear-cut differences in television viewing habits with increased age than with increased education. With age (particularly among those aged 55 and over) the number of programs watched went up irrespective of education and the percentages of news and public affairs programs watched also increased, both in absolute as well as relative terms. Steiner suggests that this increased interest in news programs may be due to increased reading difficulties, leading some people to turn to television as their principal source of news, or due to the less active schedule of older viewers, which permits them to watch their favorite newscasts more regularly. However, other studies indicate that the increased interest in news with aging also holds true for the other media—particularly newspapers and radio. A more plausible explanation, therefore, might be that elderly people are less caught up in the active affairs of their communities and the workaday world and feel a need to combat this growing disengagement by participating vicariously in world affairs via the mass media. We shall have more to say about the use of television for vicarious purposes in the discussion about Idle Haven.

In Idle Haven, every household interviewed had at least one television set, and 50 per cent had color sets. Watching television was, without question, everyone's chief leisure pursuit, and a few people even named it when asked whether they had a hobby. A few people were ambivalent about television and referred to it as the idiot box, but most were enthusiastic viewers. Almost everyone watched at least one news program a day and almost everyone watched important national events, such as the moon landing of Apollo II. One 82-year-old woman who had watched the Apollo mission on television was led to muse about the vast changes in air travel that had occurred during her lifetime; she could recall being taken out to a midwestern field to watch the Wright brothers fly their airplane. However, when people were asked to name some of their favorite programs that they watched regularly, no one specifically mentioned news or public affairs programs. The programs spontaneously named are listed below in rank order, and they reveal some interesting viewing patterns.

TABLE VIII
Favorite Television Programs of Idle Haven Residents

Type of program	Number of times mentioned
Sports events	56
Game and quiz shows	48
Variety and music shows	45
Westerns	35
Soap operas	32
Situation comedies	27
Travel and nature features	26
Movies	16
Mystery and adventure	15
Talk shows	12
Educational channel	4

The clustering of sports events, game and quiz shows, and variety shows at the top of the list reflects a common attitude in the park expressed by one man as "I don't watch nothin' that ain't real." (This man, incidentally, then went on to name *Gunsmoke* as one of his favorite programs, but it was obvious that he regarded it as a form of reality rather than as fiction.) This attitude, more strongly expressed by men than by women, is probably related to both sex and socioeconomic status. Bennett Berger argues that working-class men prefer westerns and sports events because these two types of programs are largely without middle-class content, just as with regard to comedy Berger found that their tastes ran to the rough-and-tumble comedy of Sergeant Bilko and McGraw (in Idle Haven, in 1969, it was *Hogan's Heroes* and *Hee-Haw*) rather than the more genteel family-situation comedies (1960:74-75). The aversion to programs that are not "real" no doubt has more to do with the middle-class content of most story programs than with the viewers' inability to get caught up in fictional situations, since Idle Haven residents had no trouble liking westerns (particularly *Gunsmoke* and *Bonanza*), and many retired men as well as women acknowledged that they followed various soap operas.

The working-class bias in favor of things that are "real" (or, real to *them*) is also conditioned by a vague desire to "learn something" in addition to being entertained. As all statistics indicate, most people find the purely educational programs a bore, but the great popularity of game and quiz shows stems in part from the fact that people find them educational. As Herta Herzog discovered in her early study of why people listened to *Professor Quiz* (a radio show), the focus of interest was not so much the competitive nature of the program as the fact that "many thought that such programs increased their education and were gratified to learn odd facts in this way" (in Steiner, 1963:412). Travel and nature programs (e.g., *Wide, Wonderful World*) were frequently cited by Idle Haven residents for their educational as well as entertainment value, and one man commented that he found *Let's Make a Deal* so interesting that he could watch it all day. Many residents also watched talk shows (particularly those that came on in the late afternoon) because they "learned things they didn't know."

The interest in game shows and talk shows also appeared to be linked to age and, particularly in the case of single individuals, to isolation. Such programs—where real people joke and talk with each other—take the place of social interaction for many lonely individuals. I often walked in on elderly widows watching Merv Griffin and his guests in the late-afternoon twilight and was struck by the fact that these viewers seemed to be having a silent conversation with their television sets. Many extremely elderly women also said that watching daytime soap operas gave them a similar vicarious involvement in today's world; "It keeps me current with what the younger generation's up to," one old lady remarked as she went on to list quite placidly some of the modern trends she'd learned about—adultery, drug addiction, illegitimacy, and so forth. (Of course, she could also hear about such things on news programs, but I suspect that seeing them in the context of a dramatic show gave her a better emotional understanding of why and how such things occur.) Many widows used television in a less discriminating way just to combat their loneliness: "I turn on my set just to hear the voices," or "I turn it on to keep me company." Gary Steiner, who also notes that "dependence on the medium is probably most extreme among those restricted in interests and activities —the aged, the shut-ins, the lonely," quotes a typical example of such a viewer:

> "I'm an old man and all alone, and the TV brings people and music and talk into my life. Maybe without TV I would be ready to die; but this TV gives me life. It gives me what to look forward to—that tomorrow, if I live, I'll watch this and that program" (1963:26).

The interviews in Idle Haven also supported and furnished some explanations for the often observed tendency of older people to watch fewer action programs (cf. Steiner, 1963:176). Many elderly viewers said they no longer watched such programs because violence—shootings, chases, and so forth—made them "nervous." One woman said that even talk shows made her nervous because "people always get so hostile." Such statements were often coupled with grateful references to more relaxing programs such as Lawrence Welk, Ed Sullivan, Dean Martin, and Carol Burnett.

In addition to watching television, how else did residents of Idle Haven spend their free time? As was noted in Chapter 2, 21 per cent of the households interviewed were regular church-goers and about 21 per cent of the men and 20 per cent of the women were currently active in some sort of voluntary association. However, only about 7 per cent of the residents interviewed were involved in church or lodge activities to the extent that they were occupied beyond routine participation once a month or once a week. Some of these very active participants, particularly the church members, were busy indeed—attending pot-luck suppers, choir practice, Sunday school, and other meetings—and said, with some accuracy, that the church was their whole life. A heavy schedule of lodge and club activities, although common among a few disappointed park ex-leaders (and a few who deliberately chose not to become park leaders) was not as frequent a choice as the church.

In addition to those active outside the park, we have noted that about 5 to 10 per cent of the residents were very active, either formally or informally, in the park's leadership group. There was very little overlap between those who were very active in groups outside the park and those who were very active within the park, so that individuals who enjoyed playing an active role in social groups seemed to be making a choice as to where to allocate their time and energies. Of course, for some disappointed park leaders this was a forced choice, but the fact that they went ahead and became involved in groups outside the park probably enabled them to continue living in the park despite their ostracism. There is some evidence that those who fail as leaders in the park and who do not turn to outside groups find the park so embittering and lonely to live in that they either leave or even—as in the case of the ceramics teacher who left but continued to focus her attention on the park—commit suicide.

For the 60 per cent of the park residents who participate in park events from time to time, such activities are not terribly time-consuming but they also seem to represent a partial substitution for former lodge or club affiliations. Being, predominantly, members of the working-class, most of the residents were never very active in voluntary associations; however, it should be remembered that twice as many were active at one time as are now active. Some of these affiliations were severed when residents moved into the park, and other memberships were allowed to lapse because of age or disabilities. One great advantage of planned park activities is that they are so much more accessible than activities outside the park—no one needs to drive long distances to attend them. It would be interesting to see whether, in an enclave of younger people, on-site activities could compete as successfully with outside activities—e.g., sports events, movies, dining out in restaurants—as they do among the elderly. There is no doubt that in a special setting for the elderly, on-site activities have an inherent advantage over more distant and energy consuming pursuits.

This is not to say that any activity started in a special setting for the elderly is likely to succeed simply because it is there. Aside from the personal infighting and jealousies that may sabotage various well-meant projects, socioeconomic class continues to exercise a powerful influence on people's interests. Although a few residents in Idle Haven said that they would have liked to have attended a creative writing class or a book review club in the park, there was no evidence that a sufficiently large group of residents could ever have been interested in such activities. (For example, a Spanish class was at one time attempted, but attendance rapidly dwindled and finally disappeared.)

It occurred to me that perhaps the paucity of even slightly intellectual activities in the park might be due to a lack of resources—i.e., there was no one in the park sufficiently skilled to lead such activities, and even the Spanish class was sometimes said to have failed because the park's one Spanish speaker was not sufficiently skilled as a teacher. I therefore considered, as an experiment, teaching a class in American literature or basic anthropology just to see how many residents this might draw. It soon became obvious, however, that such a test would be a better indicator of my own popularity than of any interest in the activity. When I finally managed to engineer a somewhat less biased test of cultural interest in the park—a lecture about Sino-Soviet relations by a well-known China specialist (who was, however, also my husband)—exactly the same number (thirty-six) of residents came to the association meeting who always attended. In other words, there seemed to be no great unquenched thirst for intellectual offerings, and the actual activities in the park correspond rather closely to the tastes and interests of the inhabitants. By contrast, I visited several Bay Area high-rise apartment complexes for the aged, inhabited by upper middle-class residents, that had recreation calendars which included group attendance at the San Francisco Symphony, theater parties, a book review club, and slide lectures by residents who had recently been abroad.

In addition to the impact of socioeconomic class, age, and setting on planned group activities, gender is also an important input. In Idle Haven, women participated much more extensively than men: they were often the sole participants in groups such as the card club and the ceramics and handicraft classes, and they dominated the formal and informal leadership roles of the park's association. There are various reasons why this was so. Part of the differential participation of the sexes was probably due to a subtle class difference. More of the women in Idle Haven had held white-collar jobs and were thus more comfortable in leadership roles which required some social and verbal skills. The few men whom I saw conduct association meetings were either acutely ill at ease and tongue-tied, or else overly formal and determined to run things by the book.

It is also true, of course, that many of the activities were female oriented: women were more likely to enjoy planning dinners and luncheons or participating in handicraft classes. It has also been suggested by some sociologists that retired men are not used to spending the daytime hours in such activities and feel comfortable only at evening meetings. Interestingly enough, Idle Haven did not provide much evidence for that view: the monthly luncheon—a rather female-oriented affair—was also well attended by retired men (or even just men who happened to be at home that day). However, for the men the luncheon merely constituted a good meal and a pleasant social occasion, whereas for the women it clearly had a much more important function. Since it was always a pot-luck affair to which everyone contributed something, women vied with each other to bring dishes that others would compliment. It was obvious that many women (myself included) gave considerable thought to the preparation of a dish that they excelled at, that would be "unusual" and yet not so unusual that no one would eat it. Purely aside from compliments or requests for the recipe (sometimes such recipes were so popular that they were reprinted in the monthly newsletter), the simple fact that one's dish went home clean rather than barely tasted was enough to give most women a decided sense of accomplishment. The greatest achievement of all, in the cooking realm, was to become so noted for a particular dish that people would request it on special occasions. For the "Fun Nights," which were otherwise poorly attended, some women were asked to make their special lemon cake or chocolate-cream cake, and several of them were so flattered that they obliged even though they themselves did not attend the evening or even get to taste their own cake.

The men in the park were not adept at and could not derive satisfaction from such roles, but some of them developed other special roles on which residents came to depend and for which they developed something of a reputation within the park. Some men enjoyed serving on the breakfast committee, which assisted the park's resident cook in preparing the monthly Sunday breakfast. This was a kind of short-order-house role that many of the men played to the hilt, complete with aprons, tall white hats, and the jargon of "two-over-easy-and-hold-the-bacon." Two other retired men delivered the park's newsletter to residents' homes every month, and one of these men had also become well known to numerous residents because he sold all the tickets to the monthly dinners and breakfasts and also collected money for an occasional football or baseball pool.[3]

Some retired men were also well known and often called upon in their roles as sidewalk superintendents and assistants in the actual business of installing and dismantling mobile homes. These men were often retired carpenters, mechanics, or truck drivers, and had had considerable experience in the types of tasks required, thereby saving themselves and others a great deal of money. Many of the residents in Idle Haven had leveled and hooked up their own units, installed their own skirting and awnings, and built their own porches. This do-it-yourself aspect of mobile-home living is something that will doubtlessly continue to offer greater appeal to working-class than to middle-class families; or that, at any rate, will make middle-class parks tend to be much more expensive and custom built, since in such parks residents will have to hire professionals to do the work that many working-class residents can do for themselves.

In Idle Haven, casual sidewalk-superintending and tinkering seemed to be for the men what more formal park activities were for the women. If a group of women was sitting at one end of the recreation hall playing bridge, a group of men (often the bridge-players' husbands) could be found sitting around the coffee-table talking about the latest ball-game scores, or fishing, or politics. If a group of women was busy attending the weekly ceramics class, a group of men was more likely to be found inspecting a piece of fence that had recently blown down or a camper that someone had just bought. Many of the men were well aware of the role these casual activities played in their lives and said they could never stand to live in a retirement complex consisting of apartments because it would be "too confining." "What would I do with myself

---

[3] These pools, usually on professional football games or on World Series games, were run strictly according to chance. One paid 25 or 50 cents to buy a square in a large grid, and numbers corresponding to the squares were drawn only after the entire grid had been sold. Obviously, some people had lost even before the game began—for example, those who drew tied scores in baseball, since these are played off until one or another side wins.

all day?" Women, by contrast, tended to object to apartment living
because it was too noisy, or too impersonal, or because they could
no longer climb stairs with ease. Women also enjoyed the park
because they could walk or bicycle safely, but they were much less
likely than the men merely to amble about looking for a conversation or a diversion.

In terms of private hobbies, women also seemed to be somewhat
more fully occupied than men, and their involvement with hobbies
seemed to be of longer duration. Although men cited approximately
the same number of hobbies per person as women (Table IX), their

TABLE IX

Leisure Pursuits of Idle Haven Residents

Women (N=148; 1.59 hobbies per person)		Men (N=112; 1.51 hobbies per person)	
Sewing (knitting, embroidery, crocheting)	74	Fishing	36
Reading	28	Bowling	17
Ceramics or handicrafts	18	Carpentering or tinkering	15
Cards	17	Golf	14
Camping	12	Going to ball games	12
Shopping	11	Camping	12
Cooking	10	Cards	10
Organ playing	9	Hunting	10
Travel	9	Travel	7
Bicycling	8	Gardening	7
Gardening	7	Reading	6
Bowling	7	Bicycling	5
Dancing	5	Driving	5
Driving	4	Listening to music	5
Listening to music	4	Dancing	4
Jigsaw or crossword puzzles	4	Painting (pictures)	3
Walking	3	Rug-making	2
Golf	2		
Going to ball games	2		

actual participation in private hobbies was a good deal less than
this because many of the more popular men's hobbies were occasional activities—such as fishing, camping, and hunting—which required extensive preparation and travel. Not only were such male
hobbies occasional because of these factors, but for many retired
men illness, old age, and a low income had made them genuine
ex-hobbies in which they no longer participated at all. By contrast,

half of the women cited sewing (or knitting, embroidery, or cro-
cheting) as a hobby, and in most such instances it was something
they had done for a very long time and in which they continued to
take a great deal of pleasure. The numbers of women in Idle Haven
who still made most of their own clothes, or who knitted sweaters
and socks for themselves and their families, or who crocheted af-
ghans, was truly astounding. Not only did such women's hobbies
reflect lifelong interests, but they were not much affected by age
(except for occasional complaints about arthritic fingers and poor
eyesight), and they could be pursued relatively inexpensively, at
home. Very few men were fortunate enough to have hobbies of this
sort; one man, a retired railroad engineer, had turned a passion for
tinkering into a slightly profitable hobby. He bought old, broken
appliances—toasters, radios, clocks, lamps, vacuum cleaners—which
he repaired and sold at a small profit at a local weekend flea market.
He was one of the happiest, most fully occupied "retired" men I met.

Many of the hobbies and private leisure pursuits of Idle Haven
residents also reflected their working-class status. Although nine
women and seven men mentioned that they enjoyed "travelling"
(and another four women and five men merely said that they liked
to "drive" or "go for drives"), almost no one meant by this travel
to foreign countries or overseas. Most working-class individuals,
even when they can afford it, are vaguely worried and suspicious
about leaving their own country—"I hear that people over there just
gyp you right and left"; "Mexico's too dirty for my taste"; "After
what de Gaulle said about the U. S. I wouldn't give that guy any of
my money . . ." Exceptions are those working-class individuals who
were born in Europe and who often pay a return visit to the old
country after they retire. (This motive is well understood by other,
American-born members of the working-class, one of whom commented, when I asked whether he had any desire to see Europe,
"Why should I want to do that? I haven't left anything over there.")
Of the six Idle Haven households who had visited foreign countries,
all were special cases: three had relatives abroad, either in Europe
or in Mexico, and the other three were middle-class, white-collar
families who had taken a 30-day tour of Europe or a cruise to Aca-
pulco. Cruises and automobile and travel-trailer trips to Mexico are
becoming more popular as a result of the increasingly Americanized
facilities available there, but the language barrier is still viewed
with trepidation by many, and as a result trips to Hawaii or to
Canada and Alaska are far more popular. However, for most of the

residents of Idle Haven who could afford it, travel meant a trip
by automobile or travel-trailer (less frequently by air) to another
part of the United States to visit relatives, or merely to another part
of California to fish or camp.

Trips to Reno to do a little gambling were also extremely
popular with Idle Haven residents—including one lady in her 80s
who still went once a year. Many couples went by themselves or
with another couple from the park, but in addition the twice-yearly
bus trip organized for Idle Haven residents was always sold out.
Some individuals apparently were so keen on going that they went
despite their doctor's orders (Lake Tahoe is situated at 6,000 feet
above sea level and therefore presents problems to people with high
blood pressure), since one resident had died of a heart attack on one
of these bus trips and another had become ill and died shortly
thereafter. One resident who never went to Reno confessed that it
was not because he did not care for gambling but because in his
working days he had cared a little too much: now that he was retired he felt he could no longer afford the three or four hundred
dollars that he had always managed to spend there.

Other leisure pursuits mentioned by Idle Haven residents reveal their class-based interests: e.g., attendance at ball games, bowling, and dancing. However, golf, until recently considered more of
a middle-class pastime, is gaining in popularity. Almost no one
played a musical instrument as a hobby, with the exception of nine
women who said they liked to play the organ. In all but one case,
these organs turned out to be very small chord-organs with two- or
three-octave keyboards on which—with the aid of brightly colored
keys and matching music sheets—one could play a simple hymn or
folktune.

Reading as a leisure pursuit generally increases in popularity
with age—particularly newspaper and magazine reading—but it also
appears to be strongly influenced by social class and sex. In Idle
Haven, 19 per cent of the women but only 5 per cent of the men
mentioned reading as a favorite pastime. As has been noted earlier,
some of this difference may be related to a subtle class difference
between the sexes: many of the women had had more exposure to
the white-collar world than the men and were thus more at home
with the written (and spoken) word. But even within a strictly
blue-collar context, reading appears to be a more acceptable female
pursuit; men—particularly during their working years—seem to regard with amused tolerance their wives' addiction to true romances

magazines or gothic novels, without ever discovering themselves what it means to become "lost in a book." With increasing age and a more sedentary existence for both, the two molds nevertheless tend to remain fixed: women continue to find the act of reading pleasurable whereas men don't really know how to read or how to find reading material that will hold their interest. Most of the women who mentioned reading as a popular pastime had very decided tastes and could name a number of their favorite authors or subjects: one lady was hooked on Edgar Cayce books and was deep into "mysticism" and "philosophy"; another liked religious books such as those by Taylor Caldwell; still another was chiefly a mystery fan and mentioned Agatha Christie's and Mary Stewart's books; and still another favored "family novels," which apparently included some real classics as well as the latest best-seller. Most of these women bought paperbacks—usually at a drugstore or grocery store —and several used the public library.

By contrast, the men who said they liked to read were much more vague about what it was they read. Some said they liked "history" but could not name any specific author or period of history they particularly enjoyed. One or two said that their chief reading was done in *Argosy* or *True* or mystery magazines. Most interesting, perhaps, was the fact that several men who by their own account were "real readers," when asked what it was that they read, named the encyclopedia! "Whenever I'm bored or have nothing to do, I pick up the encyclopedia, and I always learn something new." This true autodidact approach to knowledge supports our earlier statement that most of the men have had very little experience with reading or with choosing a special type of reading material; hence the encyclopedia's alphabetical, completely topical organization— and its promise of ultimately encyclopedic coverage—has great appeal. Most of the encyclopedias were either old sets of standard works—e.g., the *Britannica*—or else an encyclopedia that was then being sold (at a volume per week) in a chain grocery store.

The magazines subscribed to or read regularly by Idle Haven residents (Table X) reveal a class profile very similar to that found by Bennett Berger in his working-class suburb. As in his sample (1960:77) there is a startling dominance of *Reader's Digest* over all the other magazines mentioned. Berger suggests that the persistence of door-to-door magazine salesmen may have something to do with this, but in mobile-home parks such salesmen are generally denied access. On the other hand, the Idle Haven figures include not mere-

TABLE X

Magazines Read Regularly by Idle Haven Residents

General interest		Women's magazines	
READER'S DIGEST	55	LADIES' HOME JOURNAL	15
LIFE	17	McCALL'S	11
LOOK	15	GOOD HOUSEKEEPING	8
TV GUIDE	14	SUNSET	7
NATIONAL GEOGRAPHIC	13	BETTER HOMES & GARDENS	7
TIME	3	REDBOOK	4
NEWSWEEK	3	WOMAN'S DAY AND	
HOLIDAY	3	FAMILY CIRCLE	2

Men's magazines		Miscellaneous	
FIELD & STREAM	7	RELIGIOUS MAGAZINES	10
TRUE	7	MOVIE MAGAZINES	5
POPULAR MECHANICS	5	TRAILER LIFE	4
RIFLEMAN	3	MODERN MATURITY	2
ARGOSY	3	OFFICIAL DETECTIVE	2
MECHANIX ILLUSTRATED	2		
POPULAR SCIENCE	2		
SPORTS ILLUSTRATED	2		
"CAR" MAGAZINES	2		

ly magazine subscriptions, but also magazines read regularly, because few people seemed to distinguish between these two things.
The reason is that many of the older and poorer Idle Haven residents did not subscribe to any magazines but instead read those
that were passed on to them by a neighbor or left behind in the
laundry room or recreation hall. Thus there is a sort of multiplier
effect in a mobile-home park. Those who actually subscribe to
magazines are relatively few in number but tend to subscribe to
several at one time—one middle-class resident reeled off the names
of six magazines she subscribed to, the latest issue of each neatly
piled on her coffee-table. Such subscribers then place their old
issues in the recreation hall or in the laundry rooms, where several
more residents borrow and read them. Magazines that tend to be
kept and not donated—for example, *Holiday*, various religious and
hobby magazines, and sports magazines—have a much smaller read-
ership. And of course, there is a vast array of magazines which no
one in the park either subscribes to or reads.

If factors such as age (and physical condition), gender, socioeconomic class, and setting help determine the scope and nature of leisure activities, they also affect the values governing such activities. Thus some activities may not be deemed "appropriate" for individuals above a certain age or of a certain sex, and class mores may strongly condemn or promote certain pursuits or affect their timing and locale. As Irving Rosow has suggested, special settings—e.g., retirement communities—are still another input which may render acceptable those activities that might otherwise be frowned upon, although he does not consider the obverse possibility—namely, that special settings may also inhibit some people. For example, Calvin Trillin (1964) observed that in Sun City (Arizona), the hobby rooms and shuffleboard courts were never occupied *except* when some special class or club was using them.

In Idle Haven, I had little sense that there were strong values attached to sexual distinctions in leisure pursuits. Women whose husbands cited fishing as a hobby said that they also liked to fish (although most of these wives tended to list "camping" as their hobby while their husbands "fished"); several married couples went bowling or golfing together; and men as well as women played cards. Men were not laughed at for participating in essentially feminine handicrafts, such as hooking rugs, although previous exposure and more sex-segregated values during their younger years had obviously prepared few men to take up or enjoy such hobbies.

In non-leisure activities around the home there was also very little segregation by sex in chores: men as well as women did the grocery shopping, the laundry, and the cooking and housecleaning. Some of this shared housekeeping dated from years when both the husband and wife had held jobs; in other cases it had been brought about by the illness of one or another spouse. Thus I met one relatively young couple—both still employed—where the husband did all the cooking and the wife "kept the house"; and I met several elderly couples where the husband did almost all of the cooking and cleaning because the wife was extremely frail. Conversely, there were several women in Idle Haven who did all the driving (and much else) for their husbands because their husbands had suffered a stroke, a heart attack, or had failing eyesight.

There also seemed to be little sense that certain hobbies were inappropriate for people beyond a certain age. Even girl-watching was a recognized, if occasionally joked-about pastime; and one eighty-year-old lady, after saying that she liked Dean Martin's show because he was so handsome, added by way of explanation, "After all, one never gets too old to look!" Bicycling—not a typical sport among the elderly—is extremely popular in all mobile-home parks and is doubtless given an extra impetus not merely because parks are well suited to bicycle traffic but also because "everyone is doing it." Dancing is popular among couples of all ages.

It is in the realm of working-class values that the strongest impact on leisure is to be found, and nowhere was this more evident than in people's attitudes toward drinking. Although some extremely religious people in the park were teetotalers, it was well known that many residents of Idle Haven drank liquor, some of them to excess. (Several men, only half-jokingly, said that drinking was their chief hobby.) Nevertheless, there were very strong values surrounding where and what one drank, as well as what one would and would not admit to. Thus, it was generally considered inappropriate to drink during the day, although I visited many couples on a Sunday afternoon and found them having several highballs. (A highball, in Idle Haven, generally consisted of either bourbon or vodka and a mixer, such as 7-Up or ginger ale.) When one such couple later showed up for a Sunday-evening dinner in the recreation hall, the husband—who was quite obviously tight, and very loud-mouthed as a result—was greeted with general disapproval. One lady, sitting at the next table, remarked to no one in particular, "If that were my husband, I would put a sack over his head."

Except for dances and the New Year's Eve party, liquor was never served in the recreation hall. Occasionally a group of friends might bring some beer or a bottle of red wine to a spaghetti-feed, but this was always frowned upon by others attending the dinner. At dances, on the other hand, those who attended (and even those who stayed away) expected participants to drink heavily. Unaware of this assumption, I brought a bottle of white wine to the first dance that I attended in Idle Haven, partly because I came alone and had to drive myself home. However, my taste in liquor amazed some people so much that at the next dance several remembered me as the lady who drank only white wine! Not only was wine considered too mild by half but, as Berger also notes, working-class subjects tend to regard wine as something that only "dagos" and "winos" drink.

Life in a mobile-home park may not inhibit alcoholism but it undoubtedly makes life more difficult for alcoholics: some are evicted, others are gossiped about, and some apparently leave voluntarily rather than face social disapproval. (One woman is reputed to have sold her mobile home because her neighbor peeked at her through the curtains every time she heard another beer can being opened.) Mobile-home park life inhibits certain other pursuits—for example male hobbies that require extensive (and noisy) tools. A number of men said that they had had elaborate workshops before they bought mobile homes, and that they missed this aspect of their former lives. Several women voiced a similar complaint, but not with regard to a hobby: they said that they had had trouble getting used to a mobile home because they couldn't clean house the way they used to (shaking dust-mops and rugs outside) and missed being able to hang their laundry outside to dry in the sun.

Despite such occasional complaints, one got the impression that in terms of their leisure pursuits and life style, most Idle Haven residents were quite satisfied: the park accommodated their traditional hobbies and habits, opened up a few new opportunities, and closed off many undesirable possibilities. However, the mechanism by which mobile-home parks cater to (and profit from) their inhabitants is a delicate one, and there are some signs of trouble, to which we shall turn in the final chapter.

8. Problems and Prospects

Although we shall have to await the results of the 1970 census for exact figures, an estimated six million Americans are currently living in close to three million mobile homes. Of these, approximately one million live in California, which together with Florida leads the nation in the number of mobile-home residents. At the time of the 1960 census, there were 766,565 inhabited mobile homes. It took the industry only 6 years to build and sell another million mobile homes, and an additional 3 years to produce a million more. As of mid-1970, 450,000 mobile homes a year were being built—one out of every four new housing starts in the U. S. The government recognized this building trend in 1970 when, for the first time, it included mobile homes in a report setting forth national housing goals. Of the twenty-six million new housing units that it hopes will be built between 1968 and 1978, four million are expected to be mobile homes.

There are many reasons for this upsurge in mobile-home manu-facturing. The traditional building trades have been hamstrung by restrictive and often contradictory building codes and regulations, high union wage scales, the growing costs of traditional building materials, and on-site building methods that are not only slow but also dependent on good weather conditions. Mobile-home manu-facturers, by contrast, are not limited by traditional building codes, since they entered the field—and are still legally classified—as vehi-cles. Thus they have been free to pioneer in the use of new ma-terials, such as plastic piping and aluminum siding. Building mobile homes in a factory, on an assembly-line basis has also meant that the industry could employ semi-skilled, non-union labor and that it could operate all year, regardless of the weather.

The combination of these factors has enabled the mobile-home industry to produce dwelling units not only much more rapidly than traditional builders but also at a much lower per-unit cost. In 1970, the average mobile home could be marketed between $3,000 and $12,000 (excluding the cost of land), whereas the median price of an ordinary new home (including the lot) was $27,000. Given the fact that an estimated 65 per cent of the eligible home buyers in the nation earn less than $8,000 a year, many observers see mobile homes as a panacea for the ill-housed poor. As Edward Banfield (1970:114-31) has recently pointed out, however, there are many different kinds of poverty: some the result of old age or dis-ability, some a merely temporary poverty due to prolonged schooling or to just starting out in a job, some caused by divorce or desertion that has resulted in a family's dependency on a female head-of-household, and some "hard core" cases of lower-class poverty involv-ing what Banfield and others have called the "culture of poverty" syndrome. Are mobile homes, despite their low cost, capable of meeting the future housing needs of all these groups?

As this study has illustrated, at least one segment of the poor—the elderly, white working class—has already discovered mobile-home living, not merely because of its relatively low cost but also because of the security and companionship that mobile-home parks provide. National studies indicate that mobile homes are also popu-lar with a second low-income group—young, working-class couples—

and the industry predicts that such "young marrieds" will become an expanding segment of their market. It is less clear whether mobile homes will also become popular with young, upwardly mobile college graduates; however, a number of colleges are using clusters of mobile homes as dormitories and as married students' housing, so this market may be tapped by means of institutional rather than individual choice. But what about the two remaining low-income groups—the young, frequently Negro, mothers on welfare or struggling to support their children, and the other ghetto families that now live in deplorable slums—for whom mobile homes are also alleged to be the answer?

We have already noted that as of 1966, less than 2 per cent of the mobile-home population was Negro. In part this low percentage can be explained by the variety of means by which Negroes have been deliberately excluded from mobile-home parks. However, this is by no means the only explanation. As has also been noted, the current financing of mobile homes places them beyond the means of most ghetto families. Most banks require 20 to 25 per cent of the purchase price as a down payment, and add-on interest charges plus a relatively short loan period (in California, as of 1970, the longest loan period available was 12 years) means high monthly payments in addition to the cost of renting a space in a park. In mid-1970, a Bank of America loan for $10,000 toward the purchase of a new mobile home (at a stated interest rate of 6¼ per cent) would have cost the borrower $143.75 a month for ten years. Add to this approximately $100 a month for a space in a typical Bay Area park, and one arrives at a monthly housing cost considerably higher than most ghetto dwellers could afford, and also considerably higher than the payments on a modest tract home with a 25 or 30-year mortgage would be.[1]

Up until the present time the only experiments with mobile homes in urban ghettos have involved their use as temporary housing for residents displaced by urban renewal projects. In most of these cases no thought has been given to housing people permanent-

---

[1] For some interesting cost comparisons of mobile homes and comparably priced tract homes, see Alschuler and Betts (1970:42–55). As of mid-1970, the Federal Housing Administration began to underwrite mobile-home mortgages, but several California bank officers familiar with mobile-home financing said they did not expect this to have a major impact. The FHA terms do call for somewhat lower downpayments, but real interest rates can go up to 10.57 per cent for terms not longer than 12 years. These are the same terms already being

ly in mobile homes because land costs have dictated the need for a much greater population density. But in many cities with large Negro populations—e.g., Los Angeles, Oakland, Louisville, Jacksonville, Dallas, Washington, D. C.—the prevailing pattern of housing is single-family dwellings rather than high-rise apartment buildings, and mobile homes might well be used to replace decrepit slum housing. It seems unlikely that such an improvement in physical surroundings would spell an immediate end to the social malaise of the ghetto since, as Banfield argues, the type of poverty accompanied by a culture of poverty is in many ways self-perpetuating. However, it would be interesting to experiment with importing not merely the mobile home but also the mobile-home park into the ghetto to see whether it could survive successfully as an enclave in such an environment. Given capable and honest management, the power to evict troublemakers (hoodlums, drug-addicts, criminals), and a modicum of social cohesion, could such a park provide the safety and community spirit now so patently lacking in most urban renewal projects? Or would they succumb to a combination of depredations from without and dissension within?

These are idle speculations, but they are a good deal more concrete than the thinking done about these subjects by the mobile-home industry. Mobile-home builders are convinced that they are the wave of the future—that they hold the key to inexpensive, factory-built housing—but they have yet to think very clearly about who their new clients will be and how these new clients will be received by their present clients, the elderly and the newly married men and women of the white working class. Privately, mobile-home manufacturers seem to assume that while they may soon be building mobile homes for the Negro ghettos their actual client will be the government. Given the Nixon administration's interest in a minimum income plan and the widespread criticism of government-owned and -operated housing, this is a very large assumption indeed. The government may find it socially more desirable and simpler to make it

---

offered by large reputable banks, such as the Bank of America, to qualified mobile-home buyers. Unqualified applicants, who probably will not meet the FHA's standards either, will doubtless continue to pay the much higher interest rates charged by mobile-home dealers. It may be, however, that the FHA's move will encourage some smaller banks who have not been financing mobile homes at all (because they had limited funds to invest and more attractive investment opportunities were available) to enter this field, thereby making more mobile-home mortgage money available.

possible for large numbers of Negro poor to buy mobile homes. If this came to pass, the industry would be confronted with a challenge it is by no means prepared to meet, for there are not enough mobile-home parks available now to house all the people who want to buy mobile homes, and almost all of these parks would refuse to accept Negro residents.

The mobile-home industry is clearly betting that in the near future its present field of operations will break into two halves. On the one hand, it no doubt hopes to continue building mobile homes that will be placed in mobile-home parks. On the other hand, it foresees that it will be producing factory-built houses which will be trucked out to their sites, attached to prepared slabs of concrete, hooked up to utilities and sewage, there to become the successors to the tract homes of the 1950s. Such permanently installed mobile homes will doubtless forego the current attractions that mobile-home parks have for the elderly (no yards, a recreation hall, a fenced and controlled environment) in order to perpetuate the appeals that suburbia has always had for young families with children (private yards, no landlord or manager to control one's behavior, open space).

This newly developing second market—for factory-built non-mobile "mobile" homes—is clearly so seductive that mobile-home builders are quietly removing any obstacles that may exist between them and it. For example, they are voluntarily drafting a uniform building code that will bring their product more closely into line with conventional dwellings. More important, the industry will no doubt surrender, in the near future, any claims to producing a vehicle which is subject only to a *vehicle* but not a *property* tax. Although the notion that mobile-home park residents at the present time do not pay any sort of property taxes is ill-founded,[2] there is something of the artful dodge about their claims that they live in vehicles rather than dwellings. Whenever attempts are made to raise the motor vehicles license fees to create more revenue for highways and the like, mobile-home owners lobby to get themselves written out of the increase on grounds that their mobile homes are largely stationary. Yet when attempts are made to call their units stationary and to tax them as real property, they proudly point to

---

2 One of the most thorough discussions of the taxation issue in California is a series of editorials written by Jack Kneass and published in *Western Mobile Home News* [now *Western Mobile News*], November 27, December 4, 11, 18, 25, 1967, and January 1, 8, 15, and 22, 1968, and reprinted by *Western Mobile News* as a pamphlet. See also Alschuler and Betts (1970).

the wheels underneath and argue that they are ready to roll at a moment's notice.[3]

A more potent reason why mobile homes will sooner or later come to be taxed as real property is that county and city governments will demand it as the price for allowing more mobile-home parks to be built within their jurisdictions. At the present time many local planning boards still refuse to grant zoning permits to mobile-home park developers on the grounds that such land uses cost the local authorities more in services than they can recoup in taxes. In order to counter these arguments, and in order to open the way for the eventual creation of mobile-home tracts, the industry and park developers seem to be moving slowly in the direction of getting their future residents to pay a normal real estate tax. This is creating a good deal of friction between the industry and present-day mobile-home residents. In California, for example, the Golden State Mobilehome Owners League (GSMOL) accused that state's Western Mobilehome Association (WMA) of double dealing in supporting a bill that will increase mobile home in-lieu taxes. Wrote the mobile-home owners' lobbyist:

> "Is the WMA in the middle of a credibility gap? On the one hand Neil Nordlander [WMA's lobbyist] states that the mobile home owner pays his fair share of taxes. On the other hand, Nordlander is supporting a bill in Sacramento that will substantially raise the mobile home in-lieu tax. . . . GSMOL opposes the actions of WMA in the taxation area, and we will fight the bill at every stage" (WMN, March 30, 1970: 11).

Mobile-home owners today are beginning to clash with the industry over a number of other future-oriented moves. For example, many mobile-home park developers are beginning to operate like tract developers: they are no longer merely building a park with

---

[3] The wheels of a mobile home, although artfully hidden from view by "skirting" once the mobile home is resting on pilings in a park, are of great symbolic importance. Many residents realize that without these wheels their claim to vehicular status would be seriously weakened. Thus at many GSMOL meetings there was a great deal of criticism of elegant new parks in which residents had to install their mobile homes without wheels in order to make them look more like ordinary homes, and of dealers and installers who offer to buy a mobile home's tires (which otherwise simply rot in due course of time) once the unit has been installed in a park. "Don't let them remove your wheels!" was a frequently-heard rallying cry. "It's the first step to higher taxes."

rental spaces available to anyone with a new or used mobile home;[4] they are also selling the mobile homes to be installed within the park, and one cannot move into such a park unless one buys a new mobile home from the developer. Such parks are called "closed parks," and they pose numerous problems for the individual who buys into one, as well as for those denied access because they already own mobile homes or want to buy a mobile home on the open market.

A closed park usually offers prospective residents a choice of several different mobile homes (although these are often different models by the same manufacturer) in several price ranges. However, the price of such mobile homes is usually several hundred, and sometimes several thousand, dollars more than the buyer would have to pay if he bought the same model from an independent dealer. Closed-park developers argue that these higher prices include installation fees, patios, car-ports, and landscaping for which the ordinary mobile-home purchaser pays separately. This is partly true although, as we have seen, many mobile-home owners do much of this finishing and installation work themselves. In a closed park, the developers argue, everything is done professionally and in keeping with a master plan so that residents will not be offended by their neighbors' bad taste in landscaping or an amateurishly built porch. As one developer writes:

> ". . . [a] major advantage [of closed parks] . . . is a controlled environment. . . . every home is of the highest quality in a beautiful park. The value of a mobile home is directly related to the environment surrounding it. It stands to reason that [such] a home . . . will retain its value because of the desirability of the community as a whole" (WMN, April 13, 1970:2).

Another developer candidly notes:

> "In-park sales permits lower rents with the developer making a competitive profit on each coach sold and thus assuring the economic feasibility of the overall project. Many lenders look favorably on in-park sales to justify the construction loan.

---

[4] Of course, as was noted in Chapter 3, even such parks are not really open to everyone. Negroes and people with "old, unsightly" mobile homes are screened out and many of the spaces are rented by dealers for their prospective customers.

. . . The second problem facing the developer is zoning. Unfortunately there is still the stigma of the rundown trailer park and gypsy court image. Very few areas have outright mobile home zoning. Most require specific site plans and hearings before the local zoning body. Some cities are seriously considering in-park sales as a policy to control the park appearance. The developer must promise, as a condition of the zoning, to establish and enforce uniform regulations governing coach size, awnings, skirts, landscaping and other accessories. In-park sales is the best method of creating a socially acceptable mobile home community not only for the local zoning body but especially for the park dwellers" (WMN, January 12, 1970:18).

While it is the ostensible aim of closed parks to give residents even more security in their expertly erected homes and carefully supervised neighbors, the results sometimes fall far short of this. At several 1969 regional meetings of the GSMOL, I heard many pathetic complaints from mobile-home residents who had defective mobile homes that they had repeatedly, and without success, tried to get repaired. When someone finally suggested that one way to make a dealer honor his contract was to complain directly to the manufacturer—either of the mobile home itself or of a particular malfunctioning appliance within the home—many of these unhappy residents confessed that they were afraid to do this because they might be evicted! The explanation was that their mobile-home dealer and installer was also their landlord and that any complaints made over his head to manufacturers might provoke him into retaliating with eviction notices.

Evictions or decisions to move or sell out pose other problems in closed parks. In many of these parks the mobile homes are installed in such a way that it is not feasible to move them. Thus the "owner" of such a mobile home cannot take it with him if he chooses to move to a different park, nor—since it is located in a controlled park—can he sell it on the open market as he would an ordinary home. Instead, he must sell his mobile home subject to the park owner's approval or he must sell it back to the park's owners and they will then resell the unit to a new tenant, usually at a substantial profit to themselves.

Even in parks that are not closed, problems await the often unsuspecting resident. If he manages to find a space in an already-established park and this space has been "landscaped" by its former residents—whether with plants or with rocks—he will be charged an initial fee for this landscaping. In Idle Haven an attractive, completely fenced, rose-planted lot had changed hands four times and each time the manager had charged the new residents $200 for the landscaping, the original cost of which had been borne by the first tenant. Such unfair profits led one embittered resident of Idle Haven to claim that if he ever moved he would throw his entire rock garden into the ocean rather than leave it behind for management to sell to the next occupant.

Open parks also place restrictions on the sales of mobile homes within their confines. As was noted in Chapter 3, residents are frequently not permitted to advertise and must sell their unit through the management of the park, which withholds a commission for this service. More disturbing, many of the newer parks have a "cut-off date" on the age of a mobile home which they will permit to be sold or moved into the park. Thus in many parks (including Idle Haven) a resident who owns a mobile home more than 5 years old and who wishes to sell it will be permitted to do so *only on the condition that the new owner move the mobile home out of the park.* (In other words, while such a resident is not actually prevented from selling his mobile home, he is prevented from passing on to the new owner one of its most valuable features—namely, that it is already set up in a park.) With most mobile-home parks placing the same age restrictions on used mobile homes coming into the park, few people would be foolish enough to buy such an "over-age" mobile home since it cannot be placed anywhere.

Some mobile-home park owners sanctimoniously insist that by not allowing older mobile homes to be resold and remain in the park they are preventing tenants from making an inflated profit from people who would buy an older mobile home simply to get a space in a particular park. Of course, by prohibiting such sales the park owner is not preventing the making of a profit but merely keeping it for himself, since he usually receives a substantial kickback from the dealer who places a new unit in his park. He is also contributing to the artificial depreciation of used mobile homes.

It is often said that one of the drawbacks of owning a mobile home is that it depreciates just like a car whereas real estate generally increases in value over the years. Actually, such depreciation exists primarily on paper and is abetted by park policies such as excluding mobile homes older than 5 years. I have seen many 10-year-old mobile homes (particularly "eastern-built" models, which are generally better insulated than west coast models) which were better built and in better condition than 1- or 2-year-old mobile homes. This is not surprising when one notes that many of the older, better quality mobile homes originally cost $8,000 to $10,000 even though they were only 8 to 10 feet wide, whereas today manufacturers are building 20-foot-wide models for the same price. These newer models are undoubtedly taking advantage of some newer and cheaper materials—e.g., plastics—but they also contain much shoddy material and workmanship—e.g., thin plywood panelling with a photographically produced grain instead of the genuine hardwood panelling that one finds in many older mobile homes.

Even though there is a blue-book price for used mobile homes, just as there is for used cars, many older homes fetch much more than their blue-book value, particularly if there is no problem about their remaining in or being moved to a particular park. In Idle Haven, for example, three used mobile homes that remained in the park were sold for the following prices:

	Original Price	Age	Resale Price
A	$9,200	4 years	$10,000
B	$9,000	4 years	$ 9,500
C	$9,000	5 years	$ 9,000

The blue-book value on each of these homes was approximately $3,500. One problem connected with having a blue-book price for used mobile homes is that, regardless of what a unit actually sells for, banks will loan the buyer no more than the blue-book price. Thus, one must be more able to pay in cash when buying a used mobile home than when buying a new one. Of course, one compensatory advantage of treating a mobile home like a car is that license fees on it decline over the years. To the elderly individual who has no intention of selling or moving his mobile home it probably does not matter much that his unit is technically worth only $1,000 so long as his license fees are commensurately low. However, if mobile homes are eventually taxed as real property, then park restrictions against older units and artificially low blue-book values should be abandoned, so that resale prices can find their true level and the owner actually owns (and can sell) what he is being taxed for.

Because of the restrictions placed by parks on over-age mobile homes, owners who want to move rather than sell their older units

will often have great difficulties in finding parks that will accept
them. This is often the dilemma faced by elderly people who buy
a mobile home just as they retire and who will never again have
enough money to buy a newer, more expensive model. Some of these
people may spend their 60s in a mobile-home park in a semi-rural,
recreation area but find that in their 70s or 80s they want to move
back to an urban area in order to be closer to their children or to
hospital and shopping facilities. One elderly couple in Idle Haven
had spent 10 years in a mobile-home park near the ocean before
they discovered that their mobile home was rusting due to the salt
air—a problem they hadn't foreseen and which contributed to their
decision to move back to the Bay Area. They spent 6 months looking for a park that would be willing to take them, and they believe
the only reason the manageress of Idle Haven finally did so was
that she "took pity" on them.

Not only do age restrictions on mobile homes affect people's
chances of selling and moving them, but they create a climate of
insecurity for people who have no intention of doing either. Many
of the elderly residents in Idle Haven who were living in old
mobile homes speculated with foreboding about the possibility of
being evicted because their units no longer measured up. Nor were
these fears always groundless. In several documented cases in California, park owners have issued mass eviction notices to 20 or 30
residents of older mobile homes in their parks merely in order to
make these spaces available to dealers of new mobile homes. The
lure for the park owner is not just an entrance fee—sometimes paid
in the form of a rake-off by the dealer or sometimes paid directly
to the park by the new resident—but also the distinct possibility
than an old eight- or ten-foot-wide mobile home can be replaced
with a slightly larger one for which more rent can be charged.

Elderly residents of mobile-home parks are also being squeezed
by rent increases, particularly in newer parks located in urban areas.
Many individuals are thus caught squarely between the difficulty
of paying more rent and the greater difficulty—if not impossibility—
of moving to another, cheaper park. Even when such moves are not
ruled out by the restrictions parks maintain against older mobile
homes, they are often stymied by the expense of moving a mobile
home. There are still a number of smaller, older mobile-home parks
which, like old hotels that cater to the elderly, are a refuge for
those who can neither afford nor qualify for the newer mobile-home
parks. Unfortunately, many of these older "trailer parks" are located

in semi-rural areas and so the decision to move to one may run directly counter to other needs of the elderly—e.g., the need to be near stores, hospitals, or members of one's family. There are some older "trailer parks" in urban areas, but these are generally under enormous pressures from planning commissions who want to zone them out of existence on grounds that they are substandard "hobohemias."

These older trailer parks have a number of disadvantages but, generally speaking, not the ones cited by city planners who want to get rid of them. They are often rather run-down in appearance, but they are not havens of crime or sin. To an even greater extent than Idle Haven, they are inhabited by retired, working-class individuals, some of them living in ancient and miniscule trailers, who are trying to remain independent on small pension or social security payments. Many Idle Haven residents who had lived in such parks liked them even better than Idle Haven because "we were all like one big family."

One drawback to many of these older parks is that they have no piped natural gas; hence residents must cook and heat their mobile homes with tanks of butane, which are expensive and heavy for an elderly person to install. However, utilities pose a problem in many newer parks as well. Underground utilities in parks such as Idle Haven are often installed and owned by the park developer, who pays the city or county for gas and electricity based on a flat rate for the park as a whole. The park owner, rather than the utility company, then reads the individual meters within the park and charges residents for their monthly use of gas and electricity at a higher, individual rate—making a profit on the difference. While the state utilities control commission officially sets the rates a park owner may charge his residents for gas and electricity, many residents in Idle Haven were convinced they were being overcharged for their utilities or that their meters "ran faster" than ordinary meters.[5] Residents were also annoyed by the fact that under this arrangement utility companies are no longer willing to check a resident's stove for leaks or to reignite a pilot light.

Given some of these drawbacks to mobile-home park life, it is

---

[5] One Idle Haven resident also pointed out that when the state utilities control commission had ordered a Bay Area utilities company to give customers a substantial across-the-board refund, residents of the park had not received their share of this refund from the park owner.

not surprising that some residents are turning to "own-your-own-lot" parks and developments. In California, however, such mobile-home lots generally cost about $5,000 or more—a price well beyond the means of many retired individuals. Also, because of the high cost of land in urban areas, parks where one can buy a lot are usually located in smaller towns or in rural, recreation areas. Even if such parks were more widely available in urban areas, many older residents of mobile homes would not want to own the property their mobile home occupies because of the possibility of rising property taxes and the inability to control who their neighbors would be. (There is actually a good deal of confusion among mobile-home residents over "own-your-own-lot" parks, with some people arguing that since one is still "controlled" by management—e.g., with regard to landscaping, selling, and so forth—one may as well pay rent rather than buying, and other people convinced that owning one's own lot destroys a park's control over the environment and hence is undesirable.)

The real dilemma of most mobile-home park residents is that they want to live in a controlled environment without having to pay the sometimes steep price that such control entails. Slightly authoritarian in outlook, justifiably fearful of urban violence, and anxious to maintain all the visible outward signs appropriate to "decent people," the retired working-class mobile-home resident wants to live in a park that is neat, attractive, quiet, safe, all-white, and friendly. In order to attain these ends he is willing to pay a monthly rent to someone who will control his neighbors, but he is deeply incensed if his own freedom is curtailed or if he discovers that the park owner who is supposed to protect him from the outside world may, in fact, also be exploiting him. The ambivalence this dilemma creates in mobile-home park residents is a constant feature of their complaints. One group of tenants in a California park recently complained to the city council that the owner of their park had decided to ban all pets.

> " 'I was told that I could keep a pet when I moved in here,'
> said one woman, 'so I put a lot of money into landscaping
> my place. Now they tell me I have to move if I want to keep
> my pet. That pet means a lot to me. Where am I supposed
> to get the money to move?' "

However, another pet owner and former resident of this same park, who had sold his mobile home in response to the pet ban, was quoted as saying, "We should have been asked our opinions before many of us sold our coaches. *The people whose pets were offending should have been evicted,* before we were forced to move" (WMN, March 23, 1970:4; italics supplied).

Similarly, in a recent series of informal interviews about the advantages and disadvantages of mobile-home life, some residents complained about their park's "restrictions not normally found in a regular home, such as . . . pet restrictions and [restrictions on] late party noise . . ." and suggested that "the mobile-home owners who live in the park and are paying all of the bills should have more of a say as to what the rules and regulations should be." Others, however, complained that some mobile-home owners in the park did not landscape their yards within a reasonable length of time and suggested that "there should be stricter rules for keeping up the property around each home. Some people try so hard to make their surroundings attractive, while others still have their frontage overrun with weeds. . . . If management would strictly enforce all of the present rules of the park, mobile-home living would be all that I had expected it would be" (WMN, January 19, 1970:14).

In California, a bill was passed by the state legislature (although subsequently vetoed by Governor Reagan) prohibiting mobile-home park owners from evicting tenants "1) for failure of the tenant to pay any charges other than rent or utilities; 2) for the purpose of making the tenant's space available for a person who purchased a mobile home from the owner of the park or his agents; and 3) because the tenants hold a meeting in the recreation hall" (WMN, April 13, 1970:1). The last-stated reason grew out of a year-long conflict between one northern California park owner who prohibited his tenants from using the park's recreation hall in order to form a chapter of the Golden State Mobilehome Owners League and who threatened to evict the organizers of the park's new chapter. The legal adviser of the GSMOL, in turn, threatened to bring the park owner into court for infringing on his tenants' civil rights. At the time of this conflict, there was a great deal of talk at GSMOL regional meetings about tenants' civil rights, stressing the fact that a park owner could not institute rules that infringed upon these rights, none of which took note of the fact that most mobile-home residents are only too ready to see the rights of *others* abrogated so long as it is to their own advantage.

These remarks are not intended as a criticism of mobile-home parks or as a rallying cry for their forcible racial integration. The word "integration" in this context is, in fact, misleading since most mobile-home parks at the present time are highly integrated communities in the sense that social scientists use this term. To "integrate" them in terms of forcing them to accept a greater variety of residents might well lead to their social disintegration. As this study has tried to demonstrate, mobile-home parks such as Idle Haven are genuine small communities, with all the advantages and disadvantages that such communities enjoy. Residents trust one another, help one another, and enjoy each other's company; at the same time—given the nature of small groups—they also gossip about each other, watch to see that no one gets more than anyone else does, and occasionally bicker among themselves. Given the financial and social needs of the elderly, such communities clearly serve an important purpose. To force them to take in all applicants would be to destroy the social fabric of the parks and to turn them into ordinary working-class neighborhoods, with their greater potential for anomie, indifference, and crime.

It may be, of course, that mobile-home parks such as Idle Haven are transitory phenomena that will disappear naturally in the normal course of urban development. The ability to control admissions to parks—as well as many of the abuses that stem from it—is largely the result of a scarcity of mobile-home parks in relation to the great number of people who already own or want to buy mobile homes. Presumably, once park spaces have caught up with the demand for them, park owners will not be so quick to evict older units, demand (and get) entrance fees from new ones, and exclude Negroes and others deemed "undesirable" on grounds that the park is full. There is also a growing tendency toward building larger and larger parks—500-, 700-, and 1,000-unit parks are now being built in the Bay Area—which will dilute much of the social solidarity found in a park the size of Idle Haven. Finally, the likelihood that mobile homes will soon become factory-built homes permanently installed in ordinary suburban tracts may eliminate the "park" concept altogether.

Even if mobile-home parks such as Idle Haven should disappear within the next few years, the needs of the people to whom they now appeal are not so likely to fade away. It is true that in the future more of the elderly will be covered by social security payments, and Medicare has already eased the financial and health burdens of many. But transportation difficulties and the need for safety and community among the elderly are likely to grow in our increasingly more populous, heterogeneous, and sprawling metropolises.[6] These needs are already being met by a variety of retirement communities, apartments, and hotels, each catering to residents with certain incomes and class backgrounds. Mobile-home parks should be counted among these retirement communities, and their appeal to white, elderly, working-class individuals should not be ignored. Perhaps no better illustration of this appeal can be found than a parody of "The Night Before Christmas" which has become an item of folklore among mobile-home residents. The present version appeared in *Western Mobile News,* December 23, 1968.

'Twas the night before Christmas and all thru the park
The trailers were quiet, each one of them dark;
The moon tried to shine through the haze in the sky,
But looked like the color of fresh pumpkin pie.

The folks were all snuggled quite warm in their beds
With blankets turned on and pulled up to their heads.
When out on the street there rose such a clatter,
I dashed from my coach to see what was the matter.

And what to my trifocaled eyes should appear
But poor old St. Nick in a red Marketeer.
His coat looked familiar, his hat looked the same,
And I sighed with relief as I saw how he came.

Thank Heaven no deer with sharp little hoof
Would poke any holes in my soft metal roof.
I watched the old man as he readied his pack
With capsules and ointment and pills for the back.

He put in a carton of health food or two
And new fangled diet foods, costly and new.
He started away to distribute the stuff
And learned very soon that the going was rough.

The windows were cranky and most of them small,
There were queer-looking doors and no chimneys at all.

---

6 An acquaintance whose 75-year-old mother lives in a Los Angeles retirement community where a daily jitney takes residents to the grocery store said to me ruefully, "You know, you could starve to death in L.A. if you didn't have a car or couldn't drive on the freeways."

He seemed quite confused as he wandered around,
At the strange unconventional houses he found.

And then he decided that something was wrong
With the sort of a job he had followed so long.
So he stopped playing Santa Claus right on the spot
And started away while the notion was hot.

He didn't go back to his regular place
But went to the office and rented a space.
He bought a new coach about fifty by ten
And started to dress like the rest of the men.

He got a butch hair cut and shaved off his beard,
And because of his size it was just as he feared.
He was forced on a diet of things that you boil,
Of soy beans and carrots and safflower oil;
No sugars or starches, no butter or jelly
In order to shrink off that round little belly.

Now he lives like a senior with nothing to do
But practice his form on a shuffleboard cue.
With a home so complete and neighbors so dear
It seems just like Christmas each day of the year.

APPENDIX I: *The*
Wally Byam Club:
Community Plus Mobility

Mobile-home parks are not the only settings in which retired individuals are finding a sense of community and experimenting with life styles built around leisure pursuits rather than work. Retirement communities and retirement "towers" are springing up in all parts of the country, and through a variety of devices—including cost, location (within an urban center versus a suburban or rural area), sponsorship (e.g., by religious institutions), and the variety of services and amenities offered—most of these communities manage to draw fairly homogeneous populations, not merely in terms of age and social class but also in terms of religious affiliation and range of social sophistication and interests. For example, it is today possible to find luxurious retirement communities catering to upper-middle class WASPs—retired executives, doctors, lawyers—whose chief leisure pursuits consist of sports (tennis, golf, horseback riding, sailing), and equally luxurious retirement communities aimed at the same sociological group but with a slight difference—including perhaps a few more retired professors and other professionals with advanced degrees—whose leisure pursuits are largely sedentary and urban-centered (the opera, the theater, the museums).

In addition to this profusion of residential arrangements there are, of course, voluntary associations that bring together people of similar backgrounds, interests, and ages. Many of these associations are organized around a specific activity rather than making their appeal directly to a particular social status. In fact, it seems unlikely that a voluntary association with *only* age as its focus can ever be very successful, because in American society today, being old is a disvalued status which not many claim willingly, and also because too many cross-cutting statuses (religious, ethnic, socioeconomic) divide the elderly into disparate groups.[1] Such cross-cutting statuses make it equally unlikely that women—*qua* women—will ever become a united social movement; and the current women's liberation groups tend, in fact, to be highly homogeneous in terms of social characteristics other than gender alone.

All this is by way of introduction to a voluntary association which, like the mobile-home park, is highly homogeneous in terms of social class, ethnicity, and age, but which ostensibly bases its appeal solely on a certain shared leisure pursuit: ownership of a travel trailer. Travel-trailering as an activity tends to appeal to white working-class families, many of whom in their younger years find it an inexpensive way to take the children camping or to go fishing or hunting. However, travel-trailer clubs appeal primarily to older working-class couples who are seeking, in addition to some travel and recreation, companionship, social support in developing new

---

[1] It might be argued that the "Ham and Eggs" Movement and the George McLain Movement are examples of associations based wholly on the status of old age, but these associations appealed primarily to a special segment of the aged—those receiving welfare payments. Among McLain's followers, for example, only 11 per cent came from professional and managerial occupations. See Pinner, *et al.* (1959:57–64).

leisure life styles, and perhaps a chance to continue acting out their work roles.

There are many travel-trailer clubs throughout the country—some of them purely local groups of travel-trailer owners who make short trips together during the summer months and who plan restaurant parties and dances during the winter months. The largest travel-trailer club of all, the Wally Byam Club, is somewhat differently organized. On the one hand, it is broader in scope, being nation wide, and on the other hand it is narrower, being open only to owners of Airstream trailers—an expensive all-aluminum trailer whose models are currently priced at $5,000-$10,000. These two aspects of the Wally Byam Club—its broader geographical base plus its narrower sociological base—give its members a strong sense of group identity and exclusivity.

Wally Byam, the original designer and builder of the Airstream trailer, did not deny the fact that he started the club primarily for his retired customers, many of whom had bought his trailers but were not "getting as much out of trailering as [they] could" (Byam, 1960:15). According to Byam the idea of limiting the club to owners of Airstream trailers developed only after Byam-sponsored caravans to Mexico began to draw too many participants and when he concluded that his own make of trailer was the only one sufficiently well built to withstand some of the rugged terrain. However, the advertising and promotion aspects of a club exclusively for Airstream owners cannot have been lost on him, and today the company's president refers to the club frankly as part of its "after-purchase benefit program."

> "We took this unique type of product [the Airstream trailer] that would appeal to a specific market and added a unique merchandising program designed not only to encourage the purchaser to use the product, but also to have fun after he bought it. This is known as our "Way of Life" program. It is available only to owners of our product. In other words, when the consumer buys an Airstream, it is only the beginning. We take them from there and provide them with activities that open up a new way of life for them—a way of seeing new places, meeting new friends, enjoying new meaningful experiences" (Speech by Mr. Arthur R. Costello, President of Airstream Inc. before the New York Society of Security Analysts, April 11, 1967).

It is, in fact, difficult to sort out the commercial, company-sponsored aspects of the Wally Byam Club from the self-generated activities of its members. The company sponsors four annual rallies —in the northeast, northwest, southeast, and southwest of the United States—each of which is attended by as many as 1,500 trailers. The company also sponsors a series of "caravans"—group trips by trailer, usually to Mexico or to Canada—which are company planned and staffed with a caravan director, recreation director, caravan mechanic, and advance scout. Since caravans to Mexico have involved as many as 300 trailers and caravans to Canada have consisted of up to 400, such arrangements for overnight stops and supplies are obviously mandatory.

In addition to participating in these company-sponsored events, an Airstream owner can, for a small annual fee, become a member of the Wally Byam Caravan Club, which currently consists of approximately 100 local units with a total membership of some 10,000 households. These local units plan local rallies and social activities for their members, much as the smaller travel-trailer clubs do. However, membership in the Wally Byam Caravan Club entitles one to attend the rallies of other units, and many devoted members spend much of the year criss-crossing the country (travelling with the seasons) attending these gatherings.

Local unit rallies are usually weekend affairs held at a park or a fairground within a short travelling distance for most of the unit's members. Participants in their trailers usually assemble on a Friday night and often park in a circular formation reminiscent of covered wagons protecting themselves from Indian attack. (It is said that this formation was actually developed because it is the easiest method of parking a large number of trailers without having to back them into spots.) Activities at rallies typically include pot-luck suppers and breakfasts, square dancing, community singing, hobby displays, tours of local points of interest, and an interdenominational church service on Sunday morning, after which people depart for home on Sunday afternoon.

Since 1958, the third year of the club's existence, the largest annual activity has been the "international rally," a week-long affair always timed to coincide with July 4th, which is also Wally Byam's birthday. These mammoth rallies have been held in such places as Auburn, Washington (concurrently with the 1962 Seattle World's Fair), and Princeton, New Jersey (concurrently with the 1964 New

York World's Fair). The 1967 International Rally was held in Santa
Rosa, a small community whose sole claim to fame is that it contains
the former home and garden of Luther Burbank, but which is con-
veniently located about 60 miles north of San Francisco. The international rally sites usually have to be in or near small cities rather
than directly adjacent to large urban centers since a large tract of
empty land is required to accommodate the more than 2,000 trailers
that have been attending these annual events for the last several
years. The Santa Rosa rally, which attracted some 2,159 trailers, was
situated on a former Naval Air Base on the outskirts of the town.
Trailers were parked about 10 feet apart on either side of runways
that had been labeled "North Boulevard," "South Boulevard," and
so forth; at the juncture of the runways a group of large canvas tents
had been erected where meetings, dances, entertainment, church
services, and other events took place.

The retirement-oriented nature of the Wally Byam Club was
amply demonstrated by the sample survey I conducted at Santa
Rosa. During the four days preceding and the seven days of the
actual rally, I surveyed every thirtieth trailer as they were parked
along the former runways.[2] The total sample consisted of seventy
households: sixty-nine couples and one widower. Forty-five of the
heads of household (64.3 per cent) were fully retired, another ten
(14.3 per cent) were partially retired, and only fifteen (21.4 per
cent) were employed full time. Of the fifteen who were employed
full time, six were one or two years away from retirement and had
bought their trailers specifically with future retirement in mind.

---

[2] A comparison of the "home state" of the interview sample with the total
number of trailers from each state attending the rally indicates that the sample
was an accurate reflection of those attending the 1967 rally. Attendance at the
rally was, however, heavily weighted by club members from California (42.7
per cent of the trailers attending the rally and 35.7 per cent of the sample). A
comparison of the membership count for every unit with those attending the
rally reveals that California had a 48.2 per cent turnout, Arizona a 35.5 per
cent turnout, and Utah a 29.6 per cent turnout. Thereafter, the percentages
attending the rally declined in proportion to the distance of the state from
California, with the exception of the Deep South. Midwestern and northwestern
states' participation ranged between 15 and 10 per cent; east coast participation
was less than 10 per cent. However, the states of Louisiana and Mississippi
each had a turnout of 17.3 per cent, Georgia had a turnout of 14.6 per cent,
and Florida had 13.1 per cent of its membership at the rally. The sample is
thus somewhat affected by the geographical location of the 1967 rally, although
the homogeneity of the sample on many questions suggests that the findings of
the survey are representative for the club as a whole.

Another indication of the nature of the club is the average age of the members. Although the men ranged in age from 35 to 75, the median age was 66 and the modal age was 67. For the women, who ranged in age from 35 to 73, the median age was 60 and the modal age was 65. Moreover, 58 of the 70 households (83 per cent) stated that at the present time their usual household consisted of just the husband and wife. Eleven households (16 per cent) still included children, although only six of these had children young enough to be with them at the rally. Three other couples had brought grandchildren with them to the rally, but these children were not usual members of their households.

Compared to the residents of Idle Haven (Tables XI and XII),

TABLE XI
Comparison of Level of Education Attained
(Males Only)

Last grade completed	Idle Haven	Wally Byam Club sample
	per cent	per cent
1–8	16.5	17.1
9–11	24.7	17.1
12	44.3	30.1
Some college	7.2	14.3
College graduate	7.2	14.3
Post-graduate degree	0.0	7.1

TABLE XII
Comparison of Occupations of Males

	Idle Haven	Wally Byam Club sample
	per cent	per cent
Professional and Managerial	10.7	32.8
Clerical and Sales	16.1	27.1
Craftsmen and Operatives	66.1	31.4
Service Occupations	4.5	1.4
Students	2.7	0.0
Laborers and Farm Workers	0.0	7.1

members of the Wally Byam Club were better educated, included a larger number of professional and white-collar workers, and had somewhat higher incomes (the median income for club members was $8,000, as compared to $6,760 in Idle Haven). Nevertheless, the

TABLE XIII

Income Distribution in the Wally Byam Club Sample

Income	Retired	Partially retired	Not retired	Total number	Per cent of sample
					per cent
Less than $2,000	0	0	0	0	0.0
$ 2,001 – $ 4,000	9	0	0	9	12.9
$ 4,001 – $ 6,000	11	0	0	11	15.7
$ 6,001 – $ 8,000	12	1	0	13	18.6
$ 8,001 – $10,000	4	3	0	7	10.0
$10,001 – $14,000	3	1	6	10	14.3
$14,001 – $18,000	3	0	2	5	7.0
$18,001 – $24,000	0	1	3	4	5.7
$24,001 or above	1	4	2	7	10.0
Refused to state or not known	2	0	2	4	5.7
TOTAL	45	10	15	70	99.9

social tone of the club was very similar to that in Idle Haven: folksy, patriotic, "middle-American" in outlook. Several club members were themselves obliquely aware of this and commented to me that although there were "some real millionaires in the club, nobody knows who they are because they act just like ordinary folks." And, indeed, while the Santa Rosa survey uncovered no millionaires, the seven couples who reported annual incomes in excess of $24,000 included farmers and ranchers, the owners of a grocery store and a dairy, and a prosperous cabinet maker, none of whom had any social pretensions.

As was the case in Idle Haven, many of the white-collar participants in the Wally Byam Club appeared to have close ties to the working class: two-thirds of the professional men in the Santa Rosa sample were either engineers or technical writers, and the clerical and sales workers included a large number of people who sold construction materials or auto parts. A number of sales people also had rural ties, being involved in the sale of farm equipment and feed grains. Nevertheless, as was also the case in Idle Haven, Wally Byam Club members were not predominantly rural in origins. Thirty-three of the couples interviewed (47.2 per cent) had spent most of their adult lives in a city, or a suburb of a city, with over 100,000 population; fifteen couples (21.4 per cent) had spent most of their adult lives in cities with populations of 10,000–100,000; and twenty-two couples (31.4 per cent) had spent most of their adult lives in towns with populations of under 10,000 or on farms. These percentages approximate rather closely the population distribution of the United States as a whole; according to the 1960 Census, 34 per cent of the population lives in cities, or their suburbs, of over 100,000; 25.8 per cent lives in cities between 10,000 and 100,000; and 40.2 per cent lives in towns of under 10,000 or in rural areas.

The membership of the Wally Byam Club also resembled Idle Haven in its racial homogeneity (I did not see a single non-white face) and religious composition. The Santa Rosa sample included fifty-three Protestant households (75.7 per cent), ten Catholic households (14.3 per cent), three mixed households in which one spouse was Catholic and the other was Protestant, one Christian Scientist household, and another three households who replied or implied that "None" was the most accurate religious category for them. I came across one Jewish couple (not part of the random sample) who admitted that they knew of no other Jews in the club, although they insisted that this was not due to discrimination. This Jewish couple resembled the other club members in terms of their ages, income, and the husband's former working-class occupation, but they were atypical in that they had traveled a great deal (abroad as well as in the United States) and sheer love of travel was their chief reason for having bought an Airstream. Most of the Wally Byam Club members, like the residents of Idle Haven, considered travel abroad a form of snobbery—"Most people do it just to say they've been there"—and even their travels within the United States seemed less a form of travel than participation in a form of mobile community.

According to the Wally Byam Creed, one of the functions of the club is "To place the great wide world at your doorstep for you who yearn to travel with all the comforts of home." Undoubtedly, the phrase "comforts of home" was meant to refer to the Airstream trailer, which is indeed a very luxurious, self-contained trailer in which one can cook, take a hot bath, and read or watch television at night without being hooked up to electricity, water, or sewage lines.[3] It is evident from club rallies and caravans, however, that

---

[3] Appliances run on batteries or on butane; there is a water storage tank; and there is a sewage holding tank which must, however, be emptied every few days. At large rallies, rather than relying on their own limited water and

the comforts of home that club members are provided with extend far beyond the appurtenances of their trailers. They include such things as medical care, church services, and the kinds of friendships and community activities that solitary travelers often miss when they are away from home for extended periods. The club in fact provides its members with a sort of floating community which may be more real to many of them than the community from which they severed their ties when they retired or when they came face to face with the sorts of urban problems that caused others of their kind to move to Idle Haven.

Evidence of the community feeling that exists among club members was expressed in a variety of ways. One man said to me, "You know, we have a saying that there are no strangers in Airstream: there are only friends you haven't gotten acquainted with yet," and another man remarked that one of the wonderful things about belonging to the club was that "no matter where you pull off the road at night, another Airstream will have pulled in next to you before morning." All Wally Byam Club members are furnished with a red identification number for the front of their trailer and a directory which lists the names, addresses, and identification numbers of the club's members. The directory also indicates which club members have a free parking space (in their driveway or backyard) available to fellow Airstreamers passing through their town. Other badges of identity include a variety of club decals for one's trailer; a huge assortment of flags (American, State, club, and officer flags) which are hoisted on the front of one's trailer at rallies; and blue berets with the club's insignia, which are worn at rallies by both men and women. As in Idle Haven, many people also paint their own names on the sides of their trailers, and those who have attended numerous rallies and caravans list these, like notches on a gun. In addition some people have bestowed names on their trailers, including such noteworthy examples as: "The Livin' End," "The Ball Room," "Severance Pay," and "Our Nap Sack."

At rallies a conscious attempt is made to create instant community by turning the rally site into a kind of make-believe city. In addition to the creation of named streets, a "city jail" and a community post-office are established, and a "Police Chief" and various

---

sewage-disposal facilities, trailers are hooked up to temporary water lines and every trailer's plastic sewage pipe is inserted into the ground, into what is euphemistically called a "gopher hole" (at Santa Rosa these were dug with a special drill, probably a post-hole digger).

other officials are appointed. The press releases from the Santa
Rosa rally (as well as subsequent rallies) all made extensive use
of the theme of an "instant city":

> "Welcome to Airstream City, newest and fastest growing
> town in the world. . . . The reason the city's population took
> such a sharp turn upward today is that its gates officially
> opened at 8:30 this morning to club members, many of
> whom have been staying in trailer courts for weeks waiting
> for the signal, or travelling around the state to see the sights.
> . . . The city even has a 'jail' which is really about a four
> foot high stockade type structure built to 'punish' club
> members who fail to wear identification badges on the
> grounds, and a voluntary police force of some 200 mem-
> bers. . . . [In fact,] Airstream City is run by committees—
> volunteer committees. These range from the large parking
> and water committees, some of whose members have been
> on the grounds for a couple of weeks helping get set up, to
> the message center committee consisting of about six mem-
> bers, who see to it that emergency telephone calls and wires
> get to the residents of the temporary city. Then there's the
> post office committee headed by Ray Fortney, a former Ohio
> postmaster who estimates his office will be handling more
> than 5,000 pieces of mail a day when the rally is in full
> swing; the scooter patrol committee of about 15 members
> who also deliver messages; the hospital committee consisting
> of retired doctors and nurses, and the large police force,
> just to name a few" (Santa Rosa *Press Democrat*, June 22,
> 1967).

Not only does the creation of such a pseudo-city seem to provide participants with a kind of community environment within
which they can relate to each other, but the formal framework
described above also given many retired individuals an opportunity
to re-enact their pre-retirement roles in a "play" setting. For example, the random sample of people interviewed at Santa Rosa
included a retired doctor who spent several hours a day on call at
the first-aid trailer, a retired school teacher who spent every morning running an activity program for the pre-teenage children at the
rally, a retired minister who gave the benediction at the Sunday
church services, and several church soloists who were in the Wally
Byam Choir, which sang on Sundays. Interestingly enough, there
was a not-yet-retired police chief in the Santa Rosa sample, but he

was *not* active in policing the rally: he was on vacation. However, several retired men spent most of the rally working extremely hard and seemed to enjoy themselves thoroughly in the process.

In addition to providing individuals with a setting in which they can reenact their pre-retirement roles, the Wally Byam Club also provides many opportunities for people to learn and gain social approval for post-retirement leisure activities. The Santa Rosa rally featured square-dance classes; a hobby show; chess, golf, and bridge tournaments; and a competition for the best slides and movies taken in the course of people's trailer travels. The club itself also provides a new focus of self-identification. Many Wally Byam Club members become enthusiastic boosters of the Airstream trailer and come to identify with the parent company. They are aware that Airstream is a business enterprise run for profit and that the company garners a tremendous amount of free publicity from rallies at which some 2,000 of their trailers are assembled. At the same time, participants seem to derive a great deal of personal satisfaction from making new converts to their "way of life" and from demonstrating their solidarity to outsiders. This is, of course, not unlike the sense of community that develops within many privately run retirement communities and mobile-home parks. Given the growing number of retired individuals who can expect to live an increasing number of years in a society that provides few structured roles for them, we will probably see more such attempts to create institutions that can fill the void.

Jdle Haven Interview Schedule

I.D. No._____

Sex of
respondent(s)_____

1. What is the composition of your household at the present time?
   And may I ask the age or the year of birth for each of the people
   you have just named? (Also note whether there is a pet.)
   Members of household   *Year born or age*

2. And are you presently:
   Married_____   Widowed_____
   Divorced_____   Never married_____
   Separated_____

3. If married, how long married? (i.e., any previous marriages) If widowed, how long widowed?

4. And when did you first move into Idle Haven?

5. In what state and town were you (each of you) born?

6. Now, could you tell me the major places you have lived in throughout your lifetime, and the type of housing you lived in.
PLACE   FROM   TO   HOUSING   COMMENTS

7. Now, while we were talking about the past, could you tell me what was the last grade in school that you (and your husband/ wife) completed?

8. (For men) Are you (Is your husband) presently employed full-time, or are you (is he) either partially or fully retired?

9. (If retired) How long has it been since you (he) stopped working at your (his) last regular job?

10. What kind of work did you (he) do (have you done) most of your (his) adult life?

11. Do you (Does he) now do any work for which you get paid? No——Yes——(If yes, specify what kind.)

12. (For women) Have you (Has your wife) ever been employed during your (her) adult life? No——Yes——(If yes, specify kind of work.)

13. Was this work done: (a) only until marriage; (b) only after children were grown; (c) throughout adult life; (d) part-time; (e) some combination (specify)?

14. (For widows) What sort of work did your husband do most of his life?

15. Now when did you buy your present mobile home?

16. Have you ever moved it?

17. What is the name of the manufacturer (or brand) and what are its dimensions? How many rooms?

18. At the time that you bought this mobile home was it new or used, and what was its total selling price? How did you finance this? Is it now clear?

19. Did you buy the home fully furnished or did you furnish it with things that you already owned?

20. Have you owned other mobile homes? If so, how did you dispose of these?

21. What were the circumstances that first led you to decide to buy a mobile home?

22. Does any other member of your family live in a mobile home? If yes, did this follow or precede your own move?

23. Are there any things about mobile homes that you dislike, that you didn't know about until you had lived in one for a while?

24. Are you planning on continuing to live in a mobile home or do you plan to move into some other type of housing sometime in the future?

25. Now, I would like to ask you some questions about children. First of all, do you have any children, stepchildren, or adopted children? No_____ Yes_____.

26. If yes, for each child I would like to know:

		Marital		Location	How often		
Sex	Age	Status	Occupation	City and State	S.	W.	P.

(S—Seen; W—Written; P—Phoned)

27. Do you have any grandchildren? (If yes, probe for number, location, and extent of contact.)

28. Do you have any other close relatives living in California? (Probe relationship and extent of contact.)

29. Do you have any relatives living outside of California that you see with any regularity?

30. Now, aside from relatives and children, do you have any close friends or couples that you see with any regularity? (If yes,) would you say that most of your close friends are people here in the park, or people that you met at work, or friends from a former neighborhood, or what?

31. Could you name your three closest friends here in the park?

32. As for knowing the names of the people in the park, would you say you know: All_____, Three-quarters_____,

Half————, A quarter————, Just a few————,
None————?

33. Do you ever ask individual couples in the park into your home (a) to play cards, (b) to watch TV, (c) to have a cocktail or a beer, (d) for coffee or tea, (e) for dinner?

34. Do you ever borrow things from other people in the park? What sort of things?

35. I understand that people in the park are often helpful when someone is ill, or needs a ride, or things of that sort. Have you ever been helped in that way, and what were the circumstances? Have you had occasion to give such assistance to someone else?

36. Now, I've made a list of some things that people say they like about mobile homes and mobile-home parks. As I read them off, I want you to tell me whether this was very important, somewhat important, or not important to you in choosing mobile-home life.

	Very	*Some*	*Not*
(a) Mobile homes are easier to clean and maintain.	—	—	—
(b) Mobile homes cost less than conventional housing.	—	—	—
(c) The taxes on mobile homes are lighter than those on conventional housing....	—	—	—
(d) Mobile-home parks provide free recreation facilities such as swimming pools and shuffleboard courts.	—	—	—
(e) The people in mobile-home parks are friendlier and more neighborly than they are in ordinary neighborhoods....	—	—	—
(f) In an "adult" park one isn't troubled by young children making noise at all hours of the day and night..........	—	—	—
(g) There is not the strain by keeping up a large garden.	—	—	—
(h) A mobile-home park is a "controlled community" so that one needn't worry about undesirable people moving in next door.........................	—	—	—
(i) A mobile-home park is safer from crime			

and violence than an ordinary com-
munity. ....   —   —   —

(j) A mobile-home park isn't necessarily
free from undesirable elements, but one
can always move if need be..........   —   —   —

37. What made you choose this particular park in this particular area? (If person has lived in other parks, why did he move from these?)

38. If you had your druthers, is there a particular part of the park that you'd rather be located in? Why? Have you ever moved within this park?

39. How would you compare this park and its residents to the last ordinary neighborhood that you lived in?

40. Are you planning on remaining here, in this park, or are you thinking of moving to a different park? If the latter, why and to which park or general area? If you move, will you move your mobile home or will you sell it and buy another for the new site?

41. If you were to sell your mobile home today, what do you suppose you could get for it?

42. Are there any things about living in a mobile-home park that you dislike?

43. What do you think about mobile-home parks in which you buy a lot instead of renting one? What are some of the advantages and disadvantages?

44. Have you ever heard of the GSMOL? Are you presently a member? Are you now, or have you ever been an officer in GSMOL?

45. (If yes) About how often do you attend GSMOL meetings: (a) in your own park? (b) In the region?

46. Do you (and your wife/husband) belong to any clubs, lodges, or associations outside the park? Which ones?

47. How frequently do you attend meetings?

48. Do you attend meetings more or less frequently now than before moving into the park? More_____ Less_____ Same_____.

49. What is your religious affiliation? Protestant_____, Catholic

_____, Jewish_____, Other (specify)_____ (n.b. if religion is not the same for husband and wife).

50. Do you (and your husband/wife) attend a church in this area?

51. About how often would you say you attend church? Almost every week_____, Once a month_____, Once or twice a year_____.

52. Are you (and your husband/wife) active in any other church activities? What sort?

53. Would you say you have been more active or less active in church activities since you moved into the park?

54. What sorts of activities do you participate in here in the park?

55. About how often do you participate in a park activity? Every day_____, Once or twice a week_____, Once or twice a month_____, Once or twice a year_____.

56. Is either of you, or has either of you ever been an officer or a leader of any groups in the park? (Specify)

57. When the weather is good, about how often do you use the swimming pool in the park? Frequently_____, Occasionally _____, Never or hardly ever_____.

58. Do you own a travel trailer, a camper, or a motor home? (If yes,) about how much time a year do you spend in it? Do you belong to a travel trailer club?

59. Are there any extensive periods of time when either of you or both of you are away from the park—either on vacation or on business?

60. Do you read any newspapers regularly? What paper(s)?

61. Are there any magazines that you read more or less regularly?

62. Do you know the name of the mayor of_____[the name of the town in which Idle Haven is located]?

63. And do you know the name and the party affiliation of the man who represents this district in Congress?

64. What is your usual political affiliation? (a) Republican_____,

(b) Democrat_____, (c) Independent_____, (d) Other
(specify)_____, (e) None_____.

65. Did you vote in the last national election?

66. Did you vote for Humphrey, Nixon, or Wallace, for President?

67. Did you vote in 1964? Do you remember whether you voted
     for Johnson or for Goldwater?

68. Now I would like to ask you a few personal questions. Would
     you describe your present income as: (a) Inadequate_____,
     (b) Barely adequate_____, (c) Sufficient for your needs_____,
     (d) Sufficient with some leeway_____, or (e) Comfortable_____?

69. Compared with earlier periods of your life, would you say you
     are now better off, worse off, just about the same?

70. Are there any things that you feel you need right now that you
     can't afford?

71. Do you have any savings in the event of a serious illness or in
     the event you had to move suddenly?

72. Do you have any life insurance?

73. Do you have any medical insurance, or do you qualify for
     Medicare?

74. Do you have any major health problems at the present time?

75. Now I'm going to read off a short list of the ways people get
     their income. After each one, please say if you (or your spouse)
     had any money from that source any time during the past
     month.
     (a) Any kind of job.
     (b) Interest from investments, or rent.
     (c) Withdrawals from savings or selling real estate, or cashing
          bonds, or anything like that.
     (d) Social Security benefits.
     (e) Any other kind of government pension.
     (f) A private pension.
     (g) Old Age Assistance.
     (h) Any kind of government payment because of some injury
          you had.
     (i) Any other kind of government assistance at all.

(j) Relatives—do you get any money from them fairly regularly?

76. Now, I wonder if you would look at this card (SHOW CARD) and tell me the letter of the income group that includes you at the present time—that is, the group that includes your total yearly income from all the sources we just talked about, before taxes.

        (a) 0–$2,000
        (b) $2,001–$4,000
        (c) $4,001–$6,000
        (d) $6,001–$8,000
        (e) $8,001–$10,000
        (f) $10,001–$14,000
        (g) $14,001–$18,000
        (h) $18,001–$24,000
        (i) $24,001 or more

77. Do you have a car? Year and make?

78. Now, finally I would like to ask you a couple of questions about how you spend your leisure time. What are some of the things that you do frequently—either alone, or with someone else in or outside of the park. I am thinking of such things as sports, hobbies, handicrafts, cards, singing or playing a musical instrument, or just going out driving or shopping, or talking to people.

79. Do you have a TV set (color?)? About how many hours a day do you watch? What are some of your favorite programs?

Bibliography

Adams, Bert N.
  1968 *Kinship in an Urban Setting*. Chicago: Markham Publishing Co.
Alschuler, Karen Brecher, and Robert Stedman Betts
  1970 *Mobile Homes: Evolution of the Market, Consumer Costs, The Tax Controversy, Comparative Costs*. Berkeley: University of California, Dept. of City and Regional Planning, Working Paper No. 123.
Banfield, Edward C.
  1970 *The Unheavenly City: The Nature and Future of Our Urban Crisis*. Boston: Little, Brown and Co.
Berger, Bennett M.
  1960 *Working-Class Suburb: A Study of Auto Workers in Suburbia*. Berkeley and Los Angeles: University of California Press.
  1962 "The Sociology of Leisure: Some Suggestions," *Industrial Relations*, I(2):31–45.
  1966 "Suburbia and the American Dream," *The Public Interest*, 2:80–91.
Blau, Zena Smith

1961   "Structural Constraints on Friendship in Old Age," *American Sociological Review,* 26:429–39.

Bohannan, Paul
1958   "Extra-Processual Events in Tiv Political Institutions," *American Anthropologist,* 60:1–12.

Bott, Elizabeth
1957   *Family and Social Network.* London: Tavistock Publications.

Byam, Wally
1960   *Trailer Travel Here and Abroad.* New York: David McKay Co.

Carp, Frances M.
1966   *A Future for the Aged: Victoria Plaza and Its Residents.* Austin: University of Texas Press.

Chinoy, Ely
1965   *Automobile Workers and the American Dream.* Boston: Beacon Press, paper ed.

Construction Industries Research Inc.
1967   *An Appraisal of Mobile Home Living: The Parks and the Residents.* Los Angeles: Trailer Coach Association.

Cumming, Elaine, and William E. Henry
1961   *Growing Old: The Process of Disengagement.* New York: Basic Books.

Eichler, Edward P., and Marshall Kaplan
1967   *The Community Builders.* Berkeley and Los Angeles: University of California Press.

Etzioni, Amitai
1959   "The Ghetto—A Re-evaluation," *Social Forces,* 37(3):255–62.

Faris, Robert, and H. Warren Dunham
1939   *Mental Disorders in Urban Areas.* Chicago: University of Chicago Press.

Festinger, Leon, Stanley Schachter, and Kurt Back
1967   *Social Pressures in Informal Groups: A Study of Human Factors in Housing.* Stanford: Stanford University Press, paper ed.

Foster, George M.
1965   "Peasant Society and the Image of Limited Good," *American Anthropologist,* 67(2):293–315.

Frankenberg, Ronald
1957   *Village on the Border.* London: Cohen and West.
1966   *Communities in Britain: Social Life in Town and Country.* Baltimore: Penguin Books.

French, Robert Mills, and Jeffrey K. Hadden
1968   "Mobile Homes: Instant Suburbia or Transportable Slums?" *Social Problems,* 16(2):217–26.

Gans, Herbert J.
1962a *The Urban Villagers: Group and Class in the Life of Italian-Americans.* New York: The Free Press.
1962b "Urbanism and Suburbanism as Ways of Life: A Re-evaluation of Definitions." *In* Arnold M. Rose, ed., *Human Behavior and Social Processes: An Interactionist Approach.* London: Routledge and Kegan Paul, pp. 625–48.

1969 *The Levittowners: Ways of Life and Politics in a New Suburban Community*. New York: Vintage Books.

Gluckman Max
1963 "Gossip and Scandal," *Current Anthropology,* 4(3):307-16.

Gouldner, Alvin W.
1960 "The Norm of Reciprocity: A Preliminary Statement," *American Sociological Review,* 25(2):161–78.

HEW (U. S. Dept. of Health, Education, and Welfare)
1966 *Patterns of Living and Housing of Middle-Aged and Older People.* Washington, D.C.: Government Printing Office.
1968 *The Retirement Process.* Washington, D. C.: Government Printing Office.

Hollingshead, August B.
1953 "Class Differences in Family Stability." *In* Reinhard Bendix and Seymour Martin Lipset, eds. *Class, Status and Power.* New York: The Free Press, pp. 284–91.

Hoyt, G. C.
1954 "The Life of the Retired in a Trailer Park," *American Journal of Sociology,* 59:361–70.

HUD (U. S. Department of Housing and Urban Development)
1968 *Housing Surveys: Parts 1 and 2* (Occupants of New Housing Units and Mobile Homes and the Housing Supply). Washington, D. C.: Government Printing Office.

Jacobs, Jane
1961 *The Death and Life of Great American Cities.* New York: Random House.

Johnson, Chalmers A.
1962 *Peasant Nationalism and Communist Power.* Stanford: Stanford University Press.

Keller, Suzanne
1968 *The Urban Neighborhood: A Sociological Perspective.* New York: Random House.

Kendall, Elaine
1971 "The Invisible Suburbs," *Horizon,* 13(1):104–11.

Kleemeier, Robert W., ed.
1961 *Aging and Leisure.* New York: Oxford University Press.

Kluckhohn, Clyde
1944 *Navaho Witchcraft.* Boston: Beacon Press.

Komarovsky, Mirra
1962 *Blue-Collar Marriage.* New York: Vintage Books.

Lipman, Aaron
1961 "Role Conceptions and Morale of Couples in Retirement," *Journal of Gerontology,* 16:267–71.

Lipset, Seymour Martin, and Reinhard Bendix
1959 *Social Mobility in Industrial Society.* Berkeley and Los Angeles: University of California Press.

Litwak, Eugene
1960a "Geographic Mobility and Extended Family Cohesion," *American Sociological Review,* 25:385–94.

1960b "Occupational Mobility and Extended Family Cohesion," *American Sociological Review*, 25:9–21.

Mead, Margaret
1970 *Culture and Commitment*. New York: Natural History Press.

Miller, Stephen J.
1965 "The Social Dilemma of the Aging Leisure Participant." *In* Arnold M. Rose and Warren A. Peterson, eds. *Older People and Their Social World*. Philadelphia: F. A. Davis Co., pp. 77–92.

Nadel, S. F.
1952 "Witchcraft in Four African Societies: An Essay in Comparison," *American Anthropologist*, 54:18–29.

Neugarten, Bernice L., and David L. Guttman
1958 "Age-Sex Roles and Personality in Middle Age: A Thematic Apperception Study," *Psychological Monographs*, Vol. 72, No. 17.

Pinner, Frank A., Paul Jacobs, and Philip Selznick
1959 *Old Age and Political Behavior*. Berkeley and Los Angeles: University of California Press.

Rainwater, Lee, Richard P. Coleman, and Gerald Handel
1962 *Workingman's Wife: Her Personality, World and Life Style*. New York: Macfadden Books.

Reichard, Suzanne, Florine Livson, and Paul G. Petersen
1962 *Aging and Personality*. New York: John Wiley & Sons.

Rogin, Richard
1970 "Joe Kelly Has Reached His Boiling Point," *New York Times Magazine*, June 28, 1970:12–24.

Rosow, Irving
1962 "Retirement Housing and Social Integration," *In* Clark Tibbitts and Wilma Donahue, eds. *Social and Psychological Aspects of Aging*. New York: Columbia University Press, pp. 327–40.

Schrag, Peter
1969 "The Forgotten American," *Harper's Magazine*, 239 (August):27–34.

Shanas, Ethel, Peter Townsend, Dorothy Wedderburn, Henning Friis, Poul Milhoj, and Jan Stehouwer
1968 *Old People in Three Industrial Societies*. New York: Atherton Press.

Steiner, Gary A.
1963 *The People Look at Television*. New York: Knopf.

"The Troubled American"
1969 Special Report in *Newsweek*, LXXIV(14), October 6, 1969, pp. 29–73.

Townsend, Peter
1963 *The Family Life of Old People*. Harmondsworth: Penguin Books.
1968 "The Emergence of the Four-Generation Family in Industrial Society." *In* Bernice L. Neugarten, ed. *Middle Age and Aging: A Reader in Social Psychology*. Chicago: The University of Chicago Press, pp. 255–57.

Trillin, Calvin
1964 "A Reporter at Large: Wake Up and Live," *The New Yorker*, 40 (April 4, 1964):120–72.

Vernon, Raymond
1962 *The Myth and Realities of Our Urban Problems*. Cambridge, Mass.:

Joint Center for Urban Studies of MIT and Harvard University.

Vidich, Arthur J., and Joseph Bensman

1968 *Small Town in Mass Society: Class, Power and Religion in a Rural Community*. Princeton: Princeton University Press, rev. ed.

Walkley, Rosabelle Price, Wiley P. Mangum Jr., Susan Roth Sherman, Suzanne Dodds, and Daniel M. Wilner

1966 *Retirement Housing in California*. Berkeley and San Francisco: Diablo Press.

Werthman, Carl Shear

1968 "The Social Meaning of the Physical Environment," Unpublished Ph.D. Dissertation, Dept. of Sociology, University of California at Berkeley.

Wilensky, Harold L.

1961 "Orderly Careers and Social Participation," *American Sociological Review*, 26:521–39.

1962 "Labor and Leisure: Intellectual Traditions," *Industrial Relations*, I(2):1–12.

WMN (*Western Mobile News*, formerly *Western Mobile Home News*)

Young, Michael, and Peter Willmott

1962 *Family and Kinship in East London*. Harmondsworth: Penguin Books.

Index

74006

DATE DUE

PRINTED IN U.S.A.